STALKER

the trials and successes of a child marriage

JUANITA RAY

TOXIC THOUGHTS

a true story series

Summary: "When a fifteen-year-old foster child with a grade eight education marries a
teacher and together they relocate to isolated communities with religious borders, she has
no idea her husband will turn into a TV celebrity and she'll become an educated teen
entrepreneur whose claim to fame is building a structure that falls apart."- - Provided by
publisher.

For information regarding this publication contact:
SmorgasbordPublications@gmail.com

Toxic Thoughts Series #2
STALKED
ISBN- 978-1-936954-24-7 (Paperback)
ISBN: 978-1-936954-19-3 (Digital)

Cover art and book design by Juanita Ray

Preface

Nothing could prepare me for becoming a teen entrepreneur—but then again, most entrepreneurs . . . don't build buildings that fall apart . . .

Although I only have a grade eight education, and was raised like an animal, thanks to home economics I know how to cook a can of soup and how to feed a fake baby. So, what can possibly go wrong?

I' m a crown ward—government property, which means they typically ignore me, but that's all changing now that I'm a pregnant foster child. The government is adamant that I go to an unwed mother's home and give the baby up for adoption, while my foster mother insists I stay and have it, knowing she'll get paid to keep the baby as a foster. My roommate believes we should elope with the boys in our lives. Co-rent a cheap flat.

My boyfriend's mother wishes I would disappear from the face of the earth, which frankly at this point seems like an excellent thought. Fifteen, pregnant, Anglican, and a foster child—whose childhood was void of parental guidance—aren't great ingredients for a good wife recipe, especially considering her Catholic son is an up-and-coming teacher. She believes he can do much better than me, and welfare trash is far below her standards for any daughter-in-law. I plan to prove her wrong.

Frankly, he isn't the son she thinks he is. Weird is the best word, to describe the shy quiet boy who peers at me daily from between the chip racks. What normal person enters a store, hides behind a stand, and spends a half hour spying on somebody he doesn't know? My roommate thinks it's flattering, but then again, she believes combing Clorox through your hair and ironing it with a red hot clothing iron, are ultimate beauty tips.

Now she's teaching me how to become a good liar, because according to my future husband, I'll have to constantly lie about my age, because at fifteen I'm going to be a high school teacher's wife.

Toxic Thoughts Series

a true story memoir series
about one woman's adversities and resilience

#toxicthoughts

Battered *the monster among us* (#1)
Stalked *the trials and successes of a child bride* (#2)
Intoxicated *a true story of an add relationship* (#3)
Charmed *a true story of a second secret life* (#4)
Shattered *'til narcissism do us part, a true story memoir* (#5)
Discarded *the throw away bride, a true story memoir* (#6)
Trapped *coming soon* (#7)
Hindered *coming soon* (# 8)

For information concerning release dates for paperback, ebook, or audible formats, in regard to this series, or inquiries about any other books or series authored by Juanita Ray, contact SmorgasbordPublications@gmail.com.

Contents

It takes courage to grow up and turn out to be who you really are.

–E.E. Cummings

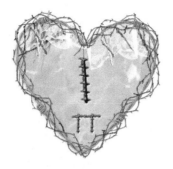

A Deranged Roommate

Everything we pass is one continuous blur. Ruby Line rolls by the passenger window at exactly the same speed it did, six months earlier, when I hopped that bus on the last day of school. The Ruby Church and a grove of trees whiz by and for brief second my heart lurches. That graveyard and church were my initiation to freedom. Now I'm saying goodbye to them and the Rubys, but I don't mind being alone, because it's all I know.

Mrs. Lolita stops humming, and points at the police station. "I don't expect any more calls from them. You can only run away so many times before you end up living in Juvenile Hall and trust me you don't want that."

"Maybe I do."

"No you don't, Juanita." She offers me a stick of gum

"I'm not kidding. You should have left me there."

"And that's exactly what scares me. If you had lived any kind of normal life, you would never say something like that. Promise me you'll give this place a decent shot. This foster mother is the complete opposite of Mrs. Ruby. She isn't a hugger, which should make you very happy, but she is a fair caregiver. You love to work for your keep and she needs all the help she can get, so you two should be as thick as thieves. I think this will be a perfect fit for both of you."

"Maybe Juvee was more perfect for me." If I knew I was only going to spend one night at Juvenile Hall, I wouldn't have spent it reading the bible. Next time, if there is a next time, I won't make that mistake again.

"You don't belong there. You need to learn some social skills and that is the last place on earth to learn them."

"Social skills?"

"How to interact with groups of people, but you need to practice with one person. You are the furthest thing away from group ready."

"I don't need to interact with a bunch of people."

"Why not? You must get lonely . . ."

"I'm good. I've gotten comfy with lonely. I was home schooled on lonely."

"Juanita the first thing you need to learn is that the house you lived in wasn't a home. Homes are different. Real homes are filled with love and comfort, like the one you just ran away from."

A short grunt escapes from between my lips. I curl my arm around the two bags on the seat beside me and sit them on my lap. My whole life is in these bags yet there's nothing in them that matters to me. "Am I going to live close to the Ruby's farm?"

"No. Unless you think several miles away is close."

I wasn't sure what a few miles meant. That's what strangers told me when I missed the school bus, after I asked how far away my house was, but no matter what shortcut I took, it always ended up to be seven or eight miles.

"What are these other people like?"

"I think they will be the perfect fit for you. You'll have an older roommate. You are going to love Denise. If she can't draw you out of your shell, nobody can. She's a foster, two years older than you."

Stalked

The other end of the Goulds has no meadows. Every acre of land is littered with houses and the further we drive, the older and smaller they get. Two lectures later the car pulls into the parking lot of a convenience store.

Mrs. Lolita sighs, dangles the keys between her fingers, and nods towards the store. It's a small shed looking building with four steps. The open sign, in the big window, to the left of a metal door, seems to be switched off. The right side of the little shop is attached to a tiny two-story house. It has one basement window and seven stairs that lead to the upper floor. A rusty Coca Cola sign dangles from the railing, clanging against the post, announcing our arrival. The side of the steps are covered with cigarette posters. It's hard to tell which entry is the main door to the store because they're both splattered with signage.

Her mustard colored sleeve pulls the metal door ajar. She swings around, removes her glasses and laughs at nothing funny.

Her blue shoes clatter towards me. "Cold feet?"

"Pardon?"

"Well you can't live in my car so grab your things and come."

"I don't have any money to buy anything."

"We're not here to shop. This is it. Come inside and meet your new foster mother."

"But-but, this is a convenience store."

"Welcome to your new home."

"Your joking right? Who lives in a store? Are you sure we're at the right address? Is that a basement window? Will I be living in the basement?"

She pivots on the edge of her navy heel, cocks her head to the side, points to our right, and says, "Not in it. Beside it, or should I say above it? The house is bigger than it looks. And no, the basement is for storage. The living quarters are on the second floor."

A bell jingles when she opens the door. A very plump woman appears at the counter. A wide smile spreads across her round face. It's the first genuine smile I've seen, since I ran away from my foster home. She waddles out from behind the counter and extends her hand to me. I fumble with the bags.

She takes them both with one hooked finger and manages to give my hand a quick squeeze. She winks, "You must be Juanita."

I nod and force a smile.

"Juanita, this is Mrs. Chafe, your new foster mother."

I glance around the store, and back at Mrs. Chafe, four times before she stops scrutinizing me.

"She's a little shy," Mrs. Lolita's voice is softer than usual.

"Well, I have no doubt we'll soon change that," smiles Mrs. Chafe, "and don't you dare call me Mrs. Chafe. It makes me feel older than the hills. Call me Molly." Mrs. Chafe holds Ms. Lolita at arm's length. "It's good to see you. I was upstairs waiting. Thought you'd use the house door. Do you have time for a spot of tea?"

"I figured you would be in here serving customers." She glances out the window at the green car parked in front of the store. "I was surprised to find this place empty."

"Oh that belongs to Frankie, Denise's boyfriend. The battery or something is dead, so he left it here for the night, over a week ago." She tucks her dark stringy hair behind her ears and steps back behind the counter. "Mind your step. The stairs are steep."

I follow Ms. Lolita and Mrs. Chafe into a backroom behind the counter. Molly's tree stump ankles jiggle in front of me. Her legs look dry and scaly. Her shins are peppered with sores that look like infected spider bites.

At the top of the steps, we come face to face with a metal security door. She unlocks it and leads the way inside. "Have you ever had a roommate?" Mrs. Chafe asks. Before I can answer, she turns to Ms. Lolita. "Tea?"

"No Mrs. Chafe—"

"If I've told you once, I've told you a hundred times, Molly or Ma, never Mrs. Chafe." She pats Ms. Lolita's arm, "Was that a yes or no for tea?" She reaches above a counter, littered with labeled baby bottles, and hovers her hand above a stack of white porcelain cups.

"Thanks but I have to say no to tea. I have a dozen or more reports to complete. I swear I need another set of arms and hands." She glances at the boxes of diapers piled in the corner and says, "And to think I consider a stack of folders overwhelming—I don't know how you manage. Well I must run." She pats my head, sighs, and scurries towards the door.

Molly raises an eyebrow and calls, "DENISE!" in a high pitched falsetto.
"WHAT?"
"STOP YELLING BACK! BEFORE YOU WAKE THE BABIES."

A skinny, tall girl struts into the kitchen, grabs an envelope from the pile of unopened mail, and fans herself so vigorously that my hair moves.

"Ma, thanks a lot for waking them up."

"See what I have to put up with around here?" Molly winks.

The girl, tosses the envelope, but it misses its mark. "Do you know how long it took me to get them to sleep?" Her short black hair, clings to her damp forehead. Something about her face looks deformed, yet cute, in a strange sort of way. Her mouth looks a little sunken in, but when she smiles, I'm surprised to see she has a full set of teeth.

"Ms. Lolita, long time no see, lucky for me," she grins. Ms. Lolita walks away, with the back of her hand, above her head. Her goodbye wave is her car keys jingling between her fingers.

"Wait! Wait! Can you give Frankie a boost before you leave? I think his battery is dead."

"How many times do I have to tell you no? It's against government policy. Christmas is around the corner and if you haven't picked up a present for Frankie yet, I suggest you buy him, or his car, a battery."

"Yadda, yadda, yadda." The girl's lips twist into a scowl.

Molly waddles towards Ms. Lolita, and accompanies her to the upstairs door. I linger behind them.

"Hello? Where do you think you're going?" Denise yanks my arm, and jerks her head towards the other end of the hall. "Get your arse back in here. C'mon, I'll show you where you're sleeping. Is that your luggage?" She grabs my plastic bags with her right hand, flicks open the cupboard with her left, grabs a box of chocolate chip cookies, and bounces across the short blue shag carpet singing, "Wake up Maggie, I think I got somethin' ta say—"

"Aren't you going to say goodbye?" Molly calls from the porch.

"BYE!" Denise opens a door to our right and ducks inside.

Further down the hall babies are crying, and behind me Molly is motioning for me to join her. She turns away for a minute, looks back and motions again. Two steps later, a hand grabs my hair and gives it a slight yank. "Go and I'll lock you out." I stand in the doorway, speechless. "Get your ass in here before Mrs. Lolita smells the smoke." Denise pulls me inside and slams the door shut. Her cheeks cave inward. Wisps of smoke drifts from her nostrils. "Want one? They're Menthol."

"I don't smoke."

"Molly does, on the side. She hides her cigarettes here, see?" She pulls out a drawer with a few red and white boxes on the left and some blue and white cartons to the right.

She picks up a blue and white box, "I don't know how she can smoke this shit! Tastes like dead farts."

She sits on the bed and pats the twin one across from her, "Sit," she orders and adds, "for Christ's sake, stop acting like a girl scout." She pulls a handful of cookies from the bag. "But they do sell good cookies. Want one? I crave chocolate when I'm on the rag but I guess it's better than being knocked up."

I sit on the edge of the bed holding my bags against my chest. She doesn't seem to need any oxygen. She chatters a mile a minute. Finally, she takes a breath. A very small breath. "Hey, Frankie and I are hitting the Hayloft. They're having a live band. Want to come?"

"What do you mean?" I ask.

"What the fuck do you think I mean? Want to come means I'm inviting you. You're not mental or anything are you? I mean you look normal, but I have a cousin, and she looks normal, except she's all messed up. Got dropped on the head when she was a baby. I think the old woman did it on purpose to get more money from welfare. She's in jail now. Had sex with a seventeen-year-old. Anyhow, I look like shit. I'm taking a nap before I get ready to go, so stop fucking talking to me."

My only experience with roommates was with the ones I met the first time I ran away from home, and this one is the complete polar opposite. I sit quietly on the edge of the bed and take in my new surroundings. This room is the complete opposite of the bedroom I had, back on the farm. It's a mess. And it smells worse than cow shit—like something died in here. Our beds are about two feet apart and it's obvious she was using mine as a wardrobe closet. Posters of the ugliest man I've ever seen, are taped to every wall in the room. His mouth is huge. It could easily hold a grapefruit.

He makes Denise look pretty. Her mouth is hung half open and her snoring sounds like a car running out of gas. Her cigarette is hanging loosely between her yellow stained fingers. I reach ahead, to slip the cigarette from her hand but an inch of gray ash falls to the floor. The dresser is full of lipstick caps, and scattered earrings, but not one ashtray anywhere. I shake an open soda. No fizz. It's half-empty. I toss the cigarette in and listen to it sputter, while the molten stench crawls from the can. The scent of burnt tobacco is coming from everywhere in the room, but largely from the clothes on my bed. I push her dirty laundry, to the foot of the mattress, and pull my top over my nose.

Lying on my side, I carefully size up Denise. She's a head taller than me, and almost as skinny as I am. Although she's sleeping like a log, she mumbles and twitches in her sleep. Is she always highly erratic, or is it merely her period that's making her act like a nut case?

Ms. Lolita is undoubtedly out of her mind to think this would be a perfect fit. Why would she place me in such a bizarre environment? And what in the world was she thinking, when she told me , I was going to love this musty-smelling, volatile human?

Armed with an Iron

The bed shakes violently. I bolt awake. For a few confused seconds, I don't know where I am.

"Get up. We have to get ready. I need you to put rollers in the back of my hair." Denise is bouncing up and down on the edge of the bed. "Hurry I forgot to set the alarm. Come on and help me."

At the end of the hall is a small bathroom with an aqua colored tub and a matching sink. "Can you believe the size of this tub? A midget could hardly fit in here," Denise complains. "Here. Stick these in my hair."

"How?"

Denise's jaw drops, "Tell me you are fucking joking. Are you serious? You don't know how to use rollers? Where have you been all your life? In a cave?"

"I've never used them."

"Look," she takes a comb with a pointy end and parts her hair in several sections. "See you make a rectangle like this, and roll it like this, then you clip it like this. Fuck it! I'll do it myself."

Molly pokes her head in the door, "Stop swearing in this house. You know what the first word out of the babies' mouths is going to be."

"Yes, I do. It's going to be shit or shitty diapers."

I cringe and wait for Molly to smack her in the head. Instead she laughs and shuts the door.

"Hello? Rollers? Use the big ones."

Denise is smearing a film of white paste on her face. If she were fat, she'd look exactly like a younger Aunt Patty.

"How many rollers do you want in the back?"

"Why? I just showed you how I wanted it done. Do however many it takes."

"Well if I do it the way you showed me you don't have enough rollers. I'll be one short."

"What did you do, count the hairs on my head?"

"No, but it's about eight inches of scalp and you only have three big rollers. Besides most of your hair is too short for the big ones. Want me to alternate? Use a skinny one first?"

"Christ I need a smoke. That's what clips are for—"

"Oh. You want me to clip two skinny ones together!"

"Yeah, but do it at the bottom in case it comes out weird."

With her help I manage to get most of the strands wound and clipped. She twists around on the toilet, examines the results and smiles at her reflection. That's when I realize how tiny her mouth is. It's the shortest I've ever seen. Not even two inches long.

"What are you going to do with your hair? You need more highlights."

"I don't highlight my hair."

"No? Well today is a good time to start. I do my own all the time. Sit." She stands and points to the toilet.

I sit, jump up, and try not to gag. "What's that putrid smell?"

"I don't smell anything."

I lift the lid. The toilet bowl is filled with dark brown fluid and a ton of toilet paper. My hand is two inches from the handle when I hear, "No! Molly will kill you if you flood this floor. We're right above her store."

"Someone forgot to flush."

"No. Someone didn't feel like rinsing out a diaper. You rinse them in the toilet twice, wring 'em out, and soak them in that bucket." Denise yanks back the plastic shower curtain, and reveals a bucket full of soiled diapers.

"After the shit falls off we toss them in there, to scrub them"

"I'm not ever doing that."

"Oh yes you will. Wait an' see."

Denise pulls a large jug from under the sink. "Sit on the toilet."

I pick up the toilet bowl brush and dip it under the diaper.

"What the fuck do you think you're doing? Put it down. I'll show you how that's done after. Now sit."

"No. I'm not sitting on the toilet with that in it."

"Well I don't know what you do, on whatever planet you're from, but here on earth, we put the lid down unless we're having a shit. Get over here. I need to wet your hair first, so put your head in the sink." She grabs a handful of my hair and says, "You've got too much hair. It's too thick." She nods at the tub. "Get under that facet." She grabs the toilet brush from me and flings it in the bathtub. It lands in the pail of soiled diapers.

"I'll take the sink, thanks."

"Fine have it your way, but you've got way too much hair—oh what the hell, I'll improvise." She fills the sink, unscrews the lid from the jug, pours a bit into the water, dips the comb in the mixture, and stirs it. Half a blink later, she yanks the comb down the right side of my head.

I jump away. "But that's Clorox. I can smell it."

"Unless you want orange hair I suggest you trust me and let me finish." I bolt out of the door. "Trust me it'll be fine. I do it all the time. If you don't come back it'll go orange on one side of your head and probably break off. Come back and let me rinse it."

"If you turn my hair orange, I swear to God, I'll kill you."

"Sit down and shut up or it will be."

I slam the toilet lid shut, sit down and close my eyes. Instantly I envision clumps of hair falling to the floor. I break out in a sweat. I tell myself Denise is not Irma and shake off the memory.

"You're not one of those epileptics, are you?"

"I'm nervous."

Seconds later she says, "I'm done." My eyes dart open. Denise is bent over the bath tub with the faucet on full blast. "I said we're done. Hurry! Duck your head under the tap."

"No way. That tub is filthy."

"Get your head under this tap right now, or I'll pour that bucket over it, shitty diapers and all."

I can tell by the glint in her eye, she is absolutely serious, and in that moment she reminds me of Irma, and dumping a bucket of smelly diapers over my head was exactly something she would do. I take a deep breath, plug my nose, and lean over the tub. She shoves my head lower below the tap and says, "Turn your—"

Water pours in my ears and her voice turns into a low gurgle. She wrenches my head left and right. I pull away and gulp for air.

She vigorously rubs the towel against my scalp, almost snapping my neck. "See? I told you! It turned out great. Look at yourself. Go on, look in the mirror."

I tilt my head from side to side. "I don't see any difference. Except it looks like a matted mess."

"That's because it's wet—I do. Wait 'til it dries."

"But my hair takes forever to dry."

"Well we don't have forever. We have to leave in an hour." She thrusts a wide tooth comb in my hair and leaves it dangling from a tangle.

"I need a brush."

"No. That shit is hard on your hair. Don't use a brush. It'll break it off. My hair used to be long—just like yours—until I started using a brush. Clorox is hard on your hair. Use the comb. I'll be back in a jiffy."

I'm getting through the last of the tangles when Denise returns with an ironing board and an iron. Maybe she's not a complete slob, after —oh yes she is—she's opening it up in the tub. Yuk.

"Here put your head on the ironing board." She gestures with the hot steaming iron.

"Hell no."

"It'll be fine. I've ironed my hair a hundred times."

My eyes widen. There's no way she could iron hair that short when I could hardly get it to wind around the rollers. "I prefer not."

"Fine! Then stay home or go out and catch pneumonia. See if I care."

"Where exactly are we going?"

"To a dance."

I have no clue what a dance is. And I can tell by the astonished look on her face that she's read my mind. She licks her index finger and taps it on the iron. The spit sizzles. Before I can back away, she grabs me by the neck and forces my head against the ironing board.

"By the time I iron all this hair, the dance will be over."

"I've never been to a dance, and I don't know how."

"Figured as much. What did ya do? Live your life under a rock?" She bends her head sideways, her dilated pupils drift from my head to my feet and rest on my eyes. "You're kidding right?"

I straighten up, rub my back and laugh.

"Care to share the joke?"

I laugh louder.

She shakes the iron at me. "What's so fucking funny?"

"You should see the look on your face."

"How can you not know how to dance? Get your head back on the ironing board. When I finish your hair, I'll teach you. It's easy."

"I'm okay with wet hair."

"Don't give me that look. It's not like I don't know what I'm doing. I used to have long hair up until two weeks ago but I cut it all off. Like it? Anyway, like I said, I ironed my hair all the time."

"What if you burn my head?"

"I won't. It's not like I've had a drink yet. Hurry up and put your ear back against the pad, I don't have all night."

Denise spends the next five minutes contorting my body into a pretzel, while the iron hisses within inches of my scalp. She pushes my head down, until my nose crunches into my belly button, while she tries to iron the underside hair, near the nape of my neck. "Now stand on the toilet and put your forehead down, like you're trying to stand on your head."

"Don't iron my hands"

"Then get them off the ironing board."

I expect the door to pop open and hear the clicking of a camera but it never happens.

"Are you done yet?"

"Do I look done to you."

"I don't know. All I can see is the bathroom counter, and, it's upside down."

"I'm done. Stand up and close your eyes." She propels me out and to my right. A door knob rattles. "You're not looking are you?"

"No."

Something creaks. "Good. Open your eyes and look in the mirror." I open one eye. She moves the ironing board, towards the door, she spins her finger and says, "Turn around . . . what do you think . . . not bad huh?"

I twist around and can't believe my eyes. "Oh my god!"

"Told you!"

"It looks so thick and rich and long! I love it."

"You know my cousin showed me how to do that before she went blind."

"Oh-h-h-h . . . uh . . . so sorry to hear that. How did she go blind?"

"Doing her hair with bleach. She had poor motor skills. You should see the burn scars on her face from the iron! But that was before she went blind. She still irons her hair and now that she can't see, she never burns herself. So, what kind of music do you like?"

Before I can respond, she says, "Fuck it. I'm the one showing you how to shake your ass, so I get to pick out the music."

For the next hour, she teaches me dance moves and I spend at least half of that time, laughing my face off.

"See? That's what hips were made for," Denise says, and bumps hers against mine. "Hurry, get dressed. Wear jeans."

I change into the outfit Adam bought me earlier this summer. Denise drools over my top and asks to borrow it.

I don't want to, but because she spent so much time helping me, I can't fathom saying no. I change the subject. "Where did you learn to dance?"

"From TV." She snaps her fingers, wiggles her butt, and gives me a smug smile. "You know you owe me. Just lend it to me once and we're even."

"Yours is really nice," I say. "I think it suits you better than this one would." I cross my arms protecting my top, as she tries to take it off me. The next thing I know I'm face down on the bed, smothering in her dirty laundry. I grab my bra through my top.

She tugs and grunts. "I know but I wore this one to the dance a couple of times now, please let go and let me have it. I look so-o-o good in burgundy and my black top will look sexy on you too. It'll bring out those highlights." She rolls away, peels off her top, and throws it at me.

"Only if we have time to wash it."

"Do I look like I have scabies? Wear it. It just came out of the wash."

I barely have it over my head when the doorknob rattles. Denise throws mine under her arm, fixes her bra, rushes to the door and flings it open. "Frankie!" She wraps her arms around his neck, sticks her tongue down his throat and winks at me over his shoulder.

I cough.

"Who's your friend? Dee?"

"Oh," Denise's lipstick smeared mouth grins and says, "This is a . . ."

"Hi, I'm Juanita."

"Juanita this is my fiancé, Frankie. Soon to be married, right baby?"

"Yep," Frankie smiles as he picks her up and swings her around. Her foot hits the ironing board, sends it flying, and the iron whips past my head and embeds into the wall.

"Holy shit!" Frankie drops Denise. Denise laughs. "Told you your muscles were getting bigger. Now move the dresser over to cover the hole and move the bed where the dresser is, quick, before Molly shows up."

I'm still sitting on the bed when he goes to move it. I jump over to Denise's, while he pulls my bed a few feet from the wall. He lifts the dresser over to the other wall and shoves it to the left of my bed. He's pushing my bed against the wall when Molly walks in the room.

"Everything okay in here?"

"Yep. Just dandy. Juanita and Dee wanted their beds further apart, sorry about the noise."

"Denise get a shirt on—Frankie when do you think you can move your car? Customers are starting to complain."

"I'll do it tomorrow Ma, I promise," Frankie kisses Molly on the cheek.

"If it's not gone tomorrow Frankie, I am going to have to get it towed somewhere."

"Ma, we'll be late for the dance, can't we talk about this later?" Denise pleads with a pout.

"How are you guys planning to get to Bay Bulls without a car? It's freezing out, and there's a wind warning."

Denise grins at Molly, sticks her thumb out, and jerks it up and down.

"You guys best be careful. Don't get in a car unless you know the driver."

"We gotta run, Ma." Denise smiles, "And don't be such a worry wart, between me and Frankie, we know everyone in the Goulds anyway."

"If the temperatures drop and we get black ice, don't hitch hike back home, find somewhere to stay in Bay Bulls okay?" Molly looks at me. "It's your job to keep her out of trouble."

As we head out the door Denise says, "Ma I am almost eighteen, I can look after myself. Go have a cup of tea and relax."

The icy wind reminds me of the years I spent in the back yard suffering from frost bite. A gust of snow hits my face, and for a minute I almost chicken out but the excitement of going to my first dance is too tempting.

Tons of cars go by but nobody picks us up. Frankie decides to lurk back in the shadows and let the two of us hitchhike. He thinks the odds of someone stopping will increase, but they don't.

"Juanita, you look like a retard, hitch hiking like that. They think your waving at them. Pull your hands out of your sleeves, and use your thumb."

My fingers are numb and white. Not because it's freezing, but because the blood won't circulate when it's cold. I tuck them back up my sleeves, pull my hood over my head and practice my dance moves. Frankie sprints from the bank, to give Denise a kiss, just as a yellow car approaches. Denise pushes him away and sticks out her thumb. The wind rips the hood from my head and my hair whips across my face. I hear the car pull over a few yards ahead.

"Hurry, hurry, we got a ride."

Frankie yanks the door open. The passenger leans against the dash, and pops her seat ahead.

"Oh there are three of you?" the driver says. "I only saw two. I don't have room for three unless one of you sits on the other's lap."

"I can stay home," I volunteer.

"Oh no you don't. You can sit on my lap." Denise shoves Frankie inside, sits beside him and yanks on my arm.

"It's okay, I don't need to go."

"Come on," Denise pulls me inside. "You're skinny as a twig, there's room on my lap. Can you believe someone finally stopped?"

"Actually, I can't," I say, as I squirm to find a spot where her knobby knees aren't digging into me. "It was awful nice of him."

Denise giggles, "Chances are, most people there will be too drunk to notice you can't dance. A bunch of people hide booze in their cars, so they can go outside and spike their soft drinks. Sometimes they sell it to people like us. Frankie, did I tell you she's never been to a dance before?"

I feel embarrassed that she's discussing my lack of dancing skills aloud but nobody seems to have heard anything. Frankie is trying to juggle having a conversation with the girl in front, with pacifying Denise who is getting more upset by the minute. Denise presses her lips against my ear. "That slut in the front seat is trying to make me jealous. I feel like popping her one."

I glance towards the front and say, "Ssshhh! If she hears you she'll have her boyfriend kick us out and we'll have to walk." The driver's eyes momentarily lock with mine. It's too dark to make out his features or eye color. Maybe I'm blocking his view. I lean my head against the window to try to stay out of his vision. Out of the corner of my eye, I see him adjust the mirror.

The front passenger pulls the mirror back towards her and snaps, "Leave it alone. I was using it to put on my lipstick." A coconut smell drifts into the back seat. I hate the smell of air fresheners. They remind me of my past. I block out the memories, close my eyes, and think about the dance, while the car slows, swerves to the right, and stops.

The female passenger is the first to get out. Maybe if she stopped locking eyes with Frankie, she would notice her boyfriend has his gaze riveted on me. "Denise, do I have anything wrong with my face?"

"Yes. You don't have enough makeup on." She laughs, grabs Frankie by the butt, and arm in arm, they saunter into the hall. I feel like a third wheel. I don't want to follow them around like a puppy but I don't want to be alone in such strange surroundings. I have no idea where to go or what to do, so I keep my distance, but stay close enough to keep them in sight.

Once a slow song plays, Denise and Frankie immediately head to the dance floor. Next, a fast song plays and Denise grabs my hand, drags me to the floor, and writhes like a snake. My movements are awkward and stiff, but after she points to a boy just shuffling his feet, and a girl who looks like she's having a seizure, I relax a little. Three songs later I'm in love with dancing. But when a slow song starts, it's obvious I'm here alone, without a date. Trying to look comfortable, turns out to be a waste of time. Everybody seems to be with somebody, except me.

Two hands cover my eyes. "Want to dance?"

I spin around. It's the security guard from the other night. The night I ran away and got caught on Signal Hill.

He takes my hand and pushes through the crowd until we are up front near the band. His smile fills a third of his face. Occasionally I smile back, but the majority of the time I study different people's dance moves. Some of them are keeping beat with the drummer, so I try mimicking them. I'm just getting the hang of it, when the song ends. As I turn to leave, he grabs my hand. "One more, okay?" That's when I notice Denise and Frankie standing a few feet away making faces and winking at me.

A slow song starts. "I'm sorry I can't do this. I'm sorry," I stammer.

"Why not? Are you here with someone?"

"Yes. I mean sort of. I am here with my roommate and her boyfriend."

"So what's the problem?"

"The problem is I can't dance."

"Yes you can I just danced with you."

"No I mean this kind of dance. I don't know how."

"You're not serious? You're joking right? All you do is hug and turn in circles, one step at a time."

I hang my head. I bet he thinks I'm the biggest moron he's ever met.

"Hey it's easy. Pretend your foot is glued to mine. Watch me." He steps from side to side. "That's it. Now keep your feet against mine."

Bad idea! I walk all over his shoes. "Sorry, I suck at this."

He holds me tighter, "Let's just go around in circles."

Half way through the song, a finger taps me between the shoulders. "Hey Frankie and I are heading outside, in case we get sidetracked we'll meet up at the end of the dance at the front door, okay?" she yells.

"Denise this is . . . this is . . ." What the heck is his name? Denise runs to catch up with Frankie just as the song grinds to an end.

He leans towards me, "My name is Gavin."

He lifts my hand to his mouth, kisses my wrist and walks me back to the spot where he found me. "I just dropped in to see who was here. I'm heading to work, got the graveyard shift, so I gotta run. Another time, okay?" His lips brush my forehead. I close my eyes, but when I open them he's already melted into the crowd.

Denise and Frankie must be still outside. I fight through the crowd to find the exit. A strong hand grips my wrist. A voice slurs, "Honey, if you got da money, I got da time." I dart back towards the dance floor and notice the restroom sign. After I move to the end of the line, for the fifth time, I spot Denise heading towards me but when she gets five feet closer, I realize it isn't her after all.

Inside the restroom cubicle, I leave my pants zipped up, sit on the toilet for five minutes, wash my hands at the sink, pretend to fix my hair, get back in line, and repeat the process. After several trips, I decide it's time for a change of plans. I venture out towards the dance floor but the hall is packed and I can't find Denise or Frankie.

Stalked

The third time I circle the dance floor, the band announces it's taking a fifteen-minute break. A huge lineup forms at the bathroom, and I join it, knowing it's going to buy me a half hour or more. While I'm in that lineup, a huge fight breaks out. Moments later the lights turn up, and the PA crackles. "We are shutting it down. You guys need to keep this alcohol free, or there won't be any more youth dances at this hall." The PA crackles and pops some more, while the crowd protests. After a second, more threatening warning, the crowd settles and slowly dissipates. Finally, I'm ushered out.

I stay near the entry watching others leave, worried Denise might be still inside, looking for me on the dance floor. I stretch my neck and scour the closest parts of the parking lot, and although everyone seems to have left the hall, Denise is nowhere in sight.

The step is slippery and one corner is covered in vomit. I slip, skid and land five feet away. I'm not the only one down for the count. Everyone is tripping or falling. Slowly, I rise up, and skid across the concrete walk to the gravel lot. Now I know what Molly meant by black ice. My feet are going where they should, or are they? Where the heck did we park? A steady stream of cars, edge out of the parking lot, onto the main road. Someone is peeing, in the bushes to my left. The last time I heard that sound was when I slept in the graveyard. But at least this time I'm not alone, and this place has outside lighting. Two boys are sitting on the curb, and a third is on his knees, throwing up.

Someone calls, "Hey baby, wanna a ride?"

My eyes are glued to my feet. I pretend I don't hear or see them. I jerk my head up, look at the stream of cars, and wave frantically to some invisible person, in the far distance. My breath is shallow and my chest hurts. The parking lot is almost empty. My prayers are sprinkled with panic. "Dear God, get me out of here. Now. Please."

A murky shadow walks towards me. As it approaches, a familiar voice says, "Juanita Rose? Is that you? Juanita?" I don't recognize the boy's voice but he knows my name, so that means he's safe. I wave at the short shadow, thinking, whoever you are, I love you. The moonlight shines and dances across the dull wrinkled skin of the biggest pest, I thought I'd never want

19

to see again. "Hey Juanita. It's me, Paul Smith. Remember me? I'm the guy you sat with on the bus ride to your Aunt Minnie's. How is she?"

"I don't know. I don't have an Aunt Minnie. I made her up."

"Ha! I knew there was no Minnie Smith in the Goulds."

"Well I was desperate, and it was a better choice than the truth."

"What was the truth?"

My mind yells, Seriously Paul, do we have to do this now? Yet I know I have to come clean if I want a ride back to my foster home.

"The truth was I ran away from home? Satisfied? God, you have to be the most persistent person I've ever met!"

"Thank you. I'll take that as a compliment. Anyhow, I lost my ride. Is there any chance I can get a lift with you, back to the Goulds?"

The Hayloft

The post office looks too bright to be closed. Paul runs towards the building and tugs at the door.

"Whoo-hoo it's unlocked. Come on. Hurry."

The wind forces the door from my hand, and slams against the side of the building. Paul wrestles it shut. In the corner, I kick my feet against the tiled wall. My toes are numb, but not as numb as my fingers. The outside entry of this small post office is worse than a freezer. I push and pull on a door that leads to a larger room, but the door won't bulge. I rub my hands together trying to warm them up.

"What the hell is wrong with your fingers, they're a light yellow, that's not freaking normal. You got jaundice or something?"

"No. Nothing's wrong. It's normal."

"No it's not."

"Yes it is. It's normal for me. I got frostbitten, a lot, as a kid."

"A lot? How does someone get frostbite even once? It's not like you guys couldn't afford to pay the electric."

"It's a long story," I sigh.

"Well I got all night unless you have somewhere to hurry off to," he chuckles.

"That's not funny," I shake my head at his sick joke. "Oh, and you can add horribly prying to your most annoying character traits." The last thing I want to talk about is my past and I find myself doing exactly what I did on that bus ride to the Goulds—I try to ignore him. "Actually I do have somewhere to go. I'm going to sleep."

In the far corner, I curl up against a cold, concrete floor.

An approaching car, jerks me to my feet. Paul pulls me down. "What did you do that for? I could have waved. You should have tried to catch their eye. We could have gotten a run." Through the window, I watch the white car swerve left, then right.

"Go on I dare you to chase it. You could probably catch it if you ran fast enough."

"You're a jerk!"

"So are you," grinned Paul, "but like it or not you're stuck with me. Keep close to the floor. At this time of night, the only people on the road, are thieves, perverts, and drunks."

I retreat to my corner and curl into a ball. A finger taps my back. "So tell me about your dad."

I roll over. Paul is sitting with his back against the concrete wall. He looks even uglier under the bright light. "Do you ever give up? You have to be the most persistent nuisance I have ever known, and no, I'm not telling you about anything."

Paul pulls a Swiss army knife from of his back pocket. My heart jumps as he opens it up. He flips out a blade and picks at his fingernails. "If anyone sees us and tries to attack us and I don't win, you use this to defend yourself, okay?" The knife reminds me of Gordon. He always carried a knife. Hurt and anger wrestle inside of my chest.

"That bad huh?"

My chin trembles.

He wipes the blade on his jeans and lays it on the floor beside me. "I don't know how anyone can sleep on cold concrete but if you can, go for it. I'll keep watch."

Paul scoots towards the front corner, and says, "I can look outside and listen at the same time, so start talking, whenever you're ready."

I don't want to talk about Dad or Irma, and I don't want to talk about me, but I do want to talk to someone about Gordon. By the time I finish, the tears break loose. "I feel so angry. I'm so mad at the world."

"Why didn't they send him to a foster home?"

"Because they have this stupid law about children under twelve. They prefer to send them back home. Even if it kills them."

"I've never found it worthwhile to get angry about the law."

"I'm mostly angry at him. Why couldn't he wait? If he hadn't committed suicide, he could have made it to thirteen, or maybe even fourteen, like I did, and then it would have been a different outcome."

Paul looks back and motions for me to sit beside him. I crawl closer, crouch against the wall, take a deep breath, and tell him all about Mr. and Mrs. Ruby, the Westvale Farm, and the boy that tried to rape me. I normally didn't share secrets and I wasn't sure why I was telling him any of these things, other than the fact I was scared, and I needed to stop thinking about Gordon.

His eyes glaze over. "You got off lucky. My girlfriend was raped for real and we're still trying to work through it." He pounds one fist into the palm of his other hand. "It's really tough on her . . . and me too. I have to be careful how I touch her hand, or how we talk. We never speak about it, but it's there between us. She's extremely distant, she doesn't want to interact with people, and she constantly tries to sabotage us. She made me go to the dance tonight, and threatened to break up with me if I didn't. She's hoping I'll meet someone else—hoping I'll ask for the ring back . . . how messed up is that?" He talks about her a little more, but after a deep sigh he stops.

I open my mouth but can't find any right words to say. She sounds pretty broken and some things he said, sounded like he was describing me. Maybe

Ms. Lolita is right. Maybe I do have more problems than I think, and maybe I could use some of that social counseling.

"I thought she was safe . . . I left her and my buddy out on the dance floor . . . then he just disappeared with her—raped her."

"You need better friends. Want to know why she wants you to go to the dance without her? She's punishing you. She wants to make sure you don't brush it aside because she can't. She wants you to revisit that night."

"Well I don't. I'd just as soon forget it ever happened. Thinking about it makes me insane with rage. Not at her, at him. He's in jail and hopefully he rots there, and gets what's coming to him, but if he doesn't, I guarantee you, when he comes out from behind those bars he will." The veins in his forehead bulge. A haze of hate hovers across his face.

"She won't discuss it with you, because she doesn't feel safe when you get like this. She thinks you're going to end up in jail and she'll be alone, so maybe she's trying to detach herself from you."

"How do you know this?"

"Because that's what I had to do with my father when I was a kid."

"You're still a kid."

"Not really. As a matter of fact, I never really got to be a kid. It's like I skipped that part of my life."

"So what could your father have done to stop you from detaching from him?"

"Nothing, but it's not the same."

"No tell me. You have no idea how much I love her. I'll try anything." His lips curl downward. "It's like Groundhog Day. Stuck reliving the past, and she's punishing me—every day, every night."

"Maybe she thinks you don't see her. Maybe she thinks she's not worthy. What if she's testing you to see if you want to choose the easy way out?" I take a deep breath and close my eyes. What could Dad have done to make me still trust him—still love him? The truth is nothing. Sometimes the damage is too great. Sometimes someone isn't worth loving. But I can't say that, so instead I ask, "Is she home all alone?"

"No she's got a great family. They have pretty well accepted me as their future son-in-law, but right now, they're doing what I'm doing. We just tiptoe around her. She started therapy three weeks ago and I think it's helping because she's stopped telling all of us, how much she hates us."

"I am so sorry Paul."

"It's okay. I love her unconditionally. She's my world. I just have to convince her, that when I look at her, I don't see damaged goods. The doctor said it was normal. Part of the healing process I guess."

"This might sound ridiculous, but hear me out, if the rapist was a young kid, mentally ill, who knew no better, would you hate him on the same level? Or would you hate him less?"

His veins pop out further than before. "This guy is not a mental case. He's a con artist. Smarter than you and I put together. So don't go there."

"I get that, but if you could think of him that way, then maybe you wouldn't get like this and you could actually have a conversation with her. A conversation she felt safe having. She needs to feel safe. Try it."

"What if I blow it?"

"Try again. Eventually you'll get good at it. You have to get past the anger, past the guilt, because it's not your fault or hers. You need to find the hurt parts, so you can heal them."

"How do you know all of this stuff?"

"It's what I tried to do with Irma. I thought she was the devil and other times I thought she was sick in the head, but either way I knew the blame didn't lie with me. I'd be really screwed up right now, if I had listened to her and believed everything was my fault."

"I wonder why all these horrible things happen to the nicer people. And the kicker is, it seems to happen to the ones who believe in God. If God, exists, why doesn't he do something? Like torture the rotten ones."

"Maybe it's a test of faith. If it was too easy, everyone would pass."

"You believe in God . . . and prayers . . . still?"

"I don't believe in much, but I do believe in that."

Paul shakes his head. "What religion are you."

"Does it matter?"

"To most people—yes."

"None of them. I don't believe in religions. The bible said pray alone in your closet. And I'm okay with that. I guess any religion is as good as the other, as long as they worship God and not a cow."

He laughs, "My girlfriend constantly refers to herself as a fat cow and I worship her, so what religion does that make me?" His voice fills with remorse, "It's not really funny actually. She gained weight after the rape, it's like she thinks it will make her unattractive to men."

"You wouldn't leave her just because she got fat would you?"

"Hell no! She can gain away. More to love."

"Paul, you have to forgive him."

"Why? Give me one good reason to forgive that piece of shit. I'll forgive him after he rots and dies in prison."

"Maybe he will. But forgiving doesn't mean you have to welcome him back into your life—or like him—no need to tell them they're forgiven. Forgiving is all about letting go."

"Nope. Not a good reason. Not happening."

"If you don't, it means he will always control you, her, and your relationship. I didn't forgive anyone because of God, I did it for me."

He turns over on his side. "How about I sleep on it?"

I spend the next hour shivering like a leaf. Paul rolls over, snores, and cuddles my arm. At first, I cringe but the louder he snores, the heavier my eyelids get, until my wakeful night ends.

"Wake up sleepy head."

I open my eyes. A wrinkled face is looming above mine. I stifle a scream.

"That ugly huh?" Paul grins, "Come on, it's getting light out. They salted the roads and traffic's started. It's safe to hitch a ride."

"What time is it?"

"Sixish," he yawns and pushes the door open.

The air is cold and brisk but there is no wind. I wonder if the police are out looking for me. What if they think I ran away again? For some strange reason I don't care. I pull my hood around my face and tie it tight.

A horn blares and toots as a blue sports car, going in the opposite direction, pulls over.

"There's my ride," Paul grins. "That fucker is eight hours late!"

The car drives away tooting his horn.

"Nice friend," I say.

"Oh he'll be back. He's just looking for a spot to turn around. He's my future brother-in-law. Live's here in Bay Bulls."

"Why didn't you go to his house last night?"

"And leave you alone? I sure as hell couldn't take you with me, not to mention it's five miles away."

The blue car slows and stops in the middle of the road. Paul scoots in beside the driver and pats the seat beside him.

"What's going on buddy?" I recognize the voice and cringe lower in my seat. "Who's your friend?"

"She's an old school mate. Where did you disappear to man? You left me high and dry."

"I take it you didn't spend the night at the house? Were you shacking up with her?" His voice sounds terse.

"No man. I spent the night sitting on an ice-cold floor at the post office scared shitless. She's a schoolmate. I couldn't leave her stranded with a bunch of leering drunks. Her friend abandoned her. Sound familiar?"

"I had to head out to work. I couldn't find you."

"I was probably taking a piss. I bet you didn't even check the bathroom."

"Sorry man. I didn't. Truth is, I ran into this girl and got distracted. Got to work fifteen minutes late and had my ass chewed but it was worth it."

"Who? Anybody I know?"

"No. Some chick named Juanita. I met her on Signal Hill."

Paul chuckles, "Wanna bet?" He shoves my head in Gavin's direction. It feels red hot. I twist and press my face against the window. Paul puts his two hands on each side of my head and laughs, "Look at him or I'll tear your head off."

I shake my head no. The vehicle lurches to a stop. It's a trick. I'm not falling for it. I keep my eyes glued to the window. Gavin's eyes appear out of nowhere. He taps on the window. I lower my head. I hear the door slam he laughs, "Don't worry I think I'm more embarrassed than you are."

"I doubt it," I mutter, and glance at him sideways.

Gavin grins, "I'm willing to bet your middle name is Trouble, and that's with a capitol T." I pull my hood further down on my forehead and yank Paul back against the seat, to block Gavin's view.

The drive feels like it's an hour long before Gavin slows down.

"Do I pull in here. Don't tell me this is the store? Yet, it's the only one that matches your description."

"Yep," I say. As soon as he parks, I jump out and slam the door. Paul reopens it, hops out and unzips his pants and attempts to fix his shirttail.

"Do you have to do that here? Now?" I groan and glance nervously towards the window.

"I sure hope you don't get in trouble because I'm tucking in my shirt. Do you want me to come in to explain what happened? Ma and I are relatives." Paul nudges me with his elbow. "A real aunt. One that isn't a figment of my imagination. And she trusts me, so I can vouch for you."

"Vouch for me?"

"Tell her what happened."

"Don't bother. I like Juvenile Hall." But Paul ignores me and strides past me, into the shop.

Molly is behind the counter. Paul jumps over it and gives her a hug and a kiss. "Well, well, well, look what the cat dragged in. I've not seen you in ages. How is Suzi doing Paul? And when is that big day going to happen?"

Molly is focused on Paul and acts like me being out for the night is something normal.

"Aww, I don't know Ma, sometimes she seems to improve, but other days it's like she's getting worse. I love her to death, but it's killing me."

"I know sweetie."

"Juanita, are you going to introduce me to your boyfriend?"

I flip a bucket upside down, and scoot towards the counter. "He's not my boyfriend. I don't have one. Apparently he's Paul's chauffeur."

Stalked

"Ma, this is Suzi's brother, Gavin. He was working the graveyard shift and just got off. Juanita spent the night because she didn't have a run home and the roads were treacherous. The only people on the road were the odd drunk so we waited for Gavin to get off work, and now we're here. She didn't know the phone number or address, and I had no clue you were her foster mother. Anyhow she's here now, safe and sound."

"Thank you Gavin. Juanita, we have one rule here regarding dances. If you get stranded, or anything bad happens, you have to call home. You should do what Denise did, after she first moved here. Tape Quarters to your tummy and write your phone number on your belly upside down. So after you say goodbye to your boyfriend, can you go upstairs, and go talk to Denise? She's been bawling like a baby ever since she got home last night."

"Honestly, he's not my boyfriend."

Gavin pulls me to my feet. "Come on girlfriend, plant me a kiss and say goodbye," Gavin grins and lurches towards me. He puckers up his lips and leans closer. I back away. A loud crash shakes the ceiling. Molly tilts her head upwards while Gavin grabs me by the shoulders.

"Fine then, I'll work on that. We can start by me picking you on Wednesday, at noon, for lunch." He plants one square on my lips.

I stand there with my mouth hung open. He bows and waltzes towards the door. "See you Wednesday."

Molly tilts her head towards the ceiling and cocks one eye at me. "That girl is going to be the death of me. See if you can't console her."

I don't remember consoling anyone in my life. How do you console someone, especially someone like Denise? The closer I get, the more fake her cries sounds. I stand outside and listen.

"I fucking hate you-hoo-hoo-hoo."

I brace myself and turn the knob. It won't open. I try again. "Go away-hay-hay, I hate you! I hate everyone," she wails.

I slide down against the door, with my back to it and knock again, from my sitting position. Nothing. I'm exhausted. All I want to do is sleep, and by the sound of her wails, I'm certain out here is a much safer place to be.

Moments later the door jerks open and I'm halfway in the room, on my back, looking up at her scowl.

"What the fuck are you doing out there?" she screams. "Do you know how long I've been waiting for you to get home? Did you ever hear of knocking? That's what fucking knuckles are for." I'm about to tell her how many times I knocked but visions of her strangling me, keeps me quiet. "I just want to fucking KIIIILLLLLLL someone."

I scramble to my feet. Is it her period? Or is this her? How does anyone get this psycho? Unexpectedly she grows quiet. I cautiously move backwards into the room, until I'm past her. She has a photo frame pressed against her chest. She lifts it to her face, slobbers all over it, then hurls it against the wall. Her eyes are bulging out of her head and a look of sheer madness blankets her face. For a minute she transforms into Irma. I blink my eyes and shake my head. Now she's back to Denise. Shit maybe I'm the insane one. No, there's Irma's back again. It's that wild look—she has Irma's eyes.

"What the fuck is wrong with you? You look like you're staring at a ghost. Haven't you seen someone fucking cry before?" She throws her arms around me and sobs hysterically. My hand softly pats the back of my burgundy top. The shoulder part reeks of smoke tinged perfume. I should have stood my ground and not lent it to her. My eyes move past her into the room and my jaw drops. Over her shoulder, lies one hot mess. The room is trashed, destroyed. A hurricane could have gone through here and done less damage. Feathers float and dance above the bed, posters are ripped to shreds, and the dresser is face down on the floor.

"I hate this fucking world and everyone in it, and yes that means you, ESPECIALLY YOU!" She bites my shoulder.

The hair stands upright on the back of my neck. Suddenly I'm glad I spent the night in a postal freezer. Right now I would rather be there, fending off a drunk stranger, than be here with Denise. Her sobs elevate to anguished screams. She lifts her head towards the ceiling and yells, at the top of her lungs, "I just want to fucking die." She backs two feet away, and hisses something inaudible. Then it raises to a sinister whisper, "That's what I'll do. I'll kill myself. That will show them! Then they'll be fucking sorry."

That's when I realize I've been holding my breath. I slowly let it out and quickly gulp a mouthful of air. At least it's not anything to do with me. Maybe I should say something. Molly said to console her, but how can I if I don't know what's wrong with her. Did she get raped? Robbed? What?

"Denise, what the heck happened? What's going on?"

Her wild glassy eyes double in size. "I'm going to do it! I'm going to kill myself! And I'm going to leave a fucking note blaming every single one of them. I hope it ruins their lives as much as they've ruined mine."

Before she can put both feet back in to crazyville, I quickly ask, "Who?"

"Frankie and that slut. That's who. Jenny Chipney. That slut stole my Frankie." Denise crawls around on the floor looking for something. "Where is it? Do you see it?"

"See what?"

"My purse," her voice is muffled. The front half of her body is slithering under her bed. Shoes, books and all kinds of junk pellet across the floor and slam against the door. Something sways above the door. My eyes lift up. A bright red purse hangs on a hook.

"Are you looking for pills or a smoke?" My eyes are peeled on Denise's butt while I grope inside her purse for pills or anything else she can use to hurt herself. Under a makeup bag, my fingers find a crumpled cigarette package and a lighter. Denise's butt shimmies backwards from under the bed. I straighten out the bent cigarette, take a long deep draw, and buckle over hacking uncontrollably. "Here," I gag, "Denise here. Have a smoke."

She swirls on the floor, lifts her sopping wet face towards me and cries, "You found my purse!" Her face reminds me of the cover of a horror book—red eyes glowing with black tears dripping from them. Careful not to touch her outstretched snotty hand, I pass her the cigarette. "Smoke it. It might help you calm down."

She looks at it disgusted. "I want my fucking purse. Where is it?"

I glance up at the door. Her eyes follow mine. "You knew it was there all along didn't you?"

"Please Denise, don't do anything crazy."

"Don't you dare call me crazy," she says, jumps up and pulls her bag from the hook.

"Hell no. I didn't. I wouldn't. I said do, not you."

She dumps the entire contents on the carpet and kicks them with her foot. She looks back in the bag, turns it upside down and shakes the crap out of it. A few coins dance across the carpet. She collapses to the floor, "No pills. Now what the fuck am I supposed to do? Smoke myself to death?"

She glares at me expecting an answer.

My New Boyfriend

It's been a week since Frankie and Denise broke up and she's still driving me nuts. I've heard the story a dozen times but she tells it again.

"I don't get it. Everything was going really good. I shouldn't have gone outside for a smoke. And the nerve of him to dance with someone without asking me. She was all over him, I got pissed and tried to rip her hair—"

"Denise, you did what? Are you making that up or did you forget about it until now?"

"Oh, I can guarantee you she has a bald spot or two. But that's no reason for Frankie to call it quits with me, and leave with her. The thought of the two of them together makes me sick. I just want to die. If I was dying in the hospital do you think he'd come visit me and break up with her?"

"Denise what do you mean break up with her? How do you know they're even dating?"

"How do I know? Here's how, I phoned him a hundred fucking times since then. I even told him I was going to kill myself if he didn't come back and he just hung up and said, don't call back."

"If he cheated on you, would you really want him back?"

"Are you nuts? Do I look like I want him back? Of course I want him back. Why the fuck, do you think I'm acting so crazy?"

"Well I don't know much about reconciliations, but I do know if I was a guy I wouldn't want to be within a thousand feet of you right now." I grab the mirror and hold it in front of her nose, "look at you. What if Frankie changed his mind and came to see you. Would you want to kiss a face like that?"

Her makeup smudged face crinkles into a smile. Her hair looks like a wig she stole from a scarecrow.

"A face only a mother could love," she laughs.

"A blind mother," I grin.

"What would you do?"

"I don't know." I look around, "not this. And I certainly wouldn't beg, as a matter of fact, I would probably find someone else as quickly as I could, so I wouldn't be stupid enough to take him back."

"Yeah, your right. I should fuck his best friend."

"No, no, I mean just clean yourself up and find someone better to hang out with. Maybe after a while you won't want him back."

"We went to the dance every Friday night. What if he took her there, last night? Everyone will know he broke up with me. If we don't get back together today, will you go to the dance with me? In case he's there?"

"No. No way. You guys would probably kiss and make up and leave me stranded again."

"We didn't just leave you. I looked for you. So did Sidney."

"Who's Sidney?"

"Sidney is . . . was Jenny's boyfriend. He asked if you needed a ride home but I told him you had a date take you home. I thought you left with that security guard guy, you know, the one you were dancing with."

"I waited until a fight broke out. They shut everything down."

"A fight?"

"Yes a fight. Wait. Was that you?"

"Probably, who cares? Sidney and I left right after Frankie left. I was trying to catch them hitchhiking but they must have got a ride right away. Fuckers!" She punches the pillow, bolts upright, knocks me out of the way and dashes for the ringing phone. Before it reaches her ear, she yells, "Frankie?"

I watch her gnaw the paint off her fingernails as she listens. "That's so sweet of you." She sticks her tongue out at me and kicks some feathers with her foot.

"Like when? How about now? I want . . . Oh okay . . . that's sounds great." She hangs up the phone and hugs herself.

"Frankie?" I ask.

"No, it was Sidney. He said he felt bad for me and asked if I needed to go for a drive or go shopping or anything to call him. So he's picking me up in ten minutes."

"Where are you going?"

"I don't know, maybe I can get him to go spy on Frankie." She looks in the mirror, "This is going to take forever. Can you help?"

I start to tidy up the bedroom.

"I'm talking about putting my face on, not cleaning up. Help me pick out a top."

I glance around the room. In the bottom of the closet I see a brown sparkly sleeve. I tug on it. It's not a sleeve, it's a sock—no it's a tube top. I hand it to her thinking there is no way she's fitting into this. "I'll bet nobody will notice the rings around your eyes if you wear this. It'll blind them."

Denise scoffs. "I'm not going for a job interview. I want something with a low cut neck."

I wave the top in front of her face. "You can't get much lower than no neck. I doubt this will cover half of your boobs."

"Good point." She yanks it over her head. It catches on her shoulders. "Help me pull it down in back."

She squeezes her breasts together. "I plan to put these puppies to work. When I'm finished with Sidney, Frankie's head will spin."

Juanita Ray

She puckers into the mirror, arches her back, and asks, "How do I look?" She lights a cigarette, leans against the window, and smirks. "I'm going to ask him to drive me to Frankie's to pick up something I need."

"Like what?"

"I don't know . . . who cares what. The point is to pick up something— not everything. I want him to get jealous, and think I'm with someone else."

She hands me her cigarette, "I gotta go—he just pulled in. You can clean this up while I'm gone if you want."

I straighten the mattress and make my bed. She can clean up her own bloody mess. I am not doing it. I kick a lipstick across the floor. It lands near the door. I step over it and head down to the shop, and find Molly emptying a rack. She asks me if I have ever used a register and when she discovers I haven't, she shows me how it works. It doesn't take long to get the hang of it. She brings back an ice cream bucket filled with clear water, and a disinfectant cleaner, leaves and returns with an armload of canned corn.

"Do you want me to practice ringing these up?"

She shakes her head, places a cloth over the opening of the disinfectant, quickly tips it upside down and places it back on the counter. The top of the lid has a price of forty-five cents written with a marker. She rubs the cloth over the top of the lid until the price disappears. She picks up the marker and scrawls fifty cents on the lid then hands the cloth to me.

"Gas prices went up. As far as I am concerned, the truck delivered these today. If a customer comes in, hide the corn under the counter. People around here gossip, so keep the marker out of plain sight. If anyone asks why some cans have different prices tell them some of it is old stock and we're happy to sell it cheaper—so mark a few of those at sixty cents."

Just when I think I'm done she fills the counter with fruit cans and grins. "Good job. Do these next."

Even though I have to use three fingers to rub off the price, I seem to be faster than she is. Probably because I poured cleaner into the lid instead of turning the bottle upside down every few seconds.

I finally finish. "Anymore?"

"No, that's it. I have a few cases, unopened, in the back office, and more down in the storage basement, but this should pack my shelves to the brim. I always do a double order, when I hear gas prices are going up."

Stacks of repriced goods cover the entire counter. I grab an armload and follow Molly, but instead of stacking them, I pile them on the floor and head back to the counter to get more. Behind my back, the door jingles and a young man with weird frizzy hair stands rooted to the spot. I squirm, expecting him to look at something other than me—or at least ask a question but he doesn't. I shift to my left, behind a taller shelf and rearrange it. I peak between the cans waiting for him to move. He finally does. He leaves.

"What did he want?" asks Molly.

"Darned if I know. He just stood there like some sort of weirdo and then he left. Maybe he's drunk or on drugs."

The shelf, I restacked, looks half-empty. I notice all the other shelves are all poorly organized. Some are a real mess. Maybe there's a reason she has cans of fruit below the sanitary napkins and beans next to the toilet paper.

Molly grabs a bottle of window cleaner and heads outside. By the time she comes back inside the store, I am rearranging the ice cream. She reaches past me, grabs two, handing me one. "Want a job? I'll pay you to help out here, but I can't afford too much."

"That's okay. I can help for free. I've got nothing better to do when schools out. By the way, I made more room on your shelves. If you want me to unpack some more boxes, I can," I suggest.

"No. I think I'll wait. Gas prices could go up again. I have to go feed the babies. Think you can watch the store for a bit?"

I nibble on a hang nail. "What if something has no price?"

Molly pulls a book from underneath the counter. "Look it up or call me. No worries, you will be fine. This is my slow time."

Not a soul comes in. But she offers to pay me anyway. It feels wrong. It's me who should be paying to be here. "No. It's okay."

She grabs a jar from under the counter and sticks the bills inside. "Whenever you need a little money for a dance or to go out with friends take it from here. Anytime you help me out I'll slip a little into the jar, but if sales are slow, it won't be much."

"You don't have to pay me. I'd rather have a bag of chips. May I?"

"Of course. But here is how I handle that sort of thing." She flips to the pages towards the back of the book until she reaches a tab marked Dee. "See all you do is write the date here, how many here, the item down here and the price in this column. But don't do it on Dee's page." She flips to the very last page and writes JR on top of the page. "Write it here. I like to keep a tab for you girls. After school starts, you may not have any money in your jar so you can work off your tab, but if you abuse it, I will cut you off. Agreed?"

I nod.

"Tonight is Saturday and everyone goes to Wards on Saturday night so you may as well take a few dollars from the jar now."

"What's Wards?" I ask.

"It's a little hangout that sells fries and sodas. All kinds of kids your age hang out there. Come here." I follow her to the door and she points to the left. "Down there about half a mile, on the right." She slips the money into my pocket.

I ask, "Can I lie down first. I'm really tired. I didn't sleep well last night."

"Sweetie you can do whatever you want. I don't own you and it took me three years to learn trust works better than control."

I look at the chip rack. It's full of different choices, all new to me. Salt & Vinegar, Smokey Sticks and they even have ketchup flavors. I take the money from my pocket and put it on the counter along with the eleven bags of chips.

"I couldn't choose," I apologize.

She looks at me and grins. "You could use a few extra pounds. You are as skinny as a skeleton. Your last foster mother must have starved you to death."

"I gained a few pounds there. I was worse."

She purses her lips together and shakes her head. For a minute, her eyes soak me in, from head to toe. She tosses the money back into the jar and opens the book. "Go ahead and grab something decent from the fridge. I'll write it on your tab and the fridge is full of cans of soda, help yourself."

I sit on my bed, open every bag of chips, and taste one. I eat the Salt & Vinegar, the ones that look like toothpicks followed by the Cheese Balls. I put the rest on Denise's bed and flop onto my mattress licking my orange fingers. I roll over on my stomach and close my eyes.

Two legs straddle my hips. Two hands are shoving my shoulders into the mattress. I smell her before she says, "Well aren't you even going to ask?"

Denise climbs off me and flops down beside my shoulder.

"Okay, I'm asking you. What?"

"I'm going to make you guess?"

I rub at the orange drool stain on my pillow. "Guess what?"

"That's what you have to guess."

Fully awake I realize she's back from her date. "You're in love with what's-his-face—the guy who picked you up."

"No but close."

"You and Frankie made up?" I turn my head away to go back to sleep.

"Yes. Frankie and I are getting back together!"

"That's nice," I mumble.

"Didn't you hear what I said? Frankie and I are back together again!"

I try to sound more excited than I feel, "That's great. Now can I go back to sleep."

"You weren't asleep. I know you were faking it. Anyway, I have to tell you everything that happened. Get up."

I open one eye to see if she is serious.

"Get up!"

"Please I need to sleep just for a few more minutes."

"You can sleep tonight."

I roll over so my back is against her. The bed shuffles to the right. I'm flying over the edge of it and she is laughing hysterically. I stay there and pretend to snore. She tugs at my foot and threatens to use me, to sweep the floor.

"Fine. You win."

"Come on help me get rid of this mess while we talk."

I must be still asleep and dreaming because Denise never cleans up anything other than shitty diapers. She yaps and yaps, for two hours straight. She talks faster than normal about every single millisecond of her day.

". . . And, when we stopped at Wards to get some fries, Frankie was standing there and he saw us and waved. I think he thinks I was dating someone else already and when we drove away he stared at us jealous as hell."

I hold myself up with the broom while she hangs the last broken picture back on the wall.

She stares back.

"What?" She twirls her hair. "Are you going to answer me or just keep staring at me like I have ten heads?"

"I'm waiting for the part about you guys getting back together."

"I told you. Didn't you even listen?" She proceeds to tell me the whole thing again.

"Stop. Stop. Just start at the part where you drive into the parking lot at Wards."

"Sidney pulled into the parking lot. Frankie was standing with his back against the wall. He waved at us. Sidney backed out of the parking lot and we drove away while Frankie stared at us the entire time."

"What happened when you got out of the car to order the fries?"

"We didn't get out to order fries."

"Then why did you go there? Because you saw Frankie?"

"No. I didn't see Frankie until we were parked."

"So how did you guys get back together?"

"I told you at Wards."

"Denise do you do drugs?"

"Fuck no! Anyway I decided the best thing to do is not call him anymore."

"Who? That Sidney guy?"

40

"No Frankie. When he calls, tell him I don't want to talk to him."

"Why not?"

"Because he's a jerk."

"Denise, if you ever look for a job, you should try to get hired, on a commission basis, by a psychiatrist."

"What? Why?"

"You could make a bunch of money getting him some patients."

"What the fuck are you talking about?"

"You should get paid for driving people nuts, like you're doing to me right now. You say you're back together—he's a jerk—you're not talk—"

She slams her torn up pillow at my face. I pull some feathers from my nose. Her eyes squint into angry slits. "I'm pissed at him for not apologizing. Get it now?"

I know the safest thing to say is nothing.

"Well? Say something."

The phone rings. I nod at it. "It's probably Frankie."

Denise whispers, "You answer it."

"Hello?"

"Hi who's this?"

"Juanita, who's this?"

"Frankie's —"

"Hi Frankie." I grin at Denise and stick out my tongue.

Silence.

More silence.

"Are you going to say something? Or did you just call to breathe in my ear?" I ask.

More silence.

I hold the phone out to Denise. "It's for you."

She folds her arms and turns her back to me. "Not until he apologizes."

"He just did," I lie, "he said he was sorry and he is going to kill himself if you don't talk to him."

She grabs the phone from me. "Oh Frankie I forgive you. I love you. I'm sorry for not talking to you." Her eyes open wide. She shakes her fist at me, opens the closet door and shuts herself inside with the phone.

One minute later, she emerges from the closet. "You big liar, that wasn't Frankie."

"If it wasn't Frankie, who was it?"

"Frankie's friend Sidney. The guy I was with earlier." She gives me the middle finger. The phone rings again. She says, "Hi Sidney," forms her lips into a circle, mouths the word Frankie, darts back into the closet, and pulls the door shut.

Her voice starts out low, rises and lowers to inaudible. My ear is pressed against the door but anything but a muffled sound. It's hard to tell if she's laughing or crying. I sit back and watch the door, bracing myself for the worst. Five minutes I envision jamming a chair against the door knob, but instead I grab my jacket, planning to find this place called Wards and try their greasy chips.

"Hey Molly, how far away did you say Wards was?"

"Just a second, while I finish up with my customer." She turns and chats for a minute about the price of gas. A rustling over by the chip stand catches my attention and as soon as I see his frizzy hair, I know who it is, and bolt back upstairs.

The Guy with the Frizzy Hair

For several days, I keep to myself and avoid going into the store portion of the house. I pick up Denise's Harlequin Romance and flip to the bookmarked page. In the book, the girl is pouring a bubble bath. That's exactly what I need. I grab the pail of shitty diapers and put it under the sink. I lift the bottle of bleach from the tub. It triggers a memory. I pull the elastic band from my hair and wear it like a bracelet. I shake my hair loose and inspect it in the mirror. More highlights would look good. I twist the blue cap from the white jug of bleach and try to remember what portions Denise used. I water it down twice as much as she did and comb it through my dry hair. After I rinse it out, I wrap a towel around my head and plug in the iron.

Denise bursts through the door, looks at me, and laughs. "What are you doing ironing your hair when it's already straight? Anyway, a guy named Gavin is here. He's in the parking lot waiting."

I completely forgot about Gavin. "Is it Wednesday already?"

"No, it's still Saturday. Days here never fucking end." Denise sarcastically blows a bubble and cracks her gum. "Anyway you'll never believe what happened to—"

I rush out the door thinking, I'd rather take my chances with Gavin than listen to the world according to Denise. I pull my hair back into a ponytail and rush outside to find the car door ajar. Denise is running down the steps. "Hey wait."

I hop inside Gavin's car and say, "Hi, how are you, can we leave now? Please?"

Denise yanks the door open. "Sidney called and he wants to know if you and I want to go shopping?"

"What?"

"I thought you were back with Frankie?"

"I am, but Frankie's car is broken, and Sidney will take me and Frankie shopping, if you come along."

"What?"

"Are you fucking deaf?"

"No. Why do I need to go?"

"Sidney won't go unless a girl comes along."

"Tell him to get his own date the normal way, tell him she's got a boyfriend," Gavin says, "and shut the door. It's frigging cold."

"Is that true? He's your boyfriend."

"Yes," says Gavin.

Denise ignores Gavin and waits for my answer.

"I don't even know who this Sidney person is, or why he would want me to come."

"He never asked for you specifically, he just said he can't take Frankie and me shopping without a date because if he runs into Jenny, she'll think he's single and try to get back with him and getting back with her is the last thing he wants. So is this guy really your boyfriend?"

"For the last time, yes." Gavin voice sounds frustrated.

"I want to hear it from her, shit head."

"Look who's calling who shit head, you're the one who needs to clean the shit out of her ears."

"Please stop arguing. If he says he's my boyfriend, he is."

Denise slams the door and gives Gavin the finger. "Go fuck yourself rent-a-cop."

"Well," laughs Gavin as he rolls up his window, "that's what I call love at first sight. Too bad, I'm taken." He glances at me and adds, "Seems like it's official, we're an item . . . sweet."

"You do realize I only said yes to get rid of her."

"I know, but you can't simply retract something like that, so let's go to lunch and plan our next date."

————

It's deep into the fall, and I'm still dating Gavin. When his shift allows it, he drives me to school and at times meets me for lunch. Five days ago, on Thanksgiving, he asked me to go steady. I said yes assuming that's what we had been doing all this time anyway.

For once, some of the girls in school seem to admire me. They think I'm cool because I date a nineteen-year-old hockey player who drives a sports car and works full time. I'm not flattered. I couldn't care less about what kind of car he has because I know exactly what they would think of me if it broke down and I had to take the bus—which I do—most lunch times.

It's Friday, and Gavin is here to take me to lunch. He's sitting on the fender flirting with a few girls. I wave but he doesn't see me.

A city bus pulls towards the bench I'm sitting on. The door swooshes open and I think, why not another tour today?

I flash my government pass at the driver and lean back in the front seat.

"Going full circle again, Juanita?"

I wait for the sound of hissing air to stop, lean my head against the window and say, "It seems to be my new routine."

The bus smells like window cleaner and diesel fuel. The seat across from me has a wad of pink gum stuck to it. From the window above it I notice several different colored storefronts. Maybe I'll check them out. That should make him wait an hour for nothing. It serves him right for being such a flirt.

The driver pulls to the curb, and says, "Hmmm, not going back to school? Early day? Or are we playing hooky?"

"Something like that," I say.

Several suits, tons of shoes, racks of perfume bottles, and bookcases filled with books, leads to a window display of one single giant white tooth. Maybe I should get my teeth checked. I pull out my government health card and slip it under the glass partition. A set of polka dot nails picks it up.

"Do you accept this here?"

"Sure do," she says.

"First visit?"

"Yes."

"Fill this out," she slides me a clipboard with a questionnaire attached.

I glance at the questions. "Why does a dentist need to know if anyone has had prostate cancer?" I ask.

She bats her eyes at me. "You gonna fill out the form or not?"

"Not," I slide the clipboard back towards her.

"Good, then goodbye."

"I need my teeth checked."

She shoves the clipboard back at me and chants, "If you want your teeth checked, you have to fill out this form."

"Fine can I borrow a pen?"

"It's in front of you," she points to a fake flower.

I take the flower and tick no to everything. Half of the questions are none of their business and I don't read the other half.

She slips a card under the window.

"What's this?"

"It's your appointment for next Wednesday, he's fully booked today."

I take the card, slip it in my pocket, and leave the empty waiting room. The next bus, back to school, is a ten-minute wait. By the time I get there, the bell is ringing and a frantic looking Gavin is pacing back and forth across the parking lot.

Stalked

He reaches his arm in the window and blows the horn at me.

I walk towards him wondering why he's still here. "Where the hell were you?" He opens the door for me. "I waited here all afternoon."

"At the dentist."

"You could have told me. Warn me next time, okay?" He bends over in the seat and kisses me, "Missed you."

I reach into my pocket and flash the card in his face. "I have to go back Wednesday. You've been warned."

I think about him flirting with the girls, "Gavin, maybe we should start dating other people."

"Was the dentist that cute?"

"No I never saw the dentist."

"But you said you w—"

"I just did the paperwork."

"Oh." He nods, "Who drove you? That guy, the one Denise wanted you to date?"

"No. What are you talking about?"

"On our first date, that day I picked you up for lunch, that guy."

"Of course not. She hasn't mentioned him since, besides I don't even know what he looks like other than he has a pale face, an afro and drives an ugly yellow car."

"Really? So you're only with me for my car?"

"Gotta a bus pass, can travel."

"You're funny. That's one of the reasons I'm with you, I love your laugh, I love your teeth, I love your hair and I love you."

"What about when I lose my teeth, my hair, my mind and all I can do is laugh?" I grin trying to make a toothless face.

He pulls me towards him and kisses me long and hard. "I doubt you'll ever lose those lips. Where to?"

"How about home. I don't feel like detention today."

After we pull into the store parking lot, he cups my chin in his hand and murmurs, "About seeing other people, get it out of your head. I am not interested in dating anyone else. Do you get me?" His hold on my chin tightens. I push Gavin away and say, "Molly just waved me in. She must need me—I have to go."

I leave Gavin grumbling to himself and find Molly waiting for me. She jingles a set of keys in her hands and points to the pair of twins sitting in the back seat of her car. "Need help with the twins?"

"No, with the shop. Can you take over? I have to bring the babies in for their shots before the clinic closes. I should only be an hour at the most."

Three hours later, I've sold eight packs of cigarettes, twelve cases of beer, and still have a continuous flow of customers when Molly returns.

Her face is flushed. "Sorry it took longer than I thought. Just give me five more minutes to change their diapers and put them in their cribs."

"Take your time I can handle it."

An hour later, my stomach is grumbling and I have to pee. *What is taking Molly so long?*

The line is long, and the third customer from the end is the guy with the frizzy hair. Uncomfortable prickles shoot through my arms, straight to my brain. His eyes shift to and from my face. My first instinct is to run upstairs, like I normally do when he comes in, but I can't leave with other customers in line. What if they leave without paying? Every single customer, except him, is holding a case of beer and half of them looked like they'd love to get them for free.

I lean towards the stairs and yell, "Molly I need a hand," chew on my lip, and continue serving the line. I chew harder. He's next. Suddenly he leaves the line, grabs a bag of chips and gets back at the end of the line. I'm relieved, but when he does it again and grabs a second bag, I'm paranoid. Stop it. Maybe he has OCD.

For some strange reason he manages to get in front of the counter, without doing it a third time. He asks for a specific brand of cigarettes. A name I've never heard before.

"I'm sorry, I can't find that brand." I look past his shoulder and apologize to the next customer. "I'll be with you in just a second."

"Take your time. I can wait." He turns to the only customer behind him and says, "Go ahead. You can go first."

Stalked

The twenty-dollar bill shakes as I shove it in the cash register. The change I hand him falls to the floor. The frizzy headed guy bends down, picks it up and hands it to him.

"Thanks buddy," he says, and heads out the door with his beer.

He asks for a brand of cigarettes I'm not familiar with.

"May I?" he asks.

"May you what?"

"May I come around the counter and point out the cigarettes?"

"I'll get Molly. She knows where everything is. MOLLY."

He ignores me, moves around the counter, excuses himself, picks out the package and quickly returns to his spot.

A ten-dollar bill is sitting on the counter, staring at me. Molly's breath is panting behind me. "Is everything okay? I can take over if you want."

From the upper landing I hear her yell, "Is the ten ours or his?"

I open the upper door and crash inside, slam it shut, and lean my back against it. Denise and Frankie are holding hands, gobbling up each other's eyes. Without breaking her gaze, she says, "We're going to Wards, want to come?"

"I have homework."

"It's Friday night, do it later. You have to try the chips dressing and gravy, it's out of this world."

Chips dressing and gravy doesn't sound that great. "Do they serve anything else?"

"Yeah. Chips without dressing and gravy, but they're not as good."

We walk about half a mile or so down the road and I smell the place before I see it. "Hmmm," Frankie's nostrils flare open. The line wraps around the entire building and out onto the sidewalk.

Everyone's breath, looks as if they're smoking. I try to blow circles into the air and wave away the steam while, Frankie and Denise suck face. The last time I blew circles like this is when I was seven years old, talking to Irma's dead husband. Back when I thought he was going to save me from her.

When it's my turn to order I forgo the dressing and gravy, pay for them and wait. The girl brings a cardboard bowl of globs of what looks like breadcrumbs from a stuffed turkey, smothered in gravy. I stare at it. She stares at me.

"NEXT!"

I take my chips and go over to Denise and Frankie. I dig around to try to find a fry without the dressing but it's impossible. I get back in the lineup to order some plain fries and taste one while I am waiting, by the time I reach the order window, I am licking the bowl ordering another round. I love them.

"Denise these are great. I'm having this for dinner every night."

"Why can't you be like that?" Frankie asks Denise.

"Like what?"

"A cheap date?"

"Who the fuck, do you think you're talking to? Are you cheating on me or what? You must be, because it sure isn't your money we spend here."

"What the hell are you talking about?" Frankie looks bewildered.

"I'm a cheap fucking date? Idiot, I'm the one paying."

She takes my plate of fries and throws them in his face. "Come on Juanita. Let's get the fuck out of here."

"Denise! Denise. I'm sorry. I didn't mean it like that. It was a joke—we have three pizza nights a week. I love you. Come back!"

Denise raises her two arms above her head, wiggling her middle fingers at Frankie and hisses at me, "If you dare turn around and look at him I'll kill you. I want him to know he's a piece of shit and I don't want him to think we are talking about him."

"Well we are," I say.

"No we are not," she says. "And I don't get how I can love that prick so much, when he drives me so fucking nuts!"

When we reach the shop, she is still muttering about Frankie. Rocks crunch as a car pulls up and honks at us. It's that yellow car that belongs to Frankie's friend.

Stalked

The windows are tinted but as the door opens I can hear Frankie say, "Dee come on. Sidney is taking us for a spin. Please Dee."

She makes him beg for another five minutes, then drops my arm and jumps into the backseat beside him. "Come on Juanita. Come for a ride with us."

"No thanks, have fun!" I say without looking back.

I hurry inside the store and mutter under my breath, "They're like hamsters. All they do is the same thing over and over again. The last thing I want to do all night is listen to them breakup, kiss and make up."

"Who are you talking to?" Molly smiles from behind the register.

I smile back. She looks tired. "I can take over," I offer.

"No need. I'm good, go enjoy yourself, it's Friday night."

I go to my room and hop into bed. Finally, peace and quiet. I forgot what it was. I fall asleep thinking, quiet sounds so good.

I wake up to a pillow being slammed in my face. It's not the first time and won't be the last, so I pretend to sleep while I wait for the second blow, grab the pillow and slam her back.

"What the fuck?" she looks at me shocked. "Why would you hit me like that you jerk? You should thank me for saving you from wasting a beautiful morning. Get up."

I gasp at her astonished. "Me? You think I'm the one being a jerk? How does this feel?" I ask, as I thrash her again.

Denise grabs a cushion from the chair and fights back.

"Not fair, that thing is hard as a rock," I wrestle her for the cushion.

Knock, knock, knock. We both sit up out of breath. Molly looks at the floating feathers. "I swear the two of you are worse than three year olds. Dee, Sidney is at the door for you, but do not think you are stepping one foot outside of this house. You're not going anywhere without cleaning up this mess first."

I am in the bathroom brushing my teeth when Denise bursts through the door.

"Don't you ever knock?" I ask as I rinse my toothbrush off. "I could have been on the toilet."

"Next time lock the door. Anyway Sidney wants to bring his ex-girlfriend back her stuff but he wants you to come too."

"No. He's too strange."

"Actually he is a nice guy, he's been driving us around and even helped Frankie get his car to the shop. Come on, Juanita, Frankie and I are going too. Please come, I need you to do this one thing for me. It's the last favor. I promise."

I rinse my mouth and spit into the sink. "Why do I need to go anywhere with him?"

"Because he's my friend too. Please Juanita, please, he won't go unless you come."

"I said no. I don't know the guy and I want to keep it that way."

"Fuck you!" She slams the door.

I'm back in the bedroom, combing my hair when Denise appears in the doorway with her arms folded, tapping her foot. "Are you going to stand in front of that thing all day or what?"

I move away from the mirror and wait for her to use it. "Go ahead. Take your turn."

"I didn't come back to use the mirror. I came back to get you." She sits on the bed, "Hurry up. Come on."

"Denise I already told you I'm not going so don't bother waiting."

"Please, please, please," she gets on her knees and grasp her hands together. "I'm begging you. For me—just this once."

"Denise, stop begging. It's not going to help . . . I'm not going."

"Why not?"

"Because I don't want to. It doesn't make any sense. It seems like you're trying to set me up with him, or something."

"I'm not. You don't understand. This is so important to me. He is going back to give his girlfriend her things. Don't you get it?"

I stare at Denise wondering if it was she, not her cousin, who was dropped on her head as a baby. "Do you even have a cousin?" I ask.

"What the fuck has my cousin got to do with this?"

"I don't know. How much do I have to do with this?"

"You have everything to do with this. He won't go unless you come. He's afraid she'll try to get back with him and he doesn't want her back. If she sees he has a girl with him, he thinks she won't try. If the front seat is empty he's scared she'll just jump in beside him. So that's why we need you."

"You want me to pretend to be his girlfriend? No. Not on your life. Are you out of your mind? Forget it!" I dig my fists into my hips. "If he's stupid enough to take her back, after she cheated on him, that's his problem, not yours. Why don't you sit in the front seat with him?"

"What do you think I am? Stupid?"

"No. I didn't insinuate you were stupid."

"Yes you fucking did. You called me fucking stupid."

"Denise. What the heck is wrong with you? Are you on your period?"

"What exactly is that supposed to mean?"

"You're acting weird. I mean it doesn't make sense why you would want to go. What if she doesn't try getting Sidney back? What if she tries getting Frankie back instead?"

"Wait . . . You don't suppose that little slut would try to get my Frankie back do you? I swear to God if she so much as looks at him. I will kill her. I'll rip her fucking head off."

I sigh, "Maybe you should just let him go alone? Have you even thought of that?"

"No," she sneers, "how the hell is she going to see that Frankie picked me over her. I want to shove it in her face. I want her to see that we got back together. Fuck her."

"Well I'm not going. Sorry. Ask someone else, ask Molly."

"Right like that's going to make her jealous."

"Why do you want to make her jealous?"

"Pay back is a bitch."

"Denise, did it ever enter your mind that instead of being jealous of you being back with Frankie, she might get jealous of me being with Sidney?"

"That's the whole idea."

"What if she goes savage and beats the crap out of me?"

I watch Denise howl, "That would be hilarious."

I leave to hide in the bathroom. I almost have the door shut when she pushes against it. We are fighting for the door when Molly appears and says, "What the heck is wrong with both of you lately? We must be coming into a full moon."

"She wants me to go for a ride with some stranger and act like his girlfriend and she won't take no for an answer."

"Ma, Sidney is bringing Jenny back her things and he just wants Juanita to sit in the front seat and that's it. She does not have to act like anything. It's just in case Jenny tries to get him back. He just wants to pretend he has a new girlfriend. He just wants to make sure she won't jump in the car and try to make out with him or anything. Frankie's will be there with us and I can't pretend to be Sidney's girlfriend because I want Jenny to see me and Frankie are back together and he loves me not her."

"Juanita you should go. What harm can it do?"

"Denise and I could get the crap beat out of us." I grin.

"Ma, see what I mean she thinks it's a joke."

"I don't. I can't. Truth is, I'm nervous as heck. I don't even know him. It's not like the world is going to end unless I go."

"I told Frankie I wouldn't marry him until he proved to her, in front of me, that we were back together and this is our only chance to do it. Ma, Juanita is afraid of Sidney and you know he wouldn't hurt a fly. Tell her."

Molly nods her head and says, "She's right."

My eyes scan the room. Where is it? Where did Denise use the phone last? I don't care if I have to walk five miles to a payphone but I'm calling Mrs. Lolita and getting the hell out of this madhouse.

Molly throws a concerned look my way. "I don't know this Jenny but Sidney is a really nice guy and he comes from a very upstanding family. The only thing wrong with him is he is too quiet— shy—like you. I think you should go. After all you do have to live with Denise."

I glare at Denise, "If I do it, this once, you'll never ask me to do anything like this again, right?"

"I promise. Cross my heart. I will never ask you to do anything again. Hurry let's go."

Molly pats my back and gently pushes me down the hall. "This might be exactly what you need."

Then it dawns on me. Maybe Molly is Denise's cousin. An older cousin. Yep, her hair looks ironed.

"Why are you staring at my hair."

"Because it's so straight. Anyway can I go back to my room? He's probably gone by now."

Molly nods.

Denise entwines her arm around mine. "No he's not. When I told him you weren't dressed yet, he said to tell you to take your time he had all day. However, I don't, so hurry up. You look fine. Let's go."

"I need to finish combing my hair." I purposely take ten more minutes to comb my hair, while scouting for the phone. My arm is cramping by the time I agree to leave.

"When are you and Frankie getting married?" I ask Denise as we walk towards the car.

"I don't know, soon why?"

"Nothing."

She stops dead in her tracks and asks, "Why?"

"Because you should do it soon, before Frankie changes his mind."

"Soon like before we bring her things back? Wouldn't that be fucking funny if we showed up with me wearing a wedding dress."

She climbs in the car. I hesitate. "Don't be shy. Get in," Denise leans out and yanks at my pocket. I half topple into the seat. She reaches past me and yanks the door shut. "Let's go, Sidney." She crawls over the seat to join Frankie in the back.

I don't look at the driver at all. I just look out the window, huddle down low, and focus on nothing, like I did most days, back when I lived on Torbay Road, and bused it to school.

"Well you could at least say hi," Denise chimes from the back seat.

Over my dead body. I stare harder, at the drops on the window.

Juanita Ray

"Hi Juanita, thank you for coming."

I glance over at his frizzy hair. He's more nervous than I am.

Denise taps his shoulder. "Is it okay if I smoke in her?"

"No I don't smoke."

My heart drops to the seat. Why would a non-smoker wait half an hour to buy cigarettes?

He backs up, shifts the gear to drive and hits the gas.

How bad would I get hurt if I jumped from the car?

I look at his speedometer. He's doing fifty.

His Ex-Girlfriend

A house, built into the side of a cliff, isn't something I've ever seen before. I sit huddled against the door, contemplating rolling down the cliff, until I crank my head and see the drop.

Denise is smacking her lips together. This is the fourth time she's redone her lips. Why put on fresh lipstick just to kiss it off?

"Frankie, don't you dare wipe that off. I want her to know we are kissing. As a matter of fact, if she comes over to the car, I want you to start necking with me."

She takes another look in the mirror and applies more lipstick. She leans ahead and shoves me towards Sidney, but I resist and hang onto the door. "You two look like arch enemies not sweethearts. You guys, need to sit closer together, Jenny is not that stupid."

I don't bulge.

"I'm serious Sidney. Did you and Jenny sit like that when you dated?"

"No, but it's okay," Sidney drives up the road and parks in a different driveway.

"It's not okay, unless you want her back."

"Heck no. The last thing I want, is her."

"Juanita you have to move closer, before she comes out."

"Denise, you sit up here and I'll sit back with Frankie."

"No way. The whole point of us coming was to show her Frankie and I are back together. Ssshhh! She's coming."

A dark haired girl stands on her porch smiling and waving like crazy.

"Looks like she's waiting for you Sidney," Frankie says.

"She can wait all she wants, I am not stepping one foot outside of this car," says Sidney.

"Can't she see you have a girl in the car?"

"No the windows are tinted," Sidney says.

"Juanita, I hate to ask you this but could you just sit a little closer just so she can see you when I open my window?" Sidney looks desperate, his fingers are tapping against the steering wheel.

I shift to the center of the front seat. "Do I have to say anything? What if she starts yelling at me?" I ask.

"Pretend to be asleep, just put your head on his shoulder and pretend you're asleep," Denise suggests.

As she taps on the window I put my head on his shoulder and close my eyes. His arm around reaches across my back. Is hand cradles my shoulder. Denise whispers, "There, now it's believable." I try to keep a calm face as I resist the urge to wrap my hands around Denise's neck and choke her.

Denise and Frankie moan and groan from the back seat.

"Denise, Frankie hand me that bag, please." Sidney twists towards me, then back to the window, without taking his arm from around my shoulders. "Here these are the things you asked for including some things you didn't, like everything you ever bought me."

Jenny starts crying, "I don't really want my stuff back. I just want you back. Denise forgave Frankie, so you should forgive me."

"That's because Frankie loves me."

Jenny steps back from the window, "Why did you bring Denise here?"

"We're on a double date," Sidney grins.

"WHAT?" Her voice rises. "Please, please, I'm sorry. I'll never do something so stupid again."

"It's too late I've met someone else."

"I don't believe you. You're too shy. There's no way you're dating someone else. Not this soon."

"Well I am and she is right here. Look for yourself."

I slink down. Jenny sticks her head into the car.

"I don't believe you, she looks scared to death. There is no way she's dating you." The more she leans into the car, the more Sidney leans my way. "Are you really his date?"

She smells like coconuts. My mind drifts back to the night we were hitch hiking to the dance. That smell drifting from the front seat wasn't from an air freshener, it was her. Sidney must be the same guy who picked us up when we were hitch hiking to that dance. Now this all makes more sense.

"Yes," I lie.

"Prove it! Kiss him."

Sidney bends his face towards me and kisses me quickly on the cheek. "Satisfied?"

Jenny laughs, "What a joke."

Suddenly I feel Sidney's mouth come crushing down on top of mine. Just as I am about to suffocate he stops, turns away and in a quiet voice asks, "Satisfied now?"

Jenny's gasp isn't as loud as the sound of her hand slapping Sidney's face. "I didn't want you back anyway. Unlike other people, I don't take sloppy seconds."

Denise hurtles into the front.

Sidney backs out of the driveway and screeches down the road.

"Let me out. I want to rip her face off."

"Denise stop. I love you baby. Stop. She's just jealous. You wanted to make her jealous and you did exactly that. Please baby, stop."

Denise rolls down the window and yells. "Now how does it feel to have someone steal your boyfriend? Fuck you, bitch!"

Frankie says, "Settle down sweetie. Keep your cool."

"Relax Denise. She made that comment to Juanita and I. She's insinuating Juanita is getting sloppy seconds and that I would be sloppy seconds if she took me back."

Denise crawls back to be with Frankie and I scoot across the seat and huddle next to the passenger door. I hear the lock click. I jump nervously.

"I'm sorry I didn't mean to scare you, it's just your pressed so hard against that door I'm afraid you might fall out," Sidney says.

The silence sounds awkward.

After five minutes he breaks it. "Thank you for doing this for me, I know it must have been hard for you."

Ten more minutes of awkward silence goes by.

"Do you like music? I have a pretty decent collection. Is there anything you want to hear?"

I say, "No thanks, I'm fine."

"For fuck sake. I can't take any more of this!" Denise grabs me and shoves me over by Sidney. "You two know you want to be together so just fucking get over your shyness. Juanita don't dare move an inch, or I'll sit in your seat for the rest of the trip, and push you against him with my two feet."

Everyone laughs.

"Is anyone in a hurry to get home?" Sidney asks.

"No. How about a milkshake to celebrate good riddance of rubbish," says Frankie.

Denise giggles.

<hr />

For the next several weeks, I see Sidney every second day, when he drops into the store to buy cigarettes. At first, the greetings we exchange are more forced and polite. But eventually the smiles become more genuine.

"You smoke more, than she does." Denise flicks my arm. I hand him his change and Denise walks him out. When she returns, she says, "How he acts around you, is different than he acts around me."

"What do you mean?"

"He's really shy with you—almost acts weird, but that's not who he really is once you get to know him. I think he's obsessed with you and you need to put the poor guy out of his misery. If you break up with Gavin and start dating Sidney, you'll be doing both of you a big favor."

"Have you forgotten I don't plan to break up with Gavin?"

"You should. He's getting way too possessive. Even Frankie doesn't show up every single day. The day we got back from milkshakes, I thought he was going to take a crowbar to Sidney's windshield, or maybe even his face. Guys who play hockey can be brutal."

I laugh. Not at what she said, but the memory it triggered of my nine-year-old brother beating the priest with his hockey stick.

"Laugh all you want." She snorts, flips me off and leaves.

———————

I sink back against the vinyl blue seat and think about what Denise said yesterday. I know she's right. Lately I've been taking earlier and longer lunch breaks to make sure I skip both Geography and Gavin. Today is one of those extended lunch days. My lunch started at eleven and I'm riding the downtown bus on a window shopping trip. Why do people cram like sardines at exit doors? I hold my nose and rush through a black cloud of nauseating fumes. Christmas displays entice me inside several stores. My goal is to find a decent present for Gavin. I find nothing, which sucks, because Christmas is only one week away. I pass by a teenager about my age. She smiles at me, exposing her silver braces.

The dentist! I forgot about the dentist!

I race down the street towards the dentist office. Lucky for me they had a cancellation. For once, I don't have to wait.

I drool on my paper bib and listen to the drill drone away.

"I think that about does it. We have filled every molar in your mouth," the dentist smiles. "You're the only person I know who loves coming here."

"I don't love it," I grin. "I'll do anything to skip Geography."

"I'd say you've skipped more than just Geography," he laughs. "By the way, when is the last time you've see your family doctor?"

"I don't have one. Why?"

"Because I suspect you have a calcium deficiency. You need to get treated."

"What happens if I don't go?"

"Tooth loss and an easier chance of breaking bones."

"I started drinking milk a couple of months ago, when I lived on a farm."

"When you see your doctor tell him I said you need to see a nutritionist."

"More time off school. Maybe I can drop math too," I laugh.

"I'm serious," he says as I dash out the door.

After another hour of hunting through a few more shops, I give up, board the city bus, and return to school. I get back as the school bus finishes boarding its passengers. I scramble to catch it, banging on the side. I panic and scream stop.

And it does. The brake lights flash.

Why didn't this ever happen when my life depended on it? I can't count the times I ran into the street racing for a missed bus. If I could have screamed this loud back then, I might have saved myself more than a dozen beatings.

The doors roll open. I forgot the bus would be early. Forgot that school was closing for the Christmas holidays.

I stretch my numb mouth and make a few weird faces trying to wake up my jaws.

I hear people giggling, look around and see most of them are laughing, at me.

I imagine how funny I must have looked and crack up. Ironically, everyone else stops laughing and turns away. Obviously, we are not laughing at the same things.

The first people I see, when I get off the bus, are Denise, Frankie and Sidney.

"Juanita, hop in we're going shopping."

"But I've been shopping."

"Did you buy anything?"

"No-o-o."

"Were you looking for something to buy?"

"Yes-s-s."

"Then hop in."

I'm in shock. That has to be the longest conversation, Sidney and I have ever had. Every day since the day we went to Jenny's house, Denise has invited me along to go somewhere with the three of them and I always say no, but today, because I'm in the Christmas spirit, I say yes. I want to buy Molly something for Christmas and I still haven't anything for Gavin so this is perfect timing.

Sidney looks better looking than normal. I'm trying to figure out what it is when Denise says, "I love your haircut. It suits your face so much better. Aren't you glad you listened to me?"

Sidney smiles at me. "I should thank you too. Denise told me you said white men look lousy in afros and you were right."

I turn and glare at Denise. "I said no such thing. But for the record the haircut does make you look better."

"See." Denise smirks. "Told you so!"

Sidney is wearing a red sweater and dress pants. A black leather jacket is on the seat beside him.

"Sorry if it's too hot, but if I turn down the heat, the windshield fogs up."

"He's not sorry, he's trying to get Juanita to take off her coat, so he can check out her boobs," laughs Denise.

Everyone except Denise is quiet. Her constant chatter lasts for the entire trip. We finally arrive at the mall and split into pairs. Frankie and Sidney head to the lower level while we girls stay put.

"Well?" Denise murmurs.

"Well what?"

"Well admit it you like him, don't you?"

"Like who?"

"Sidney."

"Of course I like him, he's a nice guy, why?"

"See? Told you he was a really nice person. If I weren't in love with Frankie, I would date him. Are you going to buy him anything for Christmas?"

I pause at the perfume display. How does anyone make a choice? After I sniff at the first three bottles, all the rest smell the same. "For Sidney? No. Why should I. I am looking for something for Gavin though. Sidney always smells nice. What cologne does he wear?"

"I know exactly what cologne he wears. Frankie asked him earlier, weren't you listening?"

"I guess not. So tell me because I like it. I think I'll buy some for Gavin."

"It's Old Spice."

"Say what?"

"Old Spice."

"I heard what you s—"

Denise interrupts me, "Why the fuck, do you do that?"

"Do what?"

"Say what?" she mimics me, "Why do you say, that, and then make me repeat myself for nothing? It drives me fucking insane."

I look at Denise's eyes bulging out of her head and laugh, "You look insane. People probably think you are. You even have a little drool going on."

"Fuck you!"

"Why do you swear so much?"

Denise shrugs. "Bad habits are hard to break. I don't swear much, do I?"

"You swear worse than a truck driver."

"Frankie is a truck driver. He never swears much at all. As a matter of fact, I don't swear that much either."

"Say what?"

Denise reaches towards my throat and pretends to choke me.

"Say what means I heard you but I can't believe what you are saying. Get it? It's short for say that again because I don't believe what I just heard." I smile at the clerk, point to the bottle of Old Spice and pay a little extra to get it gift wrapped while Denise slips outside for a smoke. I smell Denise before I see her.

"Denise, I think the smell of smoke clings to perfume more than cologne. You should start wearing Old Spice or switch to the brand of cigarettes Sidney buys. They smell better. He doesn't smell like smoke at all."

Denise splits her sides laughing. Her mascara is running down her face. "His cigarettes smell better? How the hell would you know?" She laughs even harder.

"What's so funny? Mind sharing the joke?"

"Smells better—HAHAHAHAHA. Oh my god, I've got to pee so bad."

"Mind sharing the joke?" Frankie kisses Denise's forehead.

I can smell Sidney lurking behind me. I twist around and ask, "Sidney what brand of cigarettes do you smoke?"

"I don't smoke." His hazel eyes look deep into mine.

"But you come into the store every day and buy a pack. I've seen you come back later the same night and buy a second pack."

"They're for my sister."

"Oh."

Denise howls.

Sidney looks nervous.

She is laughing so loud people are staring at us.

"Come on Frankie. Let's go to the sex shop and find your nutty girlfriend a strait jacket."

Frankie hesitates.

I shrug. "You can stay here and watch her pee herself, or shop with me."

Denise, bent in half, with her legs crossed tight, waves for us to go away.

I'm not much help to Frankie when it comes to shopping for a gift for Denise. We look at clothes but neither of us knows her size. We look at perfume and both agree she has too much of that already. We look in a chocolate store but Frankie says he wants to keep her skinny.

"Let's go in here."

I look up at the sign, Big Toys for Adult Girls & Boys.

"Forget it Frankie I'm not going into a sex shop with you. I was joking about that."

"Come on. Don't be so square. You're worse than Sidney. And, you know he has a crush on you right?"

"No he doesn't."

"Oh yes he does. Come in with me and I'll tell you everything I know."

"Forget it." I turn my back to him. In front of me is a jewelry store.

"Frankie, I know the perfect gift for you to buy Denise."

"What?" Frankie sounds excited.

"An engagement ring!"

"A what?"

"An engagement ring. You know the thing a girl wears on her finger after you ask her to marry you?"

"Like shit."

"Say what?"

"Denise doesn't need a ring I already asked her to marry me and she already said yes. Besides I don't have enough money. I put most of it into my car."

"You should do it. It's the one gift she will never expect. She'll be shocked. See that sign, it says in-house credit."

"Credit? Me get credit?"

I drag Frankie into the store. He fills out a credit application and waits. The clerk hands him the approved amount. It's double the amount he asked for.

"I could buy a good used car for this."

I pinch his ear. "It's only good for this jewelry store."

The more we look at rings, the more excited he gets. "Wait, I don't know her size."

He holds my hand in his and strokes my fingers. "Perfect. You have the same size fingers as Denise's." He turns towards the clerk, "This is my fiancée's roommate and I think her hand is the same size but . . . but what if I'm wrong?"

"That's easy," says the clerk. "We can pick a half size or a size bigger and then at least we know it will fit her. If it ends up wrong, we can resize it for free."

"I think Denise will love this one. Try it on," Frankie urges.

"It's really loose I say."

"That's perfect," says the clerk, "you're a size six and this is a size seven, better too big than too small. Most girls rather wrap string around it for a few days, rather than get one they can't wear at all."

"Can she try it on one more time?" Frankie is beaming from ear to ear. "Yep, it's perfect. She's gonna love it." He swings me around and plants a kiss on my lips. "Thank you, and thank you again for suggesting this. I can't believe I'm getting hitched." Then, he backs away, and whispers, "Oh-no."

Gavin is outside the window. He fires me a hateful look, and stalk away.

The Wrong Mr. Right

I am glum all the way home. So is Denise. She thinks Frankie didn't find her a Christmas present especially when she checked all his pockets and found nothing but his wallet. She even counted his money and found he had not spent a cent. It was smart of Frankie to hide the box in his sock. I mean who checks a person's ankle anyway?

Sidney was extremely quiet and seemed preoccupied. Denise stops pouting for a second and says, "Why don't you guys go back to the mall and shop some more and then come back and pick us up for a date."

"That's a great idea," agrees Sidney. "I'll make sure Frankie finds you something nice."

I can't tell Denise that Gavin thinks Frankie bought me an engagement ring or it will ruin her surprise. Maybe I should stop Gavin from coming around for a while in case he ruins it. I'm scared to death he'll say he saw Frankie kissing me. She'll hate me worse than Jenny. If he talks, I won't be able to explain anything to either of them. I just need to keep them apart until after Christmas.

Stalked

By the time Frankie gets back he and Sidney are both beaming. We decide to go to a movie and watch a comedy romance. It's so funny we have to watch it twice to catch up on the parts we miss by laughing so much. Second time around, it is even funnier. For a while, I forget about Gavin and actually have a little fun.

At home, stripped down to our underwear, we sit on our beds surrounded by gifts we both purchased earlier. I wrap them and toss them to Denise to tag them. I wrap the silver and red striped paper around the cologne set and toss her the package.

She dangles the tag by its tiny red string. "Gavin or Sidney?"

I shrug.

She twists the tag back and forth and squeaks, "Sidney, Sidney. I want to be a Sidney tag."

"I can't decide. Let's leave that one for now. I'm going to sleep on it."

"Good idea." Denise yawns and hits the light switch above her bed.

Three nights later, I'm still tossing and turning, torn between the choice of who to stop seeing. Gavin is more special because I dated him first, but Sidney is so nice and verbal, about his feelings for me, that I know I'll break his heart if I reject him now.

"I . . . I can't make up my mind. I like them both equally, I don't know what to do," I look towards Denise's bed waiting for something enlightening to come out of her mouth.

Finally, she bolts upright, switches on the lamp and says, "I've got it! There are three things in the box give one of them cologne, and the other one the underarm deodorant and aftershave."

"But which one do I give two things two?"

"Fuck! Give me the underarm deodorant and I'll give it to Frankie as a stocking stuffer."

"Are you supposed to give guys a stocking too?"

"There's no way you're that naive. Every foster home I've been in celebrates Christmas and that's because they match us up according to religion. So why play so dumb? Or were your parents Jehovah Witness?"

69

"My first foster was this summer. Mom died right after I turned four. She only lived for three Christmases. Dad stopped celebrating them."

"I'm sorry. I just thought you were in one most of your life . . . like me, I'm surprised your father gave you up at fourteen, or that they took you in."

"He gave me up years ago. So they made me a crown ward."

She sighs, "I'm only a foster."

"What's the difference?"

"The government owns you, but they don't own me. My legal guardian isn't them." She smiles the smallest smile I've ever seen. I want to ask her why her mouth didn't grow with the rest of her body, but I don't. Yet I can't stop staring at it. She cracks her gum and adds, "I'd go with your heart, pick the one I liked best, give him all three things and stop seeing the other guy."

If only it were that simple. Two nights ago, Sidney's goodnight hugs turned into can't wait to see you tomorrow kisses and each time I see him he grows on me more and now he's even with Gavin. "I'm not ready to choose who to say goodbye to."

"Sidney tries to hang around you all the time, Gavin doesn't, but you should drop them both and give Frankie the gifts."

"Are you out of your mind? I haven't seen Gavin all week because he's working overtime. Be fair and help me choose for real, and I'll give you a good hint about the Christmas present Frankie bought you."

"You're a liar and you'll lie about that too."

The last time I was called a liar was over beet juice, and the first time was when Dad didn't believe me about Irma. For once in my life I get to stand up for myself. The words feel good. "How am I a liar?"

"You're lying to yourself about how much you like Sidney. Anyone blind could see it."

"I'll will tell you two hints the first hint is the name of the store we were in. If you help me, I'll tell you it."

"I am helping you. Stop seeing both of them and pick the one you miss the most."

"Stop seeing Sidney and Gavin both?"

Stalked

"Exactly. I don't get why it's such a tough decision. You're afraid of Sidney and Gavin never calls, so no loss. Now tell me the name of the shop."

I feel like shaking her. She was supposed to help me pick one.

"Well Frankie said, let's go in here, and I looked up at the sign and it said Big Toys for Adult Girls & Boys."

"No shit?"

"Truth. That's what the sign said."

"So what did he buy me? A dildo?"

"I don't know I didn't go in with him, honest."

"You waited outside?"

"I told you, I didn't go in. What did you get Frankie?"

"I bought him an engraved lighter."

"For what? Frankie doesn't smoke."

"I know, but he carries a cheap lighter around with him all the time to light my cigarettes, and he deserves something nicer." She bites her nails and studies my face. "So when are you going to break the news to them?"

"Not yet. Maybe I'll date both of them for a while more," I say.

"Juanita you can't do that. You have to pick one." She jumps out of bed and grabs the phone. "Call Gavin first, seeing he was your boyfriend before Sidney. What's his number? I have a few words for the jerk."

"Why are you calling him a jerk?"

"Tell me his number."

"I don't know it."

"Stop lying." She laughs, "I'll get it from 411."

"Hang up the phone. I know who I'm picking."

"You do? Which one?"

"I choose Gavin."

"To break up with?"

I shake my head no.

"Are you serious? Are you sure? I mean Sidney seems better."

I should tell her about her present. Just tell her the truth about why Gavin dropped me. But, I can't ruin her surprise or break my promise.

71

Part of me is glad Gavin misinterpreted everything. I had a nightmare the other night of Gavin telling Denise that Frankie got engaged to me, and her tying a rope around my neck, dragging me across the floor. This fixes that. Besides, after Christmas she'll hear the whole story. But first I need to tell Gavin, so he'll keep quiet.

"I'll call Sidney for you."

"No. Don't."

Before I can stop her she is saying, "Sidney, Juanita is too much of a chicken shit to tell you herself so I will. She doesn't want to see you again."

I bury my head under the blankets and cover my ears. This isn't fair. It's her fault. All of this is all over a stupid Christmas present.

My mind is swirling with thoughts. Confused moments, smothered in regret, come and go for hours. They swirl in between the shadows flickering across the ceiling. My nose feels like I have the flu and my heart is split in half. Close to dawn, I make a decision. I spend the day in bed, dwelling on it, and for once Denise leaves me alone because she's thinks I have the flu. By the end of the day I've made up my mind—I don't want to say goodbye to either of them—at least not yet—what if I make the wrong choice?

That night Molly taps on my door. "Gavin is waiting outside in the parking lot. Put on a coat, it's freezing out."

I still have on the same clothes I wore the day before. I don't bother combing my hair or looking in the mirror. I really don't care how I look. My coat is missing, and so is Denise but my idea and Molly's idea of freezing is a lot different, and I don't need the coat anyway.

I walk over to the car and slide in the passenger seat. "Hi, long time no see . . . you okay?"

"Hi," I say back. "Sort of."

"Look I—" we both say at the same time.

"You first," I say.

"See how much we're alike?" Gavin says. "Juanita, I told my Mom about you. She said to be sure to tell you how I feel and she wants to meet you. The day I saw you in the jewelry store, I wasn't following you. It was there because I was Christmas shopping. Seeing you with another guy shocked me. I love you. I want to marry you. If you don't feel the same way about me, I'll drive away and never bother you ever again."

I look at him shocked. "I'm sorry I had no idea. Married? I'm only fifteen. I haven't finished being a kid yet. I still don't know how to take care of me, never mind somebody else."

"That'll be my job. I'll take care of both of us."

He points to my left hand and asks, "Where's the ring?"

"It's supposed to be a Christmas present," I say. "A sur—"

"Juanita," Denise is sitting in the back seat of Sidney's yellow Camaro. Half of her body is sticking out of the window. Her hair is sprinkled with tiny particles of snow. "Get over here and hurry before the storm starts." My heart races as the yellow Camaro circles Gavin's car and pulls up beside us. The passenger door flies open. Frankie is sitting beside Denise who is grinning like a Cheshire Cat. Gavin's face flushes to a vivid red. His white knuckles grip the steering wheel.

"Gavin you have to go—I have to go," I mutter and jump out of the car. "I-I-I'm sorry."

"So am I." His voice sounds flat, defeated. A tear runs down his cheek. "Well, have a nice life, and I mean that."

He hits the gas, swerves past Sidney's front fender, barely missing it, and speeds out of sight.

Frankie glances at me, frowns, and pulls on Denise's outstretched hand. "Lovers quarrel?" Denise asks while she wraps her arms around Frankie's waist.

While they trade tongues, I use mine as a landing pad for fresh falling snowflakes.

"You look retarded right now and Sidney's watching you."

"So?"

"You'd better let me go before Sidney leaves without me. I'll call you later Dee." Frankie pinches Denise's ass, grins at me, and hops back into Sidney's car.

After they drive off Denise lifts her arms towards the sky and twirls around. "I love Christmas!" Her hands drop to her hips, "So what happened?".

"He told me he loved me and wanted me to marry him."

Denise hugs me and says, "That's why I love Christmas."

"Well I don't," I grumble, "I can't wait 'til it's over!"

She follows me inside, pestering me about the big day.

I keep on my clothes, crawl into bed and pull the covers over my face.

"What's up with you? You should be happy."

"Go away Denise."

She rips the covers from my face, "Fuck you!"

"Fuck you back!"

She stares at me in shock. I push her away from me. "It's your entire fault."

Denise gasps. She doesn't push me back. Instead, she walks towards the door. Good, she's leaving. I turn my back to the door.

"Frankie you've got some explaining to do. You best get your ass back here."

I twist around. She glares at me while she paces. I sink lower under the covers. "I don't care if he already dropped you off. Call him up and tell him you need a run back here." She shakes the phone. "Tell him Juanita is having a nervous breakdown and I don't know what to do!"

"I'm fine," I yell.

Denise's says, "How the fuck do I know what's wrong with her. She's acting weird and she's freaking me out. She's acting just like me."

I start laughing.

"No, she never said a word about you. Why the fuck would she be talking about you? You're not that special."

I laugh more.

"She's losing it. Right now, she's ogling me, howling hysterically, so get your ass back here . . . Wrapping what? She told me you went in to the sex shop and bought something . . . What do you mean you didn't? If you didn't buy me a sex toy, then who the fuck did you buy it for? I'm warning you Frankie, if there are no sex toys under that tree, I will cut your dick off. I swear to it."

I laugh even harder. Tears are running down my face. Now I'm at a point where I don't know if I'm laughing or crying.

"Frankie, fuck you for laughing at me! Don't you dare come near this place. I mean it—don't or I'll stab you with my nail file and you can stick those sex toys up your fucking ass!"

I'm curled up in the bed howling. She fires the phone at me. I duck. It lands near my head. She grabs it and punches some numbers on the keypad. "Sidney. Yes, I know what time it is . . . I'll tell you what's wrong. Juanita's lost her marbles, and Frankie's having an affair . . . What? . . . What other line . . . Don't answer it don't you dare talk to Frankie . . . Could you be any longer? Fine I won't . . .I said I won't. I'll wait until you get here."

I lie in bed and stare blankly at the ceiling. Part of me wants to call Gavin and tell him the truth. Why should I keep my word to Frankie when it's ruining my life? I know what I'll do. Tomorrow, first thing, I'm calling my social worker and I'm moving to a new foster home.

Knocked Up

I soak in the bathtub, blow bubbles from my ring, twist it around so it looks like a plain wedding band and twist it back and forth, trying to catch a beam of light shining down from the ceiling socket. Denise was the first to say it looked more like a friendship ring and she's right, because although it's only a promise ring, to us it means we're engaged.

I climb out of the tub, wrap the towel around me, and wonder what Denise is doing right now. Probably smoking in bed. That's the one thing I don't miss about her being gone. I wonder how long it will take her to burn down Frankie's apartment.

Tap. Tap. Tap.

I open the door a few inches.

"Juliette, Romeo is waiting for you on the phone. Try not to tie up the line too long."

I follow Molly down the hall into the kitchen. "Isn't the shop closed?"

"Yes. Nevertheless, I don't want you talking on the phone all night. You need to get some sleep. Tomorrow is a school day."

I squeeze past her and pick up the phone. "Hi."

"Hi sweetie, I thought I'd give you a quick call to say goodnight and tell you how much I miss you."

"I miss you too."

"Still love me?"

"Of course," I grin. "Hoping I'll change my mind? Want the ring back?"

"That's it I'm driving over and giving you a spanking!"

"Promises, promises," I laugh. "Are you still coming over, to drive me to school in the morning?"

"Wild horses wouldn't keep me away. Nite sweetie. See you tomorrow."

"Goodnight," I hang up the phone and go to bed.

I drift off, wake up and drift off again. But the same dream continues right where it left off. I dream about being back at the farm. I throw pieces of apple to the stallion but two mares trot towards me. Mom is riding one and Gordon is on the other. Gordon looks at me and smiles. Mom reaches over the fence, and I run towards her.

She kisses me and warns, "Be careful, don't run. Running can be dangerous." She caresses my face. Her hand is icy cold. Over her shoulder, I see Gordon twisting the knob on his radio. I hear a buzzing static sound. The more he plays with the knob the louder it gets.

It's my alarm clock. I reach over and shut it off.

I skip breakfast to make sure I'm not late. An hour later, I'm outside waiting and he's still not here. I'm freezing. The road is wet from the melting ice. There's hardly any snow on the ground but there is a thin film of frost over the windows of Molly's van. Each time I think about going inside and changing from shoes to boots, the next thought that follows is, the next car should be his.

Five cars later, I trudge inside to warm up.

"Aren't you already late for school by now?" Molly asks.

I look out the window, rubbing my hands together and blow on my fingertips. It's about time.

"He's here," I yell as I dash towards the door.

"Be careful, don't run," I stop. The hair stands up on the back of my neck. That sounded just like Mom's voice.

I stare at Molly. "Did you say that?"

"Of course, do you see anyone else here?"

My eyes flicker across the room.

"Juanita? Sweetheart, are you okay?"

"I'm fine, honest, I'm okay. See you after school." I rush outside and stop inside of his arms.

He stands away from the door, closing it slowly. The car is toasty warm. He gets in, leans across the seat, and kisses me.

"Good morning beautiful."

I can't stop smiling.

He smiles back and says, "How about you skip school today?"

"For how long?"

"How does all day sound?"

"Are you serious? I'm not sure that's such a great idea."

"I am. I thought you could hang out with me and see what I do all day."

"You're serious?" I ask.

"Dead serious."

"Am I allowed to do that?"

"Of course."

"Don't I need like a special pass or something?" I ask.

"No."

"How do I get in?"

"You walk in with me, after I drive you there," he grins and kisses me again. "It'll be fine, you'll see. So is it your school or mine."

"Yours."

The drive is not much farther than it is to my school. As we park and get out of the car, my nerves play havoc. "What if I get kicked out?"

"That won't happen."

"What if it does?"

"It won't," he smiles and squeezes my hand.

Stalked

We walk through an open area that leads to a brightly lit underground tunnel. I'm not sure if the lights are flickering or if I'm blinking. After we pass eight emergency phones we reach a moving walkway. Eventually we arrive at a large corridor, lined with several double doors.

"Ready?" he asks.

My throat thinks I don't need to breathe. I force a swallow and nod.

We enter into what looks like a small stadium. People are scattered. A third of the seats are vacant. An older man with thick black glasses and a white beard, briefly glances our way. For a minute, I feel like the six-year-old version of me. The one that lurked beyond the living room, not welcomed to intrude, while Dad and Irma laughed at the TV. Sidney squeezes my hand, while the professor nods and continues his lecture.

Nobody seems to care I don't belong and when the lecture is over, I feel disappointed. I want to hear more.

"I'm thirsty how about you?"

"Me too."

"Is the water fountain okay or do you want a soda?"

"Water. Where is it?"

Sidney points ahead and says, "Below the restroom signs."

"Wanna race?" Without answering me, he runs like a bullet.

By the time we reach the water fountain, I'm out of breath. He hovers above the water fountain, holding the knob at the highest level. As I bend over to take a sip, he lowers it. I bend my head lower but he lowers it more. I lower my head again but this time he turns it on full blast.

I wipe my forehead, punch his leg and say, "Knock it off." He lowers it a little and lets me drink.

"Go ahead." I grin. "Your turn."

He laughs, "I'm not thirsty are you finished?"

I bend down and take one more long sip. I pucker my lips to kiss him. He leans close then jerks away from me.

"Forget it. Your cheeks are bulging out. Don't dare try spitting that at me," he says and runs.

I run after him, trying not to swallow the water. I chase him down the hall, over the escalator and out the tunnel into the parking lot. The car is ten feet away. He opens the door and jumps inside. I am right behind him, running as fast as I can, reaching towards the open door. Without warning, I hit a patch of ice that sends me sliding towards the car. I reach for the door to catch myself, but he slams it shut. My body twirls and crashes to the ground. The pain in my ankle is so severe it makes me laugh and cry at the same time. I can't talk, can't cry, can't yell and can't breathe. All I can do is bang on the bottom of the car door.

"I am not falling for that one. Forget it. Stand up and open your mouth or I'm not opening the door."

I try but a wicked pain sears through my leg. I can't move an inch. I can't get up. I throw a piece of ice at the door. "He-he-he-helppppp me."

He opens the car window part way, looks down at me laughing and says, "Nice try, but spit somewhere else."

"I won't spit at you," I half laugh and half cry.

"Then why are you laughing?"

"I'm not laughing, I'm crying."

"You don't make weird noises like that when you cry."

"Pleeeesse," I beg.

"No I can hear the water warbling in your mouth."

The pain is so bad I start rocking back and forth on the ground.

"How long are you planning to sit there?"

"Oh my god, help me, for God's sake help me. I'm not joking."

"Swear to God you're not joking."

"I swear to God I am not joking." My voice sounds shrill.

In seconds he's at my side. "Oh my god, I thought you were playing. I'm so sorry what can I do. Can you try to stand? Can I help you get up?"

I shake my head.

"Hey you," he yells at someone walking by, "Help me lift her into the car. I think she has a broken leg." I yelp in pain as they lift me into the front seat.

I spend the next twenty minutes trying to stifle moans and groans.

"Say something, talk to me. We're almost here." He points to the emergency sign.

"How will I get inside?" I say. "I can't move." I look at his skinny frame wondering which of us weighs less.

"I'll get some help."

Within seconds, he is back with an attendant and a wheelchair. I wince as she rolls me into the room. I scream as the doctor removes my shoe. He wheels me down the hall to the x-ray department. I silently curse the x-ray technician as she positions my foot. Was she born a sadist or did this job make her that way?

"Take a deep breath, hold it, don't move, stay still, now you can breathe. Let's get you turned over on your other side."

When she finishes her torture session she hands me an envelope.

"We're all done. You can wheel her back," she instructs Sidney.

He rolls me in the opposite direction of the blue arrows. "How can someone choose a job where they hurt you so much?"

"This is a hospital. Everyone in here is hurting."

"Yeah. Except the staff. Think about it."

"Ssshhh." Sidney whispers.

The room is empty but out of nowhere, a white sleeved arm reaches for my envelope. The white coat rushes past me and slips the x-rays onto a lit up medicine cabinet.

"Well you have not only managed to break a bone and tear some ligaments but you've also managed to dislocate your ankle. Do you see that?" He points to a few areas and explains the human anatomy of a foot.

"Sorry, I have no clue what I'm looking at." Maybe if you showed me my other foot I would see some sort of difference.

"Ever have a cast before?"

"When I was a kid. For a large cut inside my inner thigh."

"That's an odd spot to cut. How did you manage that one?"

"Wires gouged my leg. The bike seat was busted."

He glances up at me from his stool. I look defiantly into his concerned brown eyes while he wraps my leg in several layers of gauze.

"Scoot to the edge of the table." I half hop while leaning on both of them for support.

I sit on the table and watch him stir a pail of white mud and slap it around my leg.

He says, "No signatures on this one until it dries. Give it two days. I should start a fundraiser for signing casts. If I could get a dollar for each one I've autographed, we could buy a new x-ray machine."

"But you didn't sign mine."

"I will next visit. Leave me a spot."

"You do need a better x-ray machine one that's like a big pot that circles your leg, so people don't have to move your foot."

"Stay off yours, and don't get the cast wet. We'll change your cast as the swelling goes down. I'll see you here in two weeks, or sooner, depending on the reduction. As soon as you notice it's loose, or getting loose, come back in."

"What if it doesn't get loose?"

"Trust me, it will."

———————

Two weeks later, my cast is loose but my biggest concern is my lips. I stare in the mirror at my horrible rash. The more I lick them the worse they get. I have a red ring around my lips and they're dried and cracked. At this point, laughing makes them bleed. They're covered in hideous scabs and I sound like an idiot when I try to talk. I can't chew or smile, and I can't open my mouth to brush my teeth.

"What have we here?"

"Suck fish."

"Suck fish?"

Sidney coughs and blushes. "She's trying to say suck face. She is joking of course. She can't move her lips to make sounds."

The doctor sits on the stool and suppresses a grin. He winks at me. "No offense, but if I was you I'd get a new boyfriend. This is strike two. Are you counting?" I laugh and immediately yelp as the skin stretches and splits.

"Just nod yes or shake your head no. Lick your lips much?"

I nod.

"So they got dry and chapped first?"

I nod.

"Did you put any lip balm on them?"

I nod.

He gives me a quick dubious look. "Are you certain?"

I pretend to put some on and smear my fingers above my lips.

"Oh-h-h, I see, you put it on and lick it off. I'm going to prescribe a cream for you. Put it on every four hours. As a matter of fact, I have several samples I can give you." He rummages through a cupboard. "The tubes should last you a week or two if you apply it properly, but I can't seem to find them. Would you care to hear some unorthodox advice that may prevent this from reoccurring?"

I nod rapidly. "Yeshhh."

"It seems this is the result of stress. A nervous habit. Try lipstick."

"Li-tick?"

"Yes, ideally a bright red color. Gnawing at it will stain your teeth red and after you spend half the day looking like a circus clown, you will stop that habit. I do have a daughter your age, and her biggest concern is body image. If you're anything like her, and start wearing lipstick, you will break that habit sooner than you think. Here they are." He drops the samples into my outstretched hands. "Until they heal, apply this ointment twice daily." He winks at me, "And you'll be back sucking face in no time."

I try not to smile but it's too late. Fresh blood bubbles through the new cracks in my lips.

The doctor hands a tube of ointment to Sidney. "This is a free sample. Make sure she uses this four times daily and use some vitamin E oil to keep the scabs moist. You are going to have to feed her liquids. Soup broth and juices, but have her use a straw, not a spoon." He bends down beside me, "Now let me look at that ankle of yours."

I watch as he uses a round blade to cut through the cast. My leg looks skinnier than the other does. After another session with the x-ray technician, he reviews the films and seems satisfied with how it's healing. I watch him slather up a new cast.

For two more weeks, Sidney stays by my side and even skips university classes. My lips take forever to heal. I am so sick of soup. My first outing is buying lipstick. If the doctor thinks this will protect my lips I'm in. Every time I look in a mirror, at my smeared lipstick I feel ridiculous. How long have I looked this way? Instead of dropping a habit, I form a new one. I can't resist the urge to look in the mirror every five minutes.

Eventually, I stop biting at my lips. No more smeared lipstick during the day. I climb into bed feeling good about myself. Now if I could just keep it from smearing while I'm asleep.

I wake up with a terrible itching. Half-awake, I bang the cast against the mattress. At first, it's my leg. I want to chew my cast off. By morning, it's my entire body. I'm completely covered in hives.

As we wait in the clinic, Sidney holds my hand and squeezes it. A woman with a small child moves to the other side of the room and huddles in a far corner.

"Maybe it's my nerves," I say.

The doctor tells Sidney to wait outside and motions me inside his office.

He looks at my arms and asks to see my stomach.

"Have you been in the woods?"

"Say what?"

"Have you been in the woods?"

No, why would I be in the woods. I look at my cast, "Do I look like I would be running around in the woods?"

He writes a prescription and hands it to me.

"I'm so itchy," I complain.

"Of course you're itchy, you're covered in fly bites," he turns and walks out the door.

"Well," Sidney smiles as he wraps his arms around me, "what did he say?"

"He's an idiot. Next time bring me to the hospital, not here."

"This is where the social worker said you have to go."

84

"Well he must have found his license in a cracker jack box."

"What did he say," Sidney looks worried.

"Just get me out of here, I'll tell you after we leave the parking lot."

"What's that?" Sidney tugs at the crumpled paper in my hands,

"Prescriptions."

"There's a pharmacy here in the building."

"No Sidney please, for God's sake I am so itchy I feel like I have fleas. Let's go."

"Did he say you had fleas?" Sidney looks horrified.

"No but you're close," I say.

As we drive to the pharmacy, I'm going crazy. I look in the glove box and find a pencil. I dig at the inside my cast. "The itchiest part is my leg. This cast is driving me crazy."

"What's that clicking sound?"

"It's my cast hitting against the door."

"What are you doing to it?"

"I'm scratching inside of it."

"With what?"

"With two fingers and a pencil."

"Is it that loose?"

"Yes Sidney! Oops."

"Oops what?"

"I dropped the pencil into my cast."

I hold onto the dash as Sidney swerves the car around in the middle of the road.

"What are you doing? Trying to kill us?"

"No. I'm getting you back to the ortho doctor."

"I go on Wednesday." He shakes his head as I try to get my fingers down into my cast. "What about my prescriptions?"

"We'll get them filled while we're there."

Within minutes after we arrive, I'm ushered to the x-ray room and then back to the waiting room.

"What did the other doctor say was wrong with you?"

"Fly bites. He kept asking me if I spent much time in the woods. I should have said, yes, I raise pet mosquitoes."

Sidney laughs, "What an idiot!"

The nurse ushers me into the doctor's office.

"Your x-rays look good, other than slight lead poisoning you're fine."

I raise my eyebrows.

"Relax. It is a joke. But, we'll have to replace the cast again."

"Doc can you tell us if these are allergy hives or what?" I lift my shirt and expose my tummy.

"Lie down." He feels my stomach presses here and there than gives me a jar to go pee in and leaves the room.

After ten minutes he returns and flips through my chart.

"Well? What did my pee tell you?"

"Plenty. You are impregnated with chicken pox and a child."

Statutory Rape

Mrs. Lolita's hands press against the arms of the chair. She tilts her body towards me and for a brief second I imagine her ejecting across the room. "Young lady there is nothing funny about the charge of statutory rape."

I force a polite smile, "I told you, he didn't rape me."

"Nobody had to get raped or forced, it just means you are a minor and he isn't and he had sex with you." She rolls her eyes at Molly.

Molly throws her hands up in the air. "Leave me out of this one."

"Molly we can't. I would if I could but you are her caregiver. You are in this whether you like it or not. None of us like this," she glares at me, "why couldn't you just date someone seventeen?"

My eyes pop wide open, "So if he was a year younger everything would be okay?"

"Well I wouldn't exactly say that but when a fifteen-year-old child gets pregnant by an eighteen-year-old man, it's called statutory rape because a child can't consent to anything. It's called justice for being irresponsible."

I feel fire rise up from my soul and spit through my eyes.

"Don't look at me like that."

I stand up and shake my finger at her. "How dare you, how dare you," I shriek.

"It's Denise," Molly apologizes as Mrs. Lolita shrinks two sizes smaller. "Denise has been a bad influence on her."

"No, Denise has nothing to do with this. Leave her out of this."

"Yeah," Denise gulps. "I didn't screw her."

"Shut up Denise," I yell. I glare at Mrs. Lolita and clench my fists. How dare she threaten my Sidney? "You know who has screwed me? The government! Go charge yourselves with statutory rape because you people screwed me over when you let Irma and Dad get away with what they did to us. Where's the justice in that? Do you actually believe that making love is more of a crime than beating the snot out of people—humiliating them publicly—messing with their minds? Screw all of you."

"Maybe I have been a bad influence," Denise mutters, as I run past her, and slam the door.

I slump by the door and listen to my heart pound out of my chest. It's beating so loud I can't hear a word they're saying. I'm scared to death.

"Come on God, tell me what to do." My whine turns into pleading, "I need help now, not tomorrow." I wait for the magic lightning bolt. It doesn't happen. Then I do something I haven't done in years. I crawl under the bed, curl into a ball and cry myself to sleep.

I feel a hand pulling at me. "Wake up. Wake up and talk to me."

I smell lavender. "Mom? Mom is that you?"

She strokes my hair. Finally, she speaks, "Juanita, when I found out I had cancer, I prayed so hard to live. I thought God would keep me alive, not because I was afraid to die, but because I wanted to stay and protect you, all six of you— especially you and Bruce. I didn't know if either of you would survive without me. Do you understand, that when we are terrified, but can work past it, we become stronger?" She turns my head towards her, waiting for an answer.

I flare my nostrils as wide as I can and soak in her scent. "How can dead people smell like lavender?"

"I'm not dead."

"You are dead. People who stop breathing and get buried are dead."

"Do you think nothing continues once you die?"

"I don't know. I only know I'm pregnant," I sob.

"This memory is happening this very moment and one day it will be a past memory. Time always leads to our demise but also surpasses death. Is something ever gone, ever dead, if you remember it. If I can live in your memory, why can't I be alive somewhere else?"

"I don't know. I'm so scared Mom, I'm more scared than I've ever been in my life."

"When I was dying I had moments of fear. During those times, I would take a bubble bath in lavender. It reminded me of when I was a child, with no worries, running through a field of flowers in my bare feet. You have to find what calms you down and do it. Find the calm and control your storms."

"You calm me down," I say. "You're my calm in the storm."

"Don't forget about God. Prayer works."

"Not always. I pray a lot and so did you, and it didn't help either of us because you're dead and Irma is still with Dad and I'm hiding under a bed again."

"I am not dead. I am just in a place different from you. And my prayers did work. I prayed I would never leave you, and I haven't."

Her lips brush against my forehead. "Watch your dreams."

I jerk awake. Denise is yelling, "I found her under the bed."

I squirm out into the room. I feel hot. Maybe I need a cold shower. I can hear voices down the hall. I know they're still talking about me. Maybe I should go apologize to Mrs. Lolita. None of this is her fault.

Denise wraps her arms around me. "It'll be okay. I can't believe anyone would accuse Sidney of rape. If anyone raped anyone I bet you raped him and where's that fucking smell of lavender coming from?" she sniffs my shirt, drops to her knees, reaches under the bed and pulls out a bottle of perfume. "I wondered where that went. Anyway . . . Frankie and I decided we're going to let you live with us. You can be my little sister." She cracks her gum, "Besides, Sidney's probably going to jail. If his mother gets him off the hook, she'll never let him let him marry you and I bet she is going to hate your guts when she hears the word rape."

"Denise you're a genius!" I kiss her on the head and bolt down the hall.

"I'll testify," I pant for breath, "I'll testify."

"Mood swings. Must be the hormones," Denise says, panting and grinning at the same time.

"Well it's a good thing I came two hours early because we still have time for the hearing," Mrs. Lolita stands up and brushes off her skirt.

"You mean like now?" I ask.

"More like half an hour ago, but now will do."

"Can Denise come?"

"Absolutely not!"

"No, I mean yeah, I should come. You know to hold her hand when it's over," Denise says.

Mrs. Lolita presses her hands against her hips and stares at Denise.

"Please, I'll be on my best behavior."

"I am not going unless Denise goes," I say.

Mrs. Lolita glances at her watch and points to the door. "There's no time to change. Get in the car. Go as you are."

Trees blur past, while Denise fix her makeup.

"If she slams on the brakes and you poke your eye out with your mascara brush is it her fault or your fault?"

"Denise put that mascara back in your purse."

"Thanks a fucking lot. Last time I help you."

"You two better not be up to something. What do you mean help her? What do you have up your sleeve?"

"Nothing but my arm," Denise grins.

"Denise you will wait in this car. Understand?"

"Then leave it running because it's fucking freezing."

"Leave my car running with you in it all alone? You must be totally out of your mind."

"Bur-r-r-r. You can't leave me out here to freeze to death." Denise shudders.

Mrs. Lolita shuts off the car.

"You stay put in the lobby. No swearing, no talking, no moving."

"What if I have to pee?"

"You won't have to pee."

"But—"

I interrupt her, "Denise just shut up and wait . . . please?"

Denise rolls down the corners of her lips. "Fine." She presses the elevator button.

"You. Over there. On that bench."

Denise skulks over to the bench

The elevator is empty and only has two buttons.

"What happened to the other floors?"

"They are over in the employee elevators. The public is restricted from those."

It stops at the next floor. There are several benches beside each door. She motions to one on our right. I twist my hair into a donut and pull the ends through.

"This may take a couple of hours or it may take thirty minutes. It all depends upon how you answer the questions. Some questions will be personal and may make you feel uncomfortable but you have to answer them. Above all else, be completely honest. Okay?"

I nod.

Within twenty minutes, Mrs. Lolita is strutting down the hall with her arms clasped tight against her chest.

I scurry after her half hopping to keep up. I stick my cast into the crack of the elevator to keep it from closing. Mrs. Lolita is inside pounding on a button.

"Do you have anything else on your mind I should know about?"

"I can't wait to get this cast off."

Denise paces across the lobby. "Did you have to take so long?"

"So long? It should have been a few hours but thanks to little Miss Wonderful here it's been less than thirty minutes."

"Well it sure felt like hours," Denise complains. "So what happened? Was his mother there? Is he going to jail?"

"Denise clam up, or you'll be walking home."

"Oh, I don't need a ride. I thought you would be longer so I called Sidney and he's waiting outside," Denise says and stalks off.

"Hey, slow down. Wait for me."

Mrs. Lolita grabs my arm. "Not so fast. You and I are about to have a little talk."

She points at Denise's back. "I thought she got married, and moved out?" Mrs. Lolita says.

"She did . . . sort of," I say.

"Sort of?"

"Frankie is working overtime trying to get enough money to pay for the wedding. Sometimes he has to work out of town. She gets lonely and stays with us. I help with the store and Denise helps with Molly's babies."

She turns around and looks at me before she unlocks the car door. "Do you know where those babies came from?"

"Of course I do?"

"Denise told you?"

"Nooooo! The school nurse did a couple of years ago. I saw a cat movie about sex and kittens. It's supposed to be the same."

"I'm talking about where Molly's babies came from."

"Her vagina."

Mrs. Lolita drops her purse. She picks it back up and brushes the snow from it, unlocks the car and tosses it inside. "Get in," she grits her teeth. "You are half right and half wrong. Actually, you are one hundred percent wrong."

Now she has my interest.

"Those babies are not hers. They are fostered?"

"Okay."

"As for the vagina part, babies don't always come out that way. Obviously, you are unaware of C-Sections."

"What's that?" I ask.

"I'll take that as a no, so I guess that's something you might want to learn considering your chances of having one at your age is fairly high."

"I've seen movies where they say push, push, but . . ."

"But what?"

"I always assumed they were coming out of the vagina."

Mrs. Lolita pulls over to the side of the road and laughs. "Tell me you're not thinking what I think you're thinking. A C-Section is when they cut your stomach open to remove the babies."

"Yuk. I'm never getting one." I rub my stomach trying to cover the baby's ears.

"So who owns those babies if Molly doesn't?"

"The government. When under aged children-in-care give birth the babies go up for adoption and into foster care."

"What happens when normal teenagers living at home have babies? Why do they get to keep them? What's the difference?"

"The difference is sometimes those kids get to influence the outcome. Some parents agree to raise them sometimes they go up for adoption sometimes relatives raise them."

"Why can't I influence the outcome?"

"Juanita this is the government. There are rules. There are no exceptions because exceptions ruin the rules. I know it doesn't seem fair but that's just the way the system works."

"Well I think the system sucks and I think they should change the rules."

"Juanita, it isn't that much different for you. The government is your guardian. They own you and they own that baby of yours. It's up to them what happens to it."

"Fine if they own this baby they can give birth to it because I'm not pushing."

"Are you saying you want an abortion?"

"No. I'm not a murderer. And if I was, I would have killed Irma long ago and wouldn't be here and wouldn't be pregnant."

"So you don't want an abortion?"

"Of course I don't, I'd give it away to someone who wanted it before I'd do that."

"So you agree. The home for unwed mothers is the best thing for you."

"No I don't agree. Not for me. Sidney wants to marry me."

"You need a parent's consent to get married and—"

"No I don't because my parents are dead or disowned so I don't need their permission."

"The government is your parent. As a matter of fact, the baby is their property."

"Really? I don't think so. There is no way they are going to own my kid. What happens if I elope?"

"What do you mean if. Didn't I just hear you tell them you planned to kidnap him and force him to elope?" She bangs on the steering wheel. Her chest rises and falls. Her sigh is long and deep. "Juanita, you are one person, you will never change the government or their rules. You will only get a reputation for being rebellious. You don't want that do you?"

"Actually I do! Rebellious sounds really good right now. Nobody is getting my baby."

"Juanita it's the governments' baby."

"Good. Then go charge them with statutory rape."

We drive the rest of the way home in silence. As I leave the car I say to her, "If anyone tries to take this baby from me I will cut off their arms and stab them in the heart," and I slam the door.

Before I get to the shop door, I hear a car door slam. I'm not going to let her brainwash me. I don't turn around.

"Hey wait up, Juanita!" Denise yells. I hear another door slam.

Two arms sweep me up and carry me to the side door. "You can't walk in slush and snow with a cast on." Inside he lowers me to the ground.

I bury my head into his shoulder.

"Hey. Everything will be okay. Please stop crying. I promise I won't let anyone hurt you or our baby. I'll protect you both for the rest of my life. I swear to it."

He gently grabs my hair and pulls my face from his shoulder. "Look at me. Promise me you won't do something stupid."

"Like what?"

"Like run away."

"Sidney, they are trying to take the baby from me. It isn't fair," I sob.

I look over his shoulder and see Denise coming through the door, followed closely by Mrs. Lolita. "Hurry up," I say. "Lock the door. Don't let her in."

Denise twists the lock in the nick of time. She giggles, "This is so fucking funny."

Mrs. Lolita bangs on the door for five minutes.

Denise whispers, "I hear her walking away, I think she's leaving."

We follow Denise towards the kitchen. Sidney stops to give me a hug. I smell his Old Spice. I remember the day I gave him that gift. The day I tore up the tag, to Gavin, and made out a new tag, to him instead.

Denise stops just inside the door. She points ahead of her, gasps and says, "Someone's sitting at the kitchen table."

"Who?"

"You don't see—"

"Well at least you're not mean enough to lock Molly from coming up the store stairs," Mrs. Lolita snaps.

She looks at the three of us and sighs. "Sit down. Let's try to be civil and discuss this like adults."

"Why bother if there's nothing to change, nothing to decide, why have the discussion? What's the point when I have no control and the government can do whatever it wants?"

"Well apparently they can't. I just got a phone call saying the charges of statutory rape were dropped."

"Thank God," Sidney's smile is a mile long.

"I take it you're the boy she raped? The one she wrapped with duct tape while he was sleeping?"

Sidney turns blood red.

I grin.

Denise hoots, "Good one Juanita!" and gives me a high five.

"They're dropped? Sidney's not in trouble?"

Mrs. Lolita eyeballs me, "I wouldn't exactly say that." Sidney grips my hand tighter. "I'd say he's got a handful of trouble. So Sidney what does your mother think of all of this."

Sidney starts to choke and do something I think is humanly impossible, he turns a reddish purple.

"So she doesn't know about the rape charges?"

"No."

"What does she think about the baby?" she asks.

"She doesn't know about the baby."

"Juanita said you guys are getting married is that correct?" Mrs. Lolita puts her fingers over my lips.

"Yes. I love Juanita and I want the baby too."

"So then what does your mother think about Juanita?"

I hold my breath and wait for his answer. I feel nervous.

"Sidney is too fucking nice to tell you the truth," Denise says.

"What truth," I ask.

"That nobody's good enough for Sidney. If I'm not fucking good enough to be his friend because I'm a foster child, then she sure as hell isn't visualizing you as a daughter-in-law."

"Sidney this is really important because of Juanita's age. Decisions are being made as we speak, I need to know is Denise telling the truth?"

"No not totally," he says.

"Sidney what do you mean by not totally," I ask. I hold my breath waiting for his answer.

"She isn't visualizing anyone as a daughter-in-law because she doesn't know I'm dating anyone."

Quitting School

The principal licks his finger, flips through my file, squints, and rereads the page. He browses through to the end and chews the corner edge of his mustache. I fix my tie and fidget with my shirt button until it's hanging by two threads.

"You are correct. You have missed a significant amount of school hours, but that does not warrant this action. Your grades are not that bad considering what little time you've spent here. Do you mind if I ask what you've been doing during those skipped classes?"

"I've been at the university."

"Doing what?"

"Sitting in on science lectures."

He strokes his beard and leans towards me. "What if I guarantee you a pass for the finals? What if I promise you will not have to worry about failing grade nine? Would you reconsider?"

"I can't, because I won't be taking any exams."

"Do you have any idea how tough the world can be when you only have a grade eight education? I think you are making . . . no, I am certain you are making a terrible mistake . . . But in the event you change your mind, feel free to come back and take my offer."

For a brief minute, I regret getting pregnant. Maybe he's right, but I can't turn back time. "I can't, I'm sorry but I can't."

I grab my jacket and almost trip over my cast as I try to run down the hall. Sidney is parked near the front of the door, in the handicapped section. The door opens and I hobble in.

"Let's get out of here."

"Well what did he say?"

"He tried to talk me out of it and he guaranteed me a passing grade if I stayed."

"Why?" Sidney turns and faces me. "Why on earth would he do that?"

I give Sidney a dirty look. "Because he thinks I'm worth it."

"I didn't mean to insult you. But I am questioning his ethics. Regardless, it is a good offer. You might want to reconsider. You're so close to finishing grade nine, with only two months to go."

"What difference does one grade make if I'm quitting school? Once I marry you, I lose transportation, and all my benefits. What happens when I don't fit into my clothes anymore? I have no choice but to quit."

"Well you're not alone." Sidney says. "My parents expected me to stay as full time student until I earned my masters. Needless to say my mother freaked when I told them I was quitting to find a job. Even though I told her I would continue with night classes, she still flipped out. I was given an ultimatum."

"Because of me . . ."

"Because of the situation. So I'm living with my sister now. She sees me as the black sheep of the family."

"Tell me exactly what she said, word for word."

"I can't."

"If I'm going to marry you I need to know what she said, especially when I'll have her in my life forever."

"You're marrying me. Not my mother."

"Molly said when you marry someone, you marry their entire family. That they will be a big part of my life."

"That's not true in my case, because when I get a teaching job, it'll be in Timbuktu, too far for her to visit."

"She hates me that much? Maybe this is all a mistake. What if I work and you could keep going to school?"

"Absolutely no, no, and no. There's no way you'll ever make enough to pay rent, never mind pay a baby sitter. My sister is a secretary and she can hardly afford hers." He shakes his head, "With a grade eight education, the only job you'll get is babysitting or serving tables."

I feel that old familiar burning in my nose. I don't blink. I know if I do, tears will spill out of my eyes. "Turn the car around. If grade nine makes such a difference, I'll take the principal up on his offer."

"I didn't mean it that way. I meant the wages would be minimum, they'll be the same with grade nine or grade ten. You'd be working to pay a babysitter. And without a Bachelor's degree and experience I will be at the bottom of the teacher's pay scale."

I wipe my face dry. "So by this fall, there is chance you could get hired if you applied to some places?"

"Maybe in some remote place out in the boonies."

"People do get pregnant." I point to my belly. "Not just students like me. Teachers do and what if someone pregnant has to quit? Anyway you never know . . . Maybe someone will drop dead of isolation, or commit suicide in some ghost town in the middle of no man's land, where you're the only applicant."

"Thanks a bunch." He playfully shoves my hand away from his.

"Can we just drive around for a while? I don't feel like going home yet—not unless you want to come in for a few minutes?"

"Actually, I have to go. There's a bunch of forms we have to complete before we can get married."

"Can I come with you?"

"You probably don't want to. Mother is going."

"You're right." I barely wait for him to put the car in park. I can't leave fast enough. I feel left out, hurt and alone. But, if he had insisted I go, I wouldn't, because I'm scared to death to meet her.

"Wait. Don't you ever forget I'm on your side. We are in this together and nothing, or nobody, is going to tear us apart. I'll be back tomorrow to take you to ortho. Where's my kiss goodbye?"

I lean back into the car and give him two.

"You're not sorry for any of this are you?" he asks.

"Actually I am. I'm sorry that I broke my ankle for nothing. It would've felt worth it if I'd gotten you with that mouthful of water," I say, stick my tongue out at him, and slam the car door.

Inside, in my room, I crawl into bed, and cry. I already dreaded meeting my future mother-in-law because she knows we had premarital sex. But knowing she hates me makes it twice as bad.

All night I toss and turn and by the time Sidney arrives I have thrown up twice. The minute I see his face I forget about his mother. His smile stretches from ear to ear every time he sees me, but this time it doesn't disappear, to make room for a kiss.

I slap his leg, "Well? What? Tell me."

"Tell you what?"

"If I knew I wouldn't be asking."

"What if you don't like what you hear?" he grins.

"Stop playing mind games with me, please?"

"I'll tell you after ortho. Is it okay if I wait out here? I have a form to fill out—for the priest—for our wedding."

"Why are you shutting off the car? You'll freeze out here."

"To save gas."

"I'll try to be quick. If you get too cold, come inside. Okay?"

"Take your time. This coat has a wool lining. I'll be fine."

I'm back within five minutes.

"That was fast," Sidney looks at his watch and at my foot. "Why didn't they change it?"

It's the same cast covered with his hand drawn hearts. I lean back and smile. "They said, my appointment isn't until tomorrow. Sorry about wasting the gas."

"How the heck did I manage that? That's not like me, I'm smarter than that." He glances at the time, and asks. "Is it okay if I drop you off, go home and pack up the rest of my things."

I snuggle next to him. "I'm okay with that, but are you going to tell me about your secret or not?"

"It's not my secret it's our secret. My sister has two boys, and her sitter, comes by day but Deborah and I worked out an agreement. If I babysit, whenever she is stuck, or during the odd evenings, I get free board. But the best part is after we're married, we get to live there free of board, providing you babysit her kids, fulltime for free and if you cook and do housework, we get free food."

"That's great . . . But what if the baby cries a lot?"

"The offer is only good until the baby is born. By then, I'll have enough saved to rent a small apartment and maybe a teaching job."

Sidney's spends twenty minutes planning out our future. Because of his sister's offer he decides to stay in school and work part time, until he gets his teachers certificate.

"I thought you said you needed a year or more to get your degree before you could teach?"

"I was talking about my master's degree. With my Bachelor's degree I'll obtain a Grade V Certificate and that will land me in a decent pay scale. As a teacher, I'll get paid to be off during the summer, and that'll enable me to pick up a few more courses."

"But you said they've hired everyone already."

"They have, but unexpected things happen, and you're right."

"Right about what?"

"Suicides in ghost towns."

"It was a joke."

"I know, but people do get pregnant or hospitalized. Their loss is my gain. I'm going to be the kind of teacher kids need. I deserve a teaching job. And, I sent off five letters last night."

He leans past me and pulls open the glove box. He pulls out a letter and drops it in my lap.

"What is it?" I ask.

"Our marriage application. Well . . . part of it. Apparently, you have to agree to raise our kids as Catholic or else we can't marry."

"I'm okay with that, but if I wasn't, why couldn't we marry? Why couldn't we just elope, like Denise and Frankie did? Why do we need a middleman who makes us predicate what religion our kid wants to be?"

"I don't think Frankie and Denise got married. I think they're pretending they eloped."

"Maybe we should do the same thing."

"We have to do things right, or I'll never get hired by the Catholic school board. I don't want to deliver newspapers forever."

"What's that supposed to mean?"

"It means, today I got a job delivering stacks of newspapers."

"How can you do that, go to university and study?"

"I pick them up fresh off the press at four in the morning and by six, I'm finished. Those two hours will give us gas and food money. School full time and no rent—we're finally getting a break."

"You're serious about your sister being okay with us living with her?"

"Juanita she's elated. Mom loves lawyers—"

"Wait did you say liars? Or lawyers?"

Sidney roars, "Haahahahahah. Haahahahahah."

"I'm serious."

"What's the difference?" He wipes his eyes. "Mom wants all of us to be doctors or lawyers and marry our fellow colleagues. She threatened to disown Deborah if she married Arthur. So half the reason she's helping us, is to spite Mom."

"Why?"

"Because Arthur is a truck driver. Mom believes all of us should be above blue collar workers."

"What does your dad do?"

"You'll never believe it. Guess."

"A doctor?" I grin.

"No."

"A lawyer?"

"No. A construction worker."

"Isn't that hypocritical?"

"No, you stand corrected, it's more ironic than anything else."

"Whatever. I consider it two-faced. It's wrong. It's like the kettle calling the pot black."

"I think it's because father may have struggled financially."

"He can't be that bad—he put you all through university. That's more than my dad did for any of us and he was supposed to be well off." I reach for the radio. "I don't want to talk about negative stuff anymore."

"Find an oldies station," he grins. "If you learn some old songs you might seem older—you know if I get a teaching job we have to lie about your age, right?"

"Let's worry about that when the time comes. Maybe you'll teach elementary kids and I'll look older to them. Do they learn math in kindergarten?"

"I'm not sure," he smiles, "But I'll make a third more money if I teach eleventh grade students. It's not the students, I'm worried about, it's the nuns." He leans over and kisses me. "Stop fretting. In two weeks we'll be together forever. I promised Deborah I would babysit tonight. You can come help me if you want?" He sits for a full minute while I fidget.

"What if they don't like me? I don't want to meet them until after we're married. That way they can't change your mind."

"Are you crazy? Wild horses couldn't keep me away from you. I'll pick you up tomorrow to get your cast changed. I'll be here bright and early." He kisses me again and whispers in my ear, "Just imagine, in two weeks we will be sleeping together. No more saying goodnight in this parking lot. Give me a sec. I'll carry you inside."

"No it's okay. See you tomorrow." I catch my balance and hop on one leg until I reach the steps. I try to keep my cast out of the snow but it's impossible. Inside the shop, I find Molly and Mrs. Lolita chatting in the back office.

Molly leans forward, and pats a nearby box. I sit on it and sigh. My emotions are in turmoil. All I can think about is how much his mother hates me. But how can she, when she's never met me? What kind of woman, other than Irma, can hate someone before getting to know them? What if she hates me enough to stop the wedding?

"I hope that isn't anything important." Mrs. Lolita nods at my fingers. The paper looks like a fat straw. Horrified, I try to untwist the form. My fingers are trembling uncontrollably. So are my shoulders. The paper drops into my lap. I cover my face and burst into tears.

Molly smooths out the form, frowns and hands it to Mrs. Lolita.

"Don't cry. This isn't personal. The canon law, is why the church discourages mixed marriages, but will accept them, under the decree of 1908, providing she signs this form, agreeing to baptize, raise and educate all children as Catholics."

"Can she stop Sidney from marrying me?"

"Who?"

"His mother."

"Maybe. I'm sure she realizes, the reason the statutory rape charges were dropped, is because you're fifteen, not under fourteen. Sidney knows if he doesn't marry you, he won't go to jail. But the question is, does she? But the age of consent is twenty-one, and anybody younger, needs parental consent to marry, but I think there's an exception relating to an expectant mother. If you're one, which you are, that section isn't applicable."

"What's that mean."

"It means she may not have any say in the matter."

A Drunk Bride

My dress is nothing fancy, just a knee length frock. It wasn't my choice but when your mother-in law is paying for your dress you don't always get a say. A long dress would have been better because I have one leg skinnier than the other. Now I'm sorry I didn't get the new cast put on. It's been two weeks, since I've had my cast removed. I was supposed to get it back on after the x-rays but I decided to walk out and not bother with it. It's their fault for taking so long to do the x-ray. If I hadn't sat there for an hour, I might have thought about how bad I'd look on my wedding day.

The stained glass entry window distorts my reflection into a fragmented shadow. I twist the floral ribbon around my finger. My knees are shaking. The more I gulp the dryer my mouth feels. There are people, sitting inside, but I don't know them. Maybe they're left overs, from the church service.

The jacket Sidney is wearing is more suited for teaching, than a wedding, which is why it was chosen. I'm not fond of the color but I can't complain. It was a gift from his mom. It seems the government doesn't have a budget for weddings or come to them. And I'm glad they don't. Truth is don't want the door to open. I'm terrified to face all of those people. Real life isn't like a fairytale. I'm still not in control of my life and I expected I would be once I ran away. But I've never been in charge. Maybe after Sidney and I are married that will change, and one day soon, we'll be able to make all of our own decisions. Up until now, everyone else has made all the decisions, except the main one. Getting married was our decision not theirs, and we both know if everyone else had it their way, there would be no wedding, no us, so maybe a change has already started.

"What are you doing Sunday baby, would you like to marry me?" I stifle a squeal. Adam sings some more, "What do you say now, if it's a fine day now?"

"I can't wait for this day to be over," I whisper to Adam.

He winks at me, then his brow furrows in a frown. "You have ink on your chin." He rubs at it with his thumb. "Lift your face up." Adam mutters and continues to try and get rid of the ink mark. "It won't come off. It's just a little round blue dot at—"

"Adam stop it's not ink. It's been there forever."

"Oh my goodness, I must be as nervous as you, I forgot," he laughs.

"Great now I'll have a red chin in all my wedding pictures."

"Do you have anyone taking pictures?"

"I don't know. I didn't get to plan anything so I doubt it."

"Do you hear that?" He cups his ear towards the organ music.

"I am so-o-o-o nervous. It's like my lungs are deflated."

"Juanita you look like someone would look if they were headed for the slaughter. Smile. Relax."

"Do you have any water? My tongue is sticking to the roof of my mouth."

"Here slip your arm through mine." He puts his lips near my ear. "You don't suppose they have a little monkey, in a red and gold jacket, playing the organ do you."

A wide smile breaks across my face. I try not to laugh.

A few strangers turn. Some politely smile back.

Stalked

I slip my arm through his and stare ahead at the reddish-pink plaid jacket Sidney is wearing. Everyone else is in black.

"Juanita, I think we must be at a funeral," Adam whispers.

I start to giggle.

It takes forever to reach Sidney.

Adam kisses my cheek and whispers, "Oh and one last thing—don't let the old farts bother you. Pretend they are all naked wearing baby diapers. If that doesn't work, picture them pooping in them. That's what I'm going to do."

He smirks, backs two steps away and folds his hands like an angel.

Most of the ceremony makes no sense to me, partly because I don't go to church and also because Adam and I are the only Anglicans here, and mass and confession is a new thing for us.

About the only thing I can identify with is the priest crossing himself and everyone else from a distance. It reminds me of my sister, Marie. That's what she always did when she was nervous or scared. Finally, we get past the bit where I sell my baby to the Catholic religion, and reach the I now pronounce you husband and wife part.

Sidney pecks me on the lips holds my hand and turns to face the crowd. I lift my eyes to look around the church. I count about thirty people but none I recognize. Adam stands out like a sore thumb, like a hippie in a suit. He winks at me, sniffs, holds his nose and grins. I am trying to hold back the giggles. The more everyone stares at me the more I shake. I tremble all the way down the aisle.

His sister drives us to her parent's place, where we find everyone sitting in a circle I sit on one of the empty chairs towards the corner. The chairs form a circle around a table with plates of sandwiches and desserts. In the middle is a small cake.

A woman sits beside me. She seems really nice, and has a calmness about her. I have no clue, how I should act, so I mimic her. I am not sure what I am supposed to say when she asks, "How do you stay so slim? I bet you're going to be one of those women who don't gain a pound after you're married."

"My doctor said I will start gaining weight after the morning sickness stops." The hum of conversation disappears abruptly.

Sidney's mom seems to be choking on a piece of cake. Her husband, Clayton, slaps her back. The more he slaps the more she chokes.

Sidney's older brother walks around talking drink orders and eventually he reaches my chair. The woman next to me orders a rum and seven, so I say, "I'll have the same."

Initially the drink tastes horrible. After a few sips the strong smell of gasoline subsides.

Half way through the drink, I am not as nervous or uncomfortable. This drink is relaxing me. I gulp down the rest and tip my glass back and forth, watching the melting ice cubes swirl into a dark spiral, until it goes black.

I wake up in a bright room. I recognize nothing. I lift the covers and see I'm wearing a pair of men's pajamas.

Tap. Tap. Tap.

"Good Morning Mrs. Simon. I'm Deborah, Sidney's sister, your sister-in-law. We met at your wedding."

"What happened? Am I at your house?"

"Hmm-mmm. We got a little tipsy. Someone must have made you a very strong drink. Did it taste strong?"

"I wouldn't know. It tasted like gasoline. It was my first drink and my last."

"Good to know," she smiles. "I'm heading out to work and I want to show you how to use the slow cooker."

How did I even get here? "Where is Sidney?"

"Sidney left for classes. He said he would call you on his first break."

Some weird pulse is hammering inside my head. I step over my crumpled dress and follow her blue and pink scrubs, to the kitchen. My stomach rolls with each step I take. I watch her add a teaspoon of pepper and salt into a chrome bowl and put it in the fridge.

"At noon put everything from that bowl into the pot and press this button. It's impossible to mess this up. The children are at their grandmothers for the day. I thought you might need to get used to the place before dealing with them. After all, it is your honeymoon. I have to run, so I'll see you at four."

After she leaves, I wander around trying to find the bathroom. The only one I can find is in the master bedroom. I sit on the toilet and glance around. I never really gave any thought to a honeymoon, but by her tone of voice, you would swear she was referring to body odor. It doesn't feel like my honeymoon, and for Sidney and everyone else today is just Monday.

And that's how it seemed to be for the next month.

I spent the first month doing exactly what I did on that Monday. I babysat, dusted some furniture and made the same meal over and over and over again. Deborah doesn't trust me to do the prep work yet. The hardest part is remembering to turn on the pot at noon. It's not too hard to open the fridge, lift the bowl of meat, potatoes, carrots and onions, remove the lid from the pot and dump everything in. The meat varied. Sometimes it was chicken, pork or fish, but every second day it was beef.

Although this is Thursday and Deborah has the day off work, the slow cooker is sitting on the counter, ice-cold, filled with the same ingredients that should have been turned on three hours before. She must have forgotten to plug it in and it looks like she forgot to add the spices.

I grab the pepper and sprinkle it on unpeeled potatoes. Unpeeled? A wave of weirdness settles over me. I stop midair and glance to my left and right. I run to the master bedroom, check the bathroom. "Deborah! Deborah!"

I glance out the window. Her car is gone. I pull the cold pot towards me. Great! If I peel away the skin, how much pepper do I put back in the pot? Maybe I should just cook it this way and remove the skin after it's cooked. Maybe for the first time ever, she wants to try eating onions with the skin on.

A car pulls into the driveway. I don't need to look to know it's Sidney. His muffler sputters like a lawnmower. I press the on button, dash outside and hop into the car. Sidney has both hands gripped to the steering wheel. One of them is holding a letter.

I twist towards him expecting a kiss, "You know you shouldn't read and drive—What is it? What's wrong?"

"I've got a job . . ." His voice trails off in disbelief.

"What kind of job, a teaching job?"

He throws the letter into the air, hops out of the car and jumps up and down several times. He runs over to my door, pulls me out and twirls me around in circles.

"Juanita I got a job, a real teaching job."

"Where?"

"I don't know. Who cares where. I didn't finish reading it."

"Well, finish reading it and find out."

"Where the heck is the letter?" he pokes his head under the car.

"It's got to be here somewhere," his voice is frantic. "I didn't get the name of the school or the address."

I get out and kneel to look under the car, "Well it's not caught under any of the tires. There's no wind. Think about where you had it last." A vision of him throwing it inside of the car flashes in my mind. I jump up and rip through the car. I find it under the back seat.

Instead of handing it to him, I sit on the side of the seat and read it. St. Lawrence? Where's St. Lawrence? Still reading I get out of the car and walk around the back of it. Sidney is sitting on his butt with his head in his hands sobbing.

I tip toe back to the passenger side and yell, "Hey. I found it."

I count to ten and join him on the ground. I press the letter into his hands, "Stop crying or the ink will run and you won't be able to read it."

"Juanita. Mother was wrong. You didn't ruin my life. I got a teaching job." He turns and shakes my shoulders. "Don't you get it? We can start our life!"

"OH MY GOD YOU GOT A JOB!"

We cling to each other sobbing. "I was so scared, so scared …" his voice breaks. He wipes his face. "I was so afraid I would be rejected—a failure." He shakes his head and stares at the letter.

"How far away is St. Lawrence?"

Stalked

"I don't know, I'll have to look it up, is that what it says?" he wipes his glasses on his shirt. "My glasses keep fogging up, I can't see. Read it to me."

I read him the letter.

"Wow grade eleven," he says. "Do you realize what this means?"

"Yes we get to move, you get to do what you love, you make more money and we're going to live happily ever after," I laugh.

His eyes are cautious. "It means you will be younger than any of my students. We are going to have to lie and say you are eighteen—no nineteen. It won't look good otherwise."

"I'm okay with that," I promise him. "We won't know a soul there, so we won't have to lie to hardly anybody."

"We will. Teachers tend to hang out together. They have each other over for dinner and stuff. We're bound to make new friends."

"How do you know?" I ask.

"I talk to teaches all the time."

"No you don't."

"Oh yes I do. Some teachers are in my classes upgrading their education. I know plenty of substitute teachers. So I have a good idea of what to expect."

Deborah yells, "What the heck!" and blows her horn. "I almost ran over you."

We scramble to our feet. Her eyes are bloodshot.

"I'll help you with the kids," I offer.

"Don't bother. They aren't here."

"Deborah what's wrong?" Sidney and I follow her up the steps. She slams the door in our face.

We stop and stare at each other for a brief second. She opens the door and gasps, "Oh my god, I am so sorry. I don't mean to take it out on you."

"Take out what on me?" Sidney asks.

"Arthur left me. He's having an affair with some sleazy server he met at the truck stop. She's half his age. I'll bet you she kicks him out in a week. I sure fixed him. Wait until he gets off work and sees what I did with those kids of his."

111

Attacked

"Deborah, what did you do with those kids?" Deborah stares blankly at the door. "Deborah?"

"The same thing I did with all his clothes," she cries uncontrollably.

Sidney rushes towards the trash bins. He slowly lifts the lids. He rushes back and shakes his sister, "Where are the kids? WHERE ARE THE BOYS! I'm calling Arthur."

"You call Arthur and I will kick your sorry ass out this very minute. My business is not your business," she threatens.

"The boys are my business, they're my nephews."

I take a deep breath, "Deborah did you take all of Arthur's clothes or just some of them."

"Everything. Even his odd socks."

"What did you do with the clothes? The Salvation Army?"

"No, oh my god I should have! Why didn't I think of that?"

I take another deep breath, "Want to go get them and—"

Stalked

The phone rings. Deborah folds her arms and glares at it. "Don't answer that. SIDNEY NO."

Sidney picks it up. He listens for a minute and looks both perturbed and relieved at the same time. He says nothing and holds it out to Deborah.

"I'm not here and I'm not talking to you!" She slams down the phone. She keeps her hand on the receiver. It rings again. "How's that for a reality check you prick! How's your little love affair now? Oh and don't bother bringing them back. BECAUSE NOBODY WILL BE HERE."

She holds the phone a foot away from her face. "He hung up on me!" She stares at the phone and taps her foot. After one minute, she redials. "If you so much as try to bring those kids back here, I will charge you with neglect and abandonment." She swings the door open. It shudders against the doorstop. I'm certain the entire block can hear her.

"Should I shut the door?"

"Not if you value your life," Sidney whispers. "Ssshhh, she's coming back."

Her foot slams the door shut. "How dare you threaten me? Hear this?" She holds the phone near the bag, and dumps the bag upside down. Packages of doorknobs and deadbolts clunk onto the counter. She lifts the phone to her mouth and screams, "That's the new locks I am putting on every single door in this house AND I bought an alarm system."

She glares at me. "Juanita will not look after the boys, she won't even be here to look after them . . . no she won't, they are moving out as we speak." She listens for a minute and sneers, "No I did not abandon them. They have a right to visit their father with his new girlfriend."

She lifts her eyebrows. "Don't bother. I'll be at the club dancing. Unlike you, I'm free as a bird. Have fun with the kids and your whore." She bangs the phone against the counter.

"Sidney, change every lock in this house. Juanita and I are going to find you your own place to live."

"Deborah, are you serious? I don't make enough money to pay rent and buy food."

"I will pay for the first month but it has to be just a room, not a whole house you rent."

We look at each other in shock and say in unison, "Why?"

"Because I don't want you guys to make it easy on him or him trying to barge in here while I am at work. If he gets back in here it will be because he broke the law, busted a door down, or smashed a window, but not because he intimidated one of you."

I sigh, "We were going to move out soon anyway. I guess we may as well—"

"What do you mean move anyway," Deborah looks shocked. "Am I the last person to know everything around here?"

Sidney grins and pulls the letter from his back pocket. "I just got the news today. We were reading this when you drove up."

Deborah scans the letter. "Sidney this is great, I am so proud of you," she smiles through her tears.

"Are you sure you'll be okay. I hate to leave you all alone."

"No. I'm fine. I'll be fine. I stripped the bank account yesterday. That's how he knew I knew. That's really why he left me."

"How did you find out?" I ask. She cocks one eyebrow at me. I realize instantly it's a stupid question.

"When you have a husband who is a tub of lard who suddenly is interested in getting in shape but doesn't want to spend any time with you because he has to constantly work overtime without getting extra pay, that's your first clue. Your second clue is when the florist phones up and says you are delinquent on your bill but you haven't gotten any flowers or ordered any!" She blows her nose.

"Well lucky for me, I'm already slim," Sidney winks at me.

"If you ever cheat on me. I won't be as nice as her."

He squeezes the front door between his knees, turns the handle, steps outside and closes the door. He rattles the knob and taps on the door. Deborah is ranting about cheaters and how all men cheat.

Sidney calls, "I'm, done. Come check it out."

"Did you ask the florist who the flowers were sent to?" I ask.

"No. I gave her the fax number for work, and told her I was Arthur's secretary and I needed a copy of the original invoices or I couldn't cut her a check." She reaches into her purse and takes out several sheets of paper. "Then I went to the address on the delivery part of the invoice and found Arthur's car parked out front."

Sidney holds out a bag filled with old doorknobs. He smiles nervously at Deborah, and asks, "And then you did what?"

"I don't want those. Did you do both doors?" Deborah fumbles with her key chain.

"Yes he did. Here let me help you get those keys off. I have short nails."

"I don't care about my nails," she sobs.

"I thought you were going out?" Sidney says. "You want to look nice don't you? Have nice nails."

"I just said that to piss him off, I'm not going anywhere. I just want him to think I'm out having fun while they're stuck babysitting. I hope the kids fight, like cats and dogs, all night."

"Maybe you should go out," I say. "It might help take your mind off of things."

"What if he is here when I get back?" Deborah looks fearful.

"We'll stay and guard the house. I can hide the car in the garage and he won't know we're here. Tomorrow, if you feel the same way about us leaving, we'll look for a boarding house. We can call some places today, pack tonight and probably move out by tomorrow."

I squeeze his hand. "It will be weird to have our own place."

Deborah opens a package of cigarettes and lights one. She takes a long slow draw and says, "You think that's weird? Wait until you get to St. Lawrence."

"What do you mean weird?" I ask. "How do you know about St. Lawrence?"

The corners of her mouth turn downwards, and so do her eyes. "From nursing. Everyone in the medical field knows about St. Lawrence. You'll soon find out." She tosses a crumpled tissue on the table. It lands next to the bag of old door locks. Deborah shoves the bag toward Sidney and says,

"Didn't you hear me say, I don't want those? Please throw them in the garbage."

"Can I keep a set?" Sidney asks, "for St. Lawrence?"

"Take them all for all I care. But locks aren't what you two are going to need in St. Lawrence."

Her smug smile is unsettling. It reminds me of how Irma shaved half of my head, stood back, and admired her handiwork.

⁕ ⁕ ⁕ ⁕

The car grunts as it climbs up Barters Hill. I have a gnawing pain in the pit of my stomach. I am not excited about moving closer towards my father and his witch of a wife. I try to console myself with the fact he's not legally my father anymore, but it doesn't seem to help.

"What are you thinking about?" I ask.

"Nothing. Just how steep the hill is. What are you thinking about?"

"The same thing."

As we park in front of a skinny townhouse, I feel excited about Sidney. This will be the first time we will have some privacy and live in our own place. I rub my swollen belly. "I don't know anything about babies, cooking or nuns."

Sidney gnaws at his bottom lip. "Are you nervous about having the baby in a strange town, with no one to help?"

"What's the difference? I don't have anyone here either."

Sidney shuts off the engine. "This isn't the greatest part of town but at least there's a store within walking distance, and downtown is just around the corner. Wait here and I'll go get the key from the landlord. He lives on the first floor. Keep the doors locked." His back disappears as an old weathered door closes behind him. The peeling blue paint reveals the door was once a barnyard red. The first story looks recently painted. The entire street consists of skinny three story houses painted bright yellow, pink, red, green, lilac, blue, peach, beige and orange. No one door matches the color of the house it's attached to. The houses across the street are the same except the paint looks fresher.

Stalked

Children are playing some sort of tag game in the middle of the road. A stocky little girl kicks her right foot behind her back and grabs it with her hand. For a moment, she wavers back and forth. After two hops, she stumbles and catches herself with her hands, while her friend continues to hop past her. Cars slowly pass them on the left and right.

Tap. Tap. Tap. Sidney is waving a set of keys. I smile at his thin back as I follow him up the steps. "You know you'll have to cut your hair before you go teaching."

"No way. Nobody is touching my hair."

"Who cuts it now?"

"Deborah."

"So what are you going to do in St. Lawrence? Turn into a hippie?"

We reach the top just before my legs give out. I expect Sidney to stop and unlock one of these two doors. Instead, we turn a corner and continue climbing another set of stairs. The steps are much steeper than those back at Molly's store. At the top are two doors without numbers.

Sidney unlocks the left door, lifts me up, and stumbles a few feet before dropping me to the ground.

He waves his arm towards a counter. "Too bad we don't have stools."

"Why?"

"We could eat at the counter if we moved the hotplate."

"Well it could be worse. At least it's a two burner hotplate."

There's a small door beside the kitchen counter. Inside, is the smallest bathroom I have ever seen. It has a toilet and a skinny plastic curtain. "Where do we brush our teeth?"

Sidney pulls open the curtain, steps inside and points to the showerhead.

"Forget it. I'm not waiting to get a shower to brush my teeth."

Sidney grins and points to the toilet.

"Not funny." I say and return to the main room.

"Come here, and give me a hug."

"No." I point to the mattress. "We need to buy a tarp."

Within twenty minutes, Sidney and I are back at Deborah's house, asking to borrow bed sheets.

117

Deborah isn't in good shape. For two hours, we listen to her cry, rant and rave. While she's sulking in the bathroom, the phone rings.

"If it's Arthur, tell him I'm out on a date. Tell him he caught you going out the door."

Sidney hands me the phone. "It's Molly for you."

"Hi Molly." I listen in disbelief. I open my mouth wide and do a little dance. "Are you sure? A check for me?" Sidney gives me a thumbs up.

"Yes, it's made out to your maiden name but you should be able to cash it just the same. I think it is your quarterly clothing allowance. It looks computer-generated. It looks like it was dated two days before your wedding."

"You have no idea how happy you made us."

"Spend it wisely. There won't be anymore. Now that you're married you're not their responsibility."

"Molly, you're truly a godsend. Is it okay if Sidney comes get it now?"

I shake my head yes at Sidney, and while I'm still on the phone, he gathers up his keys, kisses me on the forehead, and leaves. I sit at the table, doodle, make a list of things we need to buy, and doodle some more.

Deborah asks, "Was that Arthur?"

"No it was Molly. The government sent my clothing allowance check so Sidney left to go get it."

"Isn't it kind of late?"

"No," I say, "Molly lives above the store and she keeps it open until eleven pm."

"You lived above a convenience store?" Deborah looks surprised.

I nod.

"You mean that store at the end of the Goulds?"

I nod again.

"Now it all makes sense."

"What makes sense?" I ask.

"I never could figure out why Sidney took so long to pick me up a pack of cigarettes or why he was so eager to go buy them for me every night. Has he been dating you since last summer?"

"I didn't start dating Sidney until just before Christmas."

"Really are you sure? When did you first meet? I mean when was the first time you actually saw him before you dated?"

"We first met in late August or September. I was hitchhiking to a dance with Denise, my roommate."

"I knew it. We held a surprise birthday for Sidney and instead of saying thank you, or you shouldn't have, the first thing he said was, 'Do you need me to go get you any cigarettes.'"

"What's so odd about that?" I ask.

"He had just picked me up a pack the night before and he knows a pack lasts me a week."

"But I don't understand he came into the shop every night and bought a pack of cigarettes. Every night."

"He came to be with you not to buy cigarettes."

"That's not true. I never spoke to him. He would just lurk around not able to decide what chips to buy. He actually scared me a little the way he looked at me. It made me so nervous, that whenever he showed up, I ran upstairs to my room."

"Dear lord, he stalked you. I cannot believe my brother is a stalker."

"He is not a stalker," I say.

"Who is not a stalker?" Sidney asks as he places the check on the table and pulls up a chair.

"You."

"Of course not. Why? Who said I was?"

I point to Deborah.

"We were discussing why it took you so long to get me some cigarettes. And now it doesn't seem so weird that you gave me thirty packages of cigarettes for Christmas."

"What was weird about that?" Sidney raises his eyebrows at Deborah.

"They come by the carton and their cheaper that way."

Sidney grins, "Well if she had a bedroom on the first floor you would have got nothing for Christmas. Do you know how much patience it took to sit in the car and wait until you showed up in the shop, knowing you were going to dart off as soon as you spotted me?"

"You were stalking me."

"No I was infatuated with you and I still am," he smiles.

"Well this has been the most shocking day of my life and I can't take anymore. I am going to bed. A cheating husband and a stalking brother. Good Lord, what's next?"

Sidney smiles wider, "I plan to stalk you for the rest of my life."

I smile back. "Go for it."

—————+—————

Sidney is lying on the floor surrounded by a pile of books and papers, reading the morning news.

"Where did you get the newspaper from?"

"It was in the hall. I've been borrowing a section at a time. Do we have any coffee?"

I point to the box on the counter. "But we don't have a pot."

"What about the care package Deborah gave us?" We both hurtle to the corner and rip the box open. Sidney tosses a roll of toilet paper towards the bathroom, and piles my arms full of dish soap, cleaning cloths and some towels.

The cupboard is bare except for half a jar of instant coffee and a box of cereal. It was Deborah who gave us the electric frying pan, my favorite wedding present. The other present was an envelope with twenty dollars in it.

"We need to pick up mugs and stuff. Do we have enough gas to get to the Arcade?"

"Why the Arcade? Isn't that like a thrift store?"

"They cash government checks. They're just down the road. Want to walk?"

"And lug things back up this hill?" He opens the cupboard and stares at the jar. "Why did Deborah give you a jar of chopped chili peppers?"

"She said it was instant coffee but she was pretty upset, so I didn't want to say anything to make her feel worse. Hey grab that box of cereal so we can eat on the run."

"No thanks. Let's cash this check and buy real coffee and a toaster."

"We have one. We got it for our wedding."

"We did? From who?" Sidney asks, as he pulls a business card from under the wiper.

"What's that?"

"I don't know . . . garbage." Sidney tears up the card and tosses it into the ashtray.

"Should you be using that for paper? What if you pick up a hitchhiker that smokes?"

"I don't pick up hitchhikers anymore. I used to keep change in here but until we get some spare money it's going to be a trash bin."

"So where's the toaster?"

"On top of the toilet tank. There was no room on the counter." He starts the car and looks me straight in the eye. "I am not making toast in a bathroom."

"Maybe we can buy one of those things for the hotplate."

"What things?"

"The wire tent thing campers make toast on or put it in the sink."

Sidney drops me off at the door and leaves to find a parking spot. I head for the camping section to look for a tarp. Instead, I find a small dented pot on clearance. I dig through a box of odd items until I find two plastic plates and a set of aluminum mugs.

"Pick up that sleeping bag."

Sidney twists and looks behind him.

"No the one over there in the clearance bin. Never mind. Here." I dump everything into his arms. "Bring this stuff to the counter."

"Haven't you heard of a shopping cart?"

"I wasn't expecting to find so much cheap stuff. Look! That sleeping bag is on clearance. Now we don't need to buy blankets."

"Isn't this a waste of money?"

"It was only a dollar."

"But it's downright ugly. Who paints a flag on canvas? It looks like preschool art. I'm not hanging this on the wall."

"It'll cover the sink. You know . . . for the toaster to sit on."

The cashier moves a few silver hairs away from her forehead. She nods at my tummy and says to Sidney, "She's nesting."

"Nesting?" Sidney lifts the trunk of the car and tosses in the packages. He slams it shut. "Nesting? What's that supposed to mean?"

I shrug. "Maybe it means—"

"Ssshhh! Listen." He turns up the volume on the radio. 'twenty-four, was one of sixteen passengers. Despite losing three siblings and his mother, the young man managed to pull one sister and a few others to safety. A nearby schooner—'

He switches the channel. '—amidst the fiery debris and found six survivors clinging to an overturned dory. Captain—'

Sidney shuts off the radio and turns on some music. Normally when he plays music, I'll be thinking about or humming the song for half the day. Not today. All I can hear in my head is that announcer's voice, over and over and over again.

I spend the entire day reorganizing everything, several times, while Sidney crams for his upcoming exam. Sidney yawns and tosses his book to the floor. "I need to get some sleep and you, young lady, you need to stop reorganizing the room."

"Come on. Help me I need to move the bed over there. I don't want people looking in our door straight at it."

"What people."

"I don't know. The landlord or whoever lives in the other room."

"Nobody lives in the other room."

"How do you know that?" I sit on the edge of the bed.

"The landlord told me."

"When?"

Sidney says, "If you come to bed I'll tell you."

I spit the toothpaste into the kitchen sink and rinse it out.

"Okay. I'm done. Tell me."

"Get in bed."

"Tell me first."

He pretends to snore.

"Fine. Have it your way." I climb over him and lean up on my elbow. "Well? How do you know we have this floor to ourselves?"

"When I went down to the car to get the sleeping bag the landlord told me if I wanted the newspapers to take them because the guy next door was dead."

I bolt upright in bed. "DEAD? HOW? Is he still in there?"

"No of course not."

"Did you even ask?"

"Juanita relax before you scare the baby. You know he can feel all of your moods."

"Maybe it's, not a he."

"You said it was. Didn't the doctor tell you it was a boy?"

"No. I read about it. You carry them in your back if they're boys and the doctor said the reason I look smaller than normal is because I'm carrying the baby in my back."

Sidney shakes his head at me. "If it's a girl we're getting you pregnant again." He tucks the sleeping bag under my chin.

"I'm too warm." I climb out of the sleeping bag and flop on top of it. "Sidney I can't stop thinking about those poor people who drowned to death. It's been on my mind all day. I don't get it. It's not like I live where it happened and everyone is talking about it. I didn't even know them yet it's really bothering me."

"Just be glad you don't live somewhere like that."

"Why?"

"You'd never hear the end of it. I'll guarantee you the entire community is talking about it."

"What community?"

"Wherever the survivors live. Hey let it go. You can't let those things eat at you. We live on an island. People die every day."

"No they don't."

"Yes they most certainly do and you would know that if you read a newspaper once in a while. Our waters are treacherous. Look what happened to the Titanic."

I can't get the image of jumping into the ice-cold ocean out of my head, "I think I'd rather drown then burn to death."

"Ssshhh. Think of something better. Think about the baby. Try to get some sleep."

I wake up to a dreary sky, lined with dark edged charcoal clouds. Usually I can see the store from this window. Not today. People walking below, look like blurred ominous forms. If they can be out in this, so can I. I grab my coat, lock the door and head down the steps towards the fog.

This fog isn't the kind that burns off. It's a dense heavy layer that lingers close to the ground, laced with moisture. It feels like a rain storm is lingering around the corner. Maybe a little thunder. When I reach the foot of the hill I can barely see the door of the small confectionary store. A bolt of lightning flashes and lights up the metal door. I pull it open and rush inside.

An elderly man is sitting on a stool with his back to me. He groans, glances towards me, carries the stool inside the counter and sits back, facing me. "Cold out there isn't it. Weather calls for rain but it'll freeze before it hits the ground."

"Do you sell meat and vegetables?"

He crosses his arms and points his fingers in opposite directions.

I see a cooler on my left and nothing on my right.

"Where are the potatoes?"

He points to a wheelbarrow over in the right corner. I choose two small ones, place them on the counter and head towards the cooler.

A package of beef that looks exactly like what I cooked at Deborah's, catches my eye. Ouch! There's no way I'll ever be able to afford something like that. The cheapest thing in the store is eggs.

"Can't I just buy two eggs?"

His two hands grip the edge of the counter. Small red hairs curl around his wrists and extend up to his rolled up shirt cuffs. His mustache reminds me of my Molly's whiskbroom.

"No. Why two eggs? No one buys just two eggs."

Molly never sold eggs at her store. At the Ruby's farm, we collected them from the chickens, as we needed them. "How many do they buy?" I ask.

He scrutinizes my face. "Where are you from?"

I feel awkward. I focus on the bags under his eyes. His breath smells like cigarettes.

"Your first time buying eggs? You live around here?"

"Yes. We just moved into a place up the road. It's just the two of us, so I just need two eggs."

"You only going to eat them once?"

"My husband and I don't have a fridge."

"Married? You look like you just got out of diapers. I'll tell you what. If you pay me for a dozen eggs I'll keep them here in the back of the cooler and you can come, get them whenever you need them."

"I don't have enough for a dozen eggs. I need to buy a bottle of instant coffee and these potatoes."

"How much do you have? Do you have enough for half a dozen eggs? People come in and buy half a dozen all the time but it's more expensive than buying twelve. I charge fifty cents extra to cut the carton in half."

"I have five dollars."

"That'll do it."

"Okay I'll buy six eggs and leave four of them here."

He chuckles and hands me a receipt and a small plastic bag.

"Got any pockets?"

"No. Why?"

"How you going to manage the eggs?"

"In a bag?"

"They'll crack."

"I'll hold them in my hand."

"Better choice." He holds the door open for me. "Yep it's a cold front alright. Careful looks like it's black ice out there."

When I reach the apartment, I hold the bag between my teeth while I struggle with the key. I grab a dishcloth from the drawer and lay the eggs on it. I heat up the frying pan and cut one of the potatoes into slices. Everything is going good until I have to turn them. They are stuck to the pan. The more I try to turn them the more they break apart.

I unplug the frying pan, grab the two eggs and head back down the hill.

Halfway there the drizzle turns to hailstones. The faster they fall the harder I run. Out of breath, I reach for the handle of the store door. My foot slips from underneath me. My hands slam against the wall.

Cra-ack.

My left hand is covered in yellow slime.

My stomach lurches. I gag uncontrollably.

"Are you okay?" Her perfume is so strong it makes me gag harder.

"No," I groan. "I needed to bring those eggs back." I look at the yellow drips sliding down towards the ground. Bits of broken shell cling to the green siding.

She walks past me into the shop and holds the door open. A few thin beads of ice fall around her shoulders. She lifts one high-heeled boot into the shop and holds the door open wider. "Ladies first." Her smile transforms her into a chipmunk. I try not to stare at her teeth. "I've lived here all my life. After a while you'll get used to Johnnie's death trap."

"And good morning to you too Clara. How goes it?"

"Hi Johnny, it goes good. You should throw a little ice on the steps. Your customer here almost fell and broke her neck. Give her some paper towels."

He rushes over with a cloth. "Are you okay?" the storekeeper asks.

"I'm fine, I didn't fall. The wall caught me."

"Good. I'd hate to have to bury you beside Martha."

"You should still ice those steps," Clara warns him.

"Here." He hands her a box of salt. "Be a doll Clara. Do it for me."

"Ten percent discount?"

126

"Go ahead take away my grandkids' college fund."

She sprinkles salt over my broken eggs. I glance at the paper towel and back at the eggs. What if I scraped them up and made scrambled eggs?

"Back already for more eggs?"

"No sir. Actually, I was bringing back the other eggs."

"It's Johnny, not sir. Why? Change your mind about cooking them today?"

"Butter and creamer."

"Come again."

"I just needed to return them so I could buy a little butter and creamer instead."

"You can't bring back two eggs just because you changed your mind."

"Well I can't bring them back anyway now because they broke when I slipped. How much is creamer?"

"What kind of creamer."

"I don't know—whatever people use in coffee—whatever is the cheapest."

He walks around to a shelf and returns with a small jar of white powder. "This is the cheapest coffee bleach money can buy."

"How much is one potato?"

"Ten cents more than the creamer."

A gust of wind blows Clara's perfume across the counter. Clara comes back in and hands him the salt, "You owe me so I expect a discount off my tab. How much is it anyway?"

"Forty-eight dollars and fifty cents, but give me the forty-eight and we'll call it even."

"I just got a promotion at work, and they want me to be a manager."

"Good for you Clara! That's great," Johnny smiles.

"No it's not great. As a manager I get weekends off but I have to work five days a week and stay to lock up," Clara complains.

"Clara, I would give my right hand to have weekends off," Johnny shakes his head.

"My niece can only babysit weekends, and daycare closes an hour before I get off."

"I'll babysit. I need a job babysitting," I blurt out.

"Really?" Clara's eyes light up. "Do you have transportation?"

"What the heck does she need transportation for? She lives just up the road. Give the kid a break."

She scribbles on the back of her receipt and hands it to me. "Tomorrow morning, eight sharp," she quips and tosses the receipt in my bag. "And don't be late or you're fired."

Before I can tell her I can only babysit for a few weeks, she rushes past me, leaving an invisible cloud of perfume hovering in front of my face. I sneeze twice.

"Now about those eggs do you want two more or the four you left here? And do you want the creamer or not?"

"I can't afford the creamer."

"Tell you what, how about I open a tab for you and put a limit, say a limit of ten bucks on it. You pay it, as soon as Clara pays you."

"Really? Thank you so-o-o much."

"So you'll take the creamer?"

"Yes and a jar of oil, a loaf of bread and a can of spaghetti . . . and some salt. Oh, and a tomato."

"Anything else?" His gold pen bounces up and down on the tab. "Are we done?"

"Do I have enough credit to buy some mayonnaise? Nothing in the store has prices on it."

"The prices are on the edge of the shelf. Below the product."

I watch as he writes down the items and calculates the total. "No. You're already two dollars and change short."

I cringe inside. "How much do you think I'll get paid for babysitting?"

"How would I know. Last time I paid a sitter your father was knee high to a grasshopper. My guess would be if it's anything under sixteen dollars a day, she's ripping you off."

"Can you make my tab limit sixteen dollars?" I ask.

Stalked

He looks at me for a minute or two before throwing his arms up. I can see a glimpse of a faded tattoo. It looks like an anchor.

"Is there a woman alive who won't rob me blind?"

"I promise I'll pay you back."

He gets off his stool and returns with a jar of mayonnaise.

He drops it in the bag. "Anything else?"

"No not today," I say, "Thanks. See you tomorrow or the next day!"

I walk on the road, in the tire tracks, whenever I can, to make sure I don't trip on any ice. Shivering from the cold and wet, I reach the apartment, with an hour to spare, before Sidney gets home.

I can't wait to tell him about my new job.

I open a can of spaghetti, throw it in with the mushed up potato, and make what resembles a tomato sandwich. I scrape the spaghetti onto a plate and hide it in the cupboard. I wash out the frying pan and hide any evidence of my surprise dinner.

For the next half hour, I sit on the bed and wait for the doorknob to turn.

He walks in with a wrinkled brown paper bag, removes two cheeseburgers, turns on the electric frying pan. "They're colder than I am." He removes the buns and tosses the meat in the pan.

I feel disappointed. "Where did you get those?"

"I volunteer at the cafeteria for free lunches, but I saved these to share with you."

"You didn't need to do that."

"Yes I did. How could I eat knowing you're here with bare cupboards?"

I throw open the cupboard door and grin. "See we have some food."

"Where did you get all of this?" he opens the mayonnaise and spreads it on the burger buns.

I point to the spaghetti. "I made us this."

"We can have it for breakfast. The burgers will be bad by tomorrow. How did you pay for this?"

"I bought it at the store. The owner gave me a tab."

"A tab? Juanita it's not like at Molly's where you could work it off."

"Oh yes it is. While I was at the store I got a job!"

"You got a job at the store?"

"Babysitting."

"Babysitting?"

"Yes!"

"You got the job at the store?"

"Yes!"

"Babysitting what? Vegetables?"

"No!"

"What's the store got a daycare? Does the owner have kids?"

After I explain what happened, Sidney asks me where Clara's house is. I show him the address. He flips over the receipt and opens the cupboard below the sink. He turns around and says, "Okay, I give up. Where did you put it?"

"Put what?"

"Fifty dollars? You spent fifty dollars? On what? I can't believe you'd spend that much, especially when we don't have a fridge. Wait there's ketchup on that receipt and I want some on my burger so where's the rest of the groceries?"

"It's not my receipt. It's hers. She used it to give me the address, and what if I make more than fifty bucks a week"

"I wouldn't count on it. And I'll guarantee you she'll want you on weekends and that's the only time I get to spend with you."

— + — + — + —

I wait for Johnny to find my page in his tab book. Sidney turned out to be right. I make exactly fifty dollars a week and it's the most boring job in the world. Last week I reorganized her cupboards and yesterday I cleaned her fridge. The first thing I thought about this morning was the milk. I put it on her windows sill because the window was cooler than the counter and I forgot to put it back.

"Just the milk?"

"Yes and I want to close my tab."

"Are you sure you want to close your tab?"

"Yes Johnny I do, but I'll be back whenever I need something." According to his clock, it's seven-thirty. "I have to go or I'll be late for work."

I grab the bag and dash out the door. I almost bang into some hooded person lurking at the edge of the street corner. "Sorry. Excuse me," I gasp. A few minutes later, I hear a whistling noise behind me. I turn around and look. A person several feet away stops to tie his shoe.

I recognize his hood. I quicken my step. Stop acting so nervous. He probably lives nearby.

I rush up towards Clara's door. Her entry is like ours. Inside the door are a few rooms and a stairwell. She lives in the top apartment but she has the entire floor to herself. She even has a small living room. I climb up the steps, and find Clara holding the door open.

"You sound like you weigh a ton," she laughs. "I can hear you before I can see you."

"I bought you some fresh milk. I think I made yours go sour."

"I figured as much when I saw the fridge cleaned out and found it in the trash."

"No." I point to her window.

"Good Lord." she chuckles. "If you hadn't told me I guarantee you it would be there until I decorated for Christmas."

She takes the bag from me and places it on the counter.

"I'm going to miss you. I can't believe this is your last week. It seems like I just hired you. Now you're leaving for . . . for?"

"St. Lawrence."

"I've never heard of the place. Must be in the middle of nowhere. Anyway, I'm off tomorrow, so could you do me a favor and change the boys' bed? Just put the bedding in garbage bags and leave the laundry on the kitchen table?"

"Did you say on the table?"

"Yes. It will be my reminder to go to the laundry mat first thing after I make coffee. God I hate housework."

I laugh, "Would you like me to tie a dirty sock around the handle of the coffee pot?"

"No! Don't you dare. By the way, the kids are going to a birthday party right after work so I will want them dressed for that so I can pick them up and run. I'll be in a rush, so I already put your pay on the counter beside the coffee pot. See you later! Keep the door locked!" She flies down the stairs.

I close the door and lean against the kitchen wall. I don't know which is worse, her perfume or the smell of brewing coffee. Lately everything smells weird and I can't stand being in this kitchen. I take the roll of garbage bags and head towards the squealing sounds. I find the boys on their bellies playing with tiny cars. Within half an hour, I'm bored out of my mind. Maybe I'm going to be a rotten mother. Maybe it would be better if I had a little girl. I mean how many times can you pretend to crash cars and not get sick of it?

I leave the kids on the living room floor and walk down the crayon colored hallway. I peel the sheets from their beds and stuff them into a plastic bags. I sit on the mattress and wonder where she keeps the spare sheets. And what is that god awful smell? It seems to be coming from the mattress. Maybe it's just me. The doctor said not to be surprised to find certain smells repulsive. But a stench? I check the boys' closet. It's a mess. Dirty clothes are scattered everywhere. I gather up their soiled clothes and put them in a separate garbage bag.

Once the bag is half-full, I kneel by the bed and look under it for stray socks. The smell reminds me of dirty cat litter. Paper cups, toys, toes of socks, and pieces of wood are embedded in a pile of dirt. I lift the mattress from the bed and lean it against the dresser. I remove what looks like a wide ladder that supports the mattress and tilt it up against the headboard of the bed. The dirt looks like gray powder. Is it ashes?

It takes me several hours to separate the clothing and toys from the mound. The clothes are so filthy I put them in a different garbage bag, and bag it twice more.

Stalked

I even find dirty diapers and both boys are school age. I take what seems to be toys and throw them in a garbage bag.

I drag the bag around the corner into the bathroom. At least she has a bathtub. I fill the tub with hot soapy water and avoid the temptation to jump in. I dump the bag of toys into it and watch the bubbles burst.

I force myself back to their room. How long has she lived here? Does she have an adult son who moved out? She must have swept twenty years of dirt under that bed. I'm afraid to look under the other one.

Several hours later, after making the boys a sandwich, I get up the nerve to venture into her room. I see what looks like pieces of a broken chair buried in a pile of dirt. It smells as if someone dumped a bunch of ashtrays in the pile.

"Mom doesn't like anyone in her room." The two boys peer under the bed. "Look over there. That's my car," Billy tries to dive under the bed.

"Stop!" I yell. Tommy instantly recoils.

"No it's mine," Billy fights him for it.

"Liar!"

"I'm telling Mom you called me a liar."

"Both of you go back into the living room."

The oldest listens while the younger boy wiggles under the bed. I grab him by the feet and pull him out. He holds onto the leg of the bed and screams, "NOOO! I WANT MY CAR!"

"You will catch a filthy disease if you go under there. You can't have the car until I clean it."

Billy rushes into the room. "Want me to hit him?"

"No!" I snap. "But you can help me get him away from this disgusting mess."

"Tommy, she said we can sit and watch to see how many toys she finds. As long as we don't move an inch."

"Okay," Tommy claps his hands. "Where do we sit?"

"How about on the mattress? Maybe you guys can help me get this one off the bed."

We pull the mattress and box spring off the bed and angle both against the wall. "Here sit against them and sit still so they don't fall on you."

Part of a scarf hangs from her top drawer. I pull it out and tie it across my face.

Billy pokes his little brother. "Haahahahahah. She looks like a bank robber doesn't she?" I pretend to shoot them. They pretend to die. The mattress tilts forward. I jump towards them and catch it, a foot away from their heads. I drag it back up against the wall.

"You two. Over by the dresser. Now."

The boys need no further encouragement.

The youngest boy tugs my hand, "Come on. Let's do mine next. I want to find some toys too."

"Not yet."

Tommy tugs on my hand. "Now."

"Only if you sit here quiet as a mouse while I work. I have to clean this one first before we do anything else."

After I have a full bag of garbage, I say, "Follow me."

I walk to the bathtub and remove the stopper. The two boys start squealing.

I throw a towel on the floor and tell them to put every toy on the towel and wait for it to dry.

"Can we dry them?"

"Sure. But if you fight over them I'm putting them in a garbage bag and giving them to your mom." I glance around the room. I see a linen closet but no shower. "You guys don't have a shower?"

Tommy points to the linen closet. I open the door. "What? You have a tub and a shower with a separate door?" I shake my finger at the boys. "Don't move. Wait right here for me. I'll be out in one minute."

I hop into the shower. Two minutes later I open the door a crack and say to the youngest, "Tommy hand me a towel."

No answer.

I open the door wider. The toys are gone and so are the boys. I run out of the room stark naked. I lurch to a stop when I find them sitting on the couch, surrounded by toys, watching a cartoon on TV. I tiptoe back to the bathroom stare at the towel on the floor. Who knows what crawled over those toys. I get dressed without drying myself off.

I pick up the phone and call Clara at work.

"What is it," her voice sounds full of panic. "What's wrong with the kids?"

"The kids are fine I just have a bunch of garbage I need to get rid of it. Or should I leave it in the kitchen?"

"Put it in the trash can. Under the sink."

"No I'm talking about three bags of garbage, the big green bags, half-full."

"I said bag the dirty laundry not trash it."

"I cleaned under your bed."

"But why? I told you not to go into my room."

"Well I was looking under the kids beds for laundry and that's what started it. Then the kids made me do yours to find their missing toys."

"I am so embarrassed, are you calling to quit?"

"I'm calling to find out where the garbage goes once it's full."

"Oh it goes outside."

I prop the phone between my ear and shoulder and drag the bag through the door. I am halfway down the steps but I don't see any garbage cans.

I hear the kids giggling close behind me. "Your kids are not allowed outside, right?"

"Absolutely not."

I twist and say, "Get inside and lock the door until I come back and don't open it for anyone." They both take turns taunting me.

"They won't listen and the youngest is sticking his tongue out."

"Spank them."

"Your mom said if you don't listen you are getting a spanking."

They shrug.

"And she is going to cut your ears off when she gets home." They scramble inside and slam the door. I drag the bag up to the landing and check the door. I laugh, "That worked."

135

I notice broken wood jutting from the bag. I twist the torn side away from me and look past the lower landing.

"I don't see any cans. Where out—"

A shadow falls across the bottom steps. I freeze. His hooded head tilts sideways up towards me. I talk a step backwards. He turns away looks left and right. In a split second, he twists around raises his right knee and lurches forward two steps at a time. I scream and push the bag at him. The phone drops from my shoulder toppling somewhere below him.

He stops, turns back and stomps it to pieces.

I scream and rush towards the top of the stairs and beat on the door. I can hear the kids laughing. I kick at it. The laughter stops. "Let me in. NOW. OPEN THE DOOR."

"No. You said don't open the door," the oldest yells back.

He pulls my leg and pulls me down several steps. I try to reach the railing as I fly past it. Abruptly his grasp flies from my shins. I scramble to my feet while he rolls his arms and wavers backwards his foot caught on the garbage bag. I yank at the broken leg sticking out from underneath it. The bag rips and trash scatters down the steps. He grabs at the railing, his right knuckles whiten, then he pulls himself forward and lunges at me. I grab the splintered wood and ram him across the face. His eye slant shut, I can smell the alcohol. I pull back with all my might and bat him across the face a second time.

His head twists to the side and he teeters backwards. I kick my feet against his knee. A searing burn flies through my left ankle as I watch him topple to the bottom.

I pick up the chair leg I used to hit him with and sit on the top of the stairs rocking and crying. The kids are crying frantically inside and refuse to open the door. I sit on the top step trying to get up the nerve to run past the twisted body. He looks dead, crumpled face down. I'm terrified he'll wake up the moment I step over him. Maybe he's not dead. Maybe he's waiting for me to check if he is.

I look down at the busted up phone. If I was inside I couldn't even call the police—but at least I'd be safer. I stand up with my eyes riveted on him.

Stalked

I hold the broken spindle in my right hand. It wavers erratically above my head. My wrist feels like it's on a spring. I try to step away from the door but my body is seized in fear. I squeeze my left hand between my back and the door and tap quietly. If I could turn around, I could knock louder but I don't dare take my eyes off him. I see his hand twitch. I scream, "Open the door!" I scream again at the top of my lungs, "OPEN UP THE DAMN DOOR!"

Hello St. Lawrence

The past several minutes have been a blur. Carla rushes towards me, "I'm the one who called. This is my sitter. Where are the kids?"

I ignore her too afraid to move. Carla's hands are shaking more than mine are as she fumbles with the key to the door. When the kids hear the knob rattle, they scream so loud I can't hear what the officer is saying to me.

They rush into her arms. She falls to her knees crying. "Thank you, thank you, thank you."

"Mommy we didn't open the door. We didn't open the door," the youngest cries.

"Good boy," she cries, hugging him closer.

"It was me, I'm the one who made him listen," the older one brags wiping his eyes. "Juanita told us not to open the door and I listened. He wanted to open it and I stopped him."

Carla rushes down the steps. I hear Carla gasp. She runs down the steps and kicks him square in the gut.

Stalked

He groans louder.

I breathe a sigh of relief as he goes limp again. If he's dead now, at least I'm not the one who killed him.

She pulls her foot back ready to kick him again.

"You bastard!" she screams.

An officer holds her back, "You know this man?"

"He's my boyfriend, my ex-boyfriend, he's a lousy drunk, a—"

The cop with the wallet returns. He's smiling. Fear rises in my chest. Is he releasing him?

"Do you know your boyfriend is on probation?"

"Yes. He likes to fight, which is why he's my ex-boyfriend."

"Well I'd be worried about the fact that he's a pedophile."

Carla savagely kicks the lifeless man repeatedly. Suddenly she's the center of attention and not me.

The older boy clings to me for a moment then says, "Wait here." I feel dizzy, too dizzy to move. I feel an envelope being tucked into my pocket, "Mommy forgets things when she's mad. She might forget to pay you." He throws his arms around me, "You're not coming back are you?"

I hug him wondering how he knows what I'm thinking. He pats my head and frowns. "The good ones never ever come back."

The next hour is a blur. I hear the paramedic voice. "Good. She' fine."

Is she referring to me or Carla? I don't feel one bit fine. I watch the stairs replay the moments from two hours earlier. His hood flashes in and out of the stairwell. I see a broom move back and forth. Clara's voice is muffled. She stoops to pick up some debris. It falls into the bag. I know I should help her but I can't muster up the energy. I close my eyes, cross my arms and rest my head on my lap. My stomach reminds me of gym class. The time we had to roll on those huge balls. I feel the baby kick me twice. He somersaults and kicks the opposite side before settling down. It helps calm me. Two familiar hands touch my shoulders. I smell him before I look up. I wrap my arms around his neck, as he carries me down the steps.

"She's okay," Clara says nervously. "You have a brave wife." He puts his hand on my swollen tummy. "He didn't hurt the baby did he?"

"Yes—I mean no." My voice sounds hoarse. My throat feels sore. I rest my head back on his shoulder. He sits me in the driver's seat of the car.

"Scoot over a little." I move away from the driver's side. He holds a thermos to my lips.

The smell of hot chocolate drifts under my nostrils. It reminds me of the Sundays at the farm, back in Mrs. Ruby's kitchen eating gooey chocolate chip cookies, sipping hot chocolate. Maybe I shouldn't have run away. Maybe it was safer there.

I sip on the thermos. It's warm. I take two more gulps before I hand it back to him.

"It's going to be okay." He sips the hot chocolate and offers me more. I shake my head. "The cops said his alcohol level was through the roof. You're very lucky. You know that right? You'd be no match for a sober version of him." He shudders and says, "I don't want to think about what might have happened if he wasn't so intoxicated."

He flips on the heater and hovers his hand over the dash. He quickly shuts it off. I feel a gust of cool air. "Almost warmed up."

"Can you take me home now?"

"Yes, unless you think I should take you to the hospital."

"No they said I was okay. I'm just dizzy. I didn't eat all day . . . and I don't want to be anywhere near here."

"I just wish I had gotten here sooner. I saw the police but I didn't expect it to be about you." He chuckles and scratches his head, "Looking back, why am I surprised?" His smile disappears. "You know I would die if anything ever happened to you. He wouldn't have a breath lift in his body, drunk or not." His fingers stroke my cheek. "The main thing is that you're okay. That's all that really matters."

"I just need to be home."

I hear a sharp tapping on my passenger window. My door flies open.

"Juanita, what the hell are you doing with him?" Sidney pulls me gently from the front seat, and glares at Gavin. "You stay away from my wife. You hear me? She's my wife."

"One of us has to take care of her and it doesn't look like you're doing such a great job. I would never let her work in this part of town, and I sure as hell wouldn't let her or the baby live in it either."

Sidney puts his arm around my back and propels me towards his Camaro. "How did you end up in his car?" Sidney is visibly upset.

"I don't know," I watch Gavin weave his car past the vehicles. Sidney follows him and passes our house. He spends five minutes parked a block away from our street before he heads home. Why isn't he saying something?

Sidney drives around the block twice before he brings me home. As soon as he unlocks our door, I head straight to the bathroom and lock it. I turn the shower on and stand underneath it. I lather myself in shampoo from head to toe. I stare at the drain and watch the last bubbles gurgle down the drain. I strip off my clothes and kick them to the corner of the shower. I scrub myself twice more. By the time I rinse off, the water is turning cold.

I open the door a crack. "Sidney. Where did the towels go? Can you hand me one?" I shiver and shake. I turn on the shower and feel the water. It's freezing. I shut it off. "CAN YOU PLEASE HAND ME A TOWEL."

His hand appears. "Could you take any longer?" I grab the towel and slam the door in his face. "Jerk!"

I find Sidney pacing from one side of the bed to the other. He glares at me, "Why the hell didn't you tell me what happened. Clara came by. She asked if you could babysit tomorrow—"

"You must not have heard her right. She's off tomorrow." I bend my head and wrap the towel around my hair.

"Oh I heard her right. She thinks the kids are too traumatized to drag to the laundry mat AFTER WHAT HAPPENED. You could have been KILLED. I told you not to take that job. Next time you should listen to me." His hands fly through his hair and return to his hips. "I told her to find someone else. You're not going back."

It is then I notice the boxes. I see one pried open.

"What's going on?"

"You wanted a towel."

"I'm talking about all of the boxes."

"We're moving."

"To where? We can hardly afford this place."

"We're going to St. Lawrence."

"But your job doesn't start for three weeks and we're broke. Are you crazy or what? How do you think we're going to manage?"

"I don't know but I'll figure something out. The sooner we leave the better. Help me pack the rest of this stuff. Everything but the sleeping bag and the clock. I already set the alarm for five."

"Shouldn't we go to the laundry mat and do laundry? Maybe wash the sleeping bag?"

"No. Besides we need every spare cent we have."

"Oh my god, my check was in my pocket!"

"STOP."

I freeze. I have never seen Sidney this angry. I keep my back to him.

"Turn around please. I need to talk with you. Clara dropped by your check. She said it fell out of your pocket when your husband carried you down the steps. I need to see your face." His face is stern. His arms are hugging his chest. Why isn't he hugging me?

"Fine just don't yell at me anymore. I've had a hard day." For a moment, I wish I had given the Christmas cologne to Gavin.

"What are you thinking about? Right now. What?"

"Nothing. Like I told you, I had a hard day. And you're right. I shouldn't have taken the job."

"You're not thinking about Gavin?"

"No. I'm thinking about slapping you in the face."

His face relaxes. "Good. That box on the bed is empty. The only things left to pack are your clothes. I'll put this box in the bathroom, so we don't forget our toothbrushes and combs."

"How far away is St. Lawrence?"

"Three hundred and fifty kilometers."

"What's that in miles?" I ask.

"Let's put it this way, it's about a five-hour drive—actually if we head out now—"

"Go NOW?"

"No. That wouldn't work out. We'll have to leave first thing in the morning. Let's go cash some checks. You're not the only one who got paid today."

"I need to stay here, I'm tired and my hair is too wet."

"I am not leaving you anywhere alone."

"I'm safe. The police arrested the pedophile guy. He's in jail."

"It's not the pedophile I'm worried about," mutters Sidney.

The night races by and we hit the road without eating. I watch the landscape change from green and lush to barren. I wait for the barren rocky view to go away. It doesn't. It gets worst. Four hours later we reach St. Lawrence. The town looks like a ghost town. No cars until we stop at a street light across from the hospital. The parking lot is full. Not a single available spot.

"Someone famous must be sick," I say. "Everyone seems to be at the hospital."

Sidney turns at the light, drives another mile and pulls into a very wide dirt driveway, and parks in front of a big two-story house. The neighbor's house is about twenty feet away and by the tire marks, it looks like they share the driveway. "How do you know this is the right place?"

He clicks his tongue and says, "I phoned them."

"It looks lived in," I say, gazing at the closed curtains.

"Well it's supposed to be empty, wait here," Sidney says.

He checks the door. I look up at the second story. There are curtains on both of the windows. I look closely at the lower windows waiting for movement. Something catches my eye. Out of nowhere, two people have materialized and are standing on the porch talking to Sidney.

The woman repeatedly slaps her hands onto her apron. White puffs of dust scatter in the breeze.

I can see Sidney's mouth moving and he seems to be motioning for me to come over to him. I shake my head. He approaches the car and opens my door. "Come on. They've invited us in for tea."

"I can't. I don't even know them. Besides I don't drink tea."

"You do now." He mouths the words, "Our landlords."

I mouth back, "I don't care."

Sidney turns away from me, "She's shy when it comes to strangers."

The broad shouldered woman stomps towards me. "Darlin' you won't stay that way long around us. Now come on over. When I heard you were coming early, I put on a spot of tea. Come on. No need to be shy around us." Her house is ten feet away. The door is wide open. I turn to make sure Sidney is following me.

"Never mind them. Come along. We don't bite. Take a seat."

A rocking chair is wedged between the cot and the stove. "No darlin', not that chair. He'll throw a fit. Sit over here. That way you'll be right next to me. The men can sit together. No doubt they'll be talkin' business."

The white cotton tablecloth hovers above the table and falls perfectly in place. Her hands move fast as she covers the surface with plates of cookies, biscuits, buns, jams and jellies. Everything looks homemade except for a bright red box of crackers. The box is covered in clear cellophane wrap. "Don't be shy help yourself." She unties her apron, and gives it to the man. "Be a dear and go outside and give it a shake or two."

"Woman, are ya done bakin'?"

"Almost," she smiles. Her dimples remind me of Sidney's belly button. I giggle nervously.

He tosses the apron on the cot and joins us at the table. "No need to dust it off den is dere?" He pops an entire cookie in his mouth, followed by three more. He gulps down an entire cup of tea and rubs his hands together. "Ready to go? Hurry up and finish yer tea so we can read yer leaves." He winks at me, takes my cup, swishes it around and swirls his hands over it and says, "I bet yer anxious to see da house."

"Christ Arnold. She just sat down. Let the poor child eat."

"Actually I'm full. Is the house ready?" I ask.

Arnold slaps his knee. "That depends on where yer taking it."

"She meant empty—ready for us." Sidney explains.

Stalked

"Naw. I wouldn't call her empty." The old man tilts his chair backward and scratches behind his ear. Sidney's eyes open wider than mine do. Arnold chuckles. "It's full ta da brim wit' furniture."

"I washed all the curtains, all the beddings and left a fresh pile of towels. There's nothing you needs to tend to. Are you sure you wouldn't like another spot of tea first? Another scone?"

"No thanks. It was delicious. I really am full."

"You hardly ate a bite. I s'pose you're hardly a hundred pounds. You'll be lucky if that baby weighs an ounce." Her hands fly across the plates, picking up various cookies. She tosses them into a plastic container and places it on my lap. "For later. When you get some cravings. That's when the baby is telling you it's hungry. Don't forget you're eating for two. Now don't refrigerate these or they'll go stale and pick up the smell of every vegetable in your fridge. Onions are known to do that. When I was pregnant with Leonard I near hated the smell of onions."

"We don't have a fridge."

"My dear, that house comes fully loaded. What kind of landlords would we be to rent you a house with no fridge? I dear say the landlords in St. John's must be a tad stingy with their money. Well Arnold, I s'pose we ought to bring them next door and give them the keys and such."

The house is only ten steps away.

"Never seen one of those before." The woman points to Sidney's yellow Camaro. "Are all the cars in St. John's that bright?"

"Come winter and ice yer gonna need a truck unless walkin' is yer t'ing." Arnold waves his arm at the car, as though he's swatting at a fly.

He unlocks the house door and stands beside it. "Ladies before germs." I step inside. Directly across from me is a flight of stairs. To the left is the living room. "T'ree bedrooms up dere and dis here," he opens a door to our right, "is yer kitchen. Ya know Gracie I shouldn't have listened to Leonard. Dis house should be like ours and walk right in yer kitchen. If ya had a crowd come over dey would be cloggin' up dis place."

Gracie opens the kitchen door. "The fridge is new. That stove's was my mother's but it still works like a charm."

145

"You can't beat an oil stove can you Gracie? Couldn't say fer certain how many meals came out of she. I'd say enough to feed all of St. Lawrence t'ree or four times. Hadn't she Gracie?"

The stove is a giant hunk of cast iron with a shelf built into the top. The claw legs seem embedded into the linoleum floor. There is a ten-inch ring shape burned into the floor, just below the oven door. In comparison to the room, the stove looked like a child's toy oven. "This kitchen is huge. I could fit three more tables in here and about twenty in the living room."

"Now why would ya want ta go and do dat fer? I don't know how it is wit' da folks in St. John's but nary a one of us uses a living room fer company. And around here dere's bound to be a wake more often den ya wants. And dose t'ings all happen in da kitchen." His dark eyes cloud over. He points to a door just past the stove.

"I never could figger out why Leonard wanted two kitchen doors. Dere's da other one, over dere by da counter."

"He wanted it because of his flare ups. To get to the bathroom quicker. I s'pose it'll come in handy a time or two for you when that baby drops." Gracie wipes her eyes with the tail of Arnold's plaid shirt. She pauses and caresses the door.

"Well 'nuff about dat. Move on Gracie. Show her da rest of da place before she grows a batch of wrinkles."

"What's that?" I point to a giant steel grid in the floor of the living room.

"Ya never heard of a floor furnace? Ya lift dat grate and ya tosses a match in dere." I watch as Arnold shows Sidney how to light it. Instead of tossing in the match, he blows it out. "It's da easiest t'ing in da world. Go ahead. Best ya get started doin' it yerself. She's got a wee bit of oil in her. It'll do ya fer a day or two. Dere's no oil wit' da rent and ya have ta pay fer the electrical yerselves."

Sidney coughs. "Would it be okay–I'm expecting a relocation check from the school board– do we have to pay the rent now?"

The man lifts his eyebrow. "I taut you teachers made damn good money? If ya don't sleep here where do ya plan ta live? In dat yeller car?"

146

Stalked

"I don't get paid until after two weeks of teaching but I'm expecting the relocation check any day."

"I don't know. No, I don't t'ink I can do dat." I hold my breath. His eyes drop from my face to my torso. "But what I can do is give ya da first month fer free. Dat should help ya out a bit. Ya know wit' ya being in da family way and all."

Sidney is still on his knees with his head stuck into the furnace opening, "The match went out," he mutters.

I could have kissed the old man, "Oh thank you, thank you so very much sir," I shake his hand.

"No t'anks needed. Relax child. Yer not pumpin' gas or nuttin. But ya best t'ank the boss before she fires me."

I smile at his wife. "Thank you, ma'am."

Her fists fly to her hips. "You so much as call me ma'am one more time and I'll make sure he charges you double what he's s'posed to." Her right fist unfolds and slides into her pocket, retrieves a gold band and slips it on her finger. "I lost it once in a batch of dough."

I twist my ring and ask, "How did you find it?"

"Arnold show her your tooth." She lifts his top lip.

"Gracie, dere's nuttin ta see. Leave it be."

"He near hates it when I tell people he near choked to death on my wedding ring." Gracie reaches in her other pocket and slips a watch around her wrist. "Goodness time flies. I have to run to the hospital to pick up my Sally." Her face hardens. "She'll be waiting on me. God knows she's itchin' to get out of there." Her eyes rest on my belly. "Soon you'll be joining that batch. Was it packed when you drove by?"

My stomach rolls into a tight ball. "Ow ow ow owwwwww."

"I s'pose I'll take that to mean a yes then?"

"Yes. I did notice there are a lot of cars over at the hospital—at least there was when we drove by." I say.

"Not all folk have cars. Half of dem been parked dere fer months. Dey wouldn't be outta gas if dey fixed dat damn hole in da ground."

Gracie wrings her hands together. "I could fix that in no time at all. and I wouldn't have any trouble findin' a good crowd of women to help me."

"Now, now, Gracie, how would people survive wit'out dat fluorspar mine? What do ya think folks would be doin' wit'out it?"

"Breathing. That's what. Living and breathing like normal men instead of dying faster than flies."

A bright glow fills the room as an inferno rises above my head.

"Quick help me get da grate on she." Arnold yells at Sidney. Together they pull the grate across the flames. Arnold runs outside. I watch as the black grate turns to a vivid orange. Within seconds, he's panting at the door.

"I turned off da main flow. Next time ya lights dat t'ing make sure ya gets it on da first try. She needs ta light fast. Ya can't let her build up oil like dat or da house will go up in smoke. Ya got any insurance?"

"Insurance? I have car insurance," says Sidney.

"Nope. House insurance."

"Of course not. I don't own a house," says Sidney.

"Ya will, if ya burns dis one down."

Gracie runs her hand along the desk in the corner of the living room. "I left this here. Thought you might like it for correcting exams and such, but if you're going to burn the place down I'm taking Leonard's desk back home."

"Is Leonard your son?" I ask.

"Was our son. Died of lung cancer. Worked at that mine . . . Arnold built this house for him . . . and his bride."

"Where does she live?"

"Up da road at da cemetery. She up and committed suicide after her brudder up and died. Passed one year to da day Leonard did. Guess she wanted ta be wit' both of dem more den live here beside us. Her brudder worked wit' Leonard, and the t'ree of dem were tight as a drum. Dat's how dey all met. Such a sad t'ing. Nuttin but t'ings like dat goin' on here now."

"I am so sorry." Somehow those words don't seem good enough but I can't find anything better to say.

"You know that's not half the story child. Do you want to know the full of it?"

I say nothing. I don't want to know. I can see by her twisted face that whatever is coming isn't good.

A small voice behind me says, "Not many fathers or big brothers around here anymore. All I can say is good luck hanging onto your man."

I turn around. A young freckle-faced boy, maybe twelve, is standing grinning in the door. "Don't worry if one of the widows steals him," he points a blood red finger at Sidney, "you can come live with us. Can't she Mom?"

Gracie grabs the boy by the ear, "Bobby, mind your tongue, and get your butt back to the house this very minute! And how many times have I told you to keep your fingers out of the cherry jar?"

"Don't put nuttin near dat grate and keep it off fer a bit. But I'll turn yer oil back on right now."

Sidney and I are exhausted. As soon as they leave we bolt upstairs. The bedroom is huge. I pull the patchwork quilt away from the pillows. It's heavier than it looks. The white crisp sheets smell like fresh air. The pillow cases have creases across them.

Sidney strips down to his boxers. His body is bonier than mine. "I need to learn to cook. You looked starved to death. Skin and bones."

"So do you."

I rub my belly, "Haahahahahah. Not funny."

"I'm serious. You look like you already had the baby."

"I wish." I take a deep breath and suck in my stomach. A bump pokes out, moves across my belly and disappears.

Sidney climbs in bed and traces my left cheek bone with his fingertips. "When I get paid we'll buy an iron."

"What for?"

"I can't go to class with wrinkled shirts."

"The only thing I've ever ironed is hair. What if I ruin them?"

The only answer I get is Sidney snoring in my left ear.

It takes three weeks for Sidney's check to arrive. And it takes the same length of time to run out of oil. I huddle over the boiling water wondering if I move away from the steam will a film of ice form over my face. The house is freezing and we have barricaded ourselves in the kitchen since yesterday. Both kitchen doors are closed and this is the third time I've filled, and boiled, the electric frying pan dry.

"Did you ask Arnold why your check was delivered to them and not us?"

Sidney's teeth chatter. "He said the mailman is used to delivering any mail related to this house to Arnold's mail box and their son always checks the box on his way home from school."

"But school is out at three."

"Apparently he doesn't go straight home. Maybe he had detention."

"I can't stay here one minute longer. I think I'd rather be in labor than deal with this." I pull my hands up inside my coat. "We need to go to the hospital—"

"Are you in labor?"

"No. Of course not. But we can go to the hospital and volunteer. We can get warm and help people at the same time. I'm serious—is that someone knocking on our door or is it the wind banging something around?"

"I'll go check it out."

"No don't open that door it will freeze—"

A gust of wind pushes the open door into the wall.

"Watch out for dat dere wind. Da gust is strong 'nuff ta blow da socks off ya." Arnold walks past Sidney into the kitchen. His eyes dart from the counter to the stove.

"Gracie and me are having us a game of cribbage and we taut it would be handy ta have two more players, but I see ya have yer coats on. Ya headin' out somewheres or warmin' up yerselves?"

"No. Just trying to stay warm. We ran out of oil."

"Den come on over. Gracie is puttin' on quite da spread."

Stalked

We follow him across the yard. Although it's snowing, and the wind is blowing, it feels much warmer outside. The sun is beating down on his doorstep, melting the snowflakes as they hit the ground.

"Dis will turn ta rain 'fore you know it."

A gorgeous blast of heat hits us as we enter their kitchen. Plates of food surround the most bizarre toothpick holder I have ever seen. It's a long block of wood with double rows of holes drilled along the edges. Four colored toothpicks protrude out of the holes on the far end. Arnold pulls a worn deck of cards from a crevice in the wood. "By da size of yer eyeballs, I take it dat ya never laid eyes on a cribbage board before." He pats the block of wood. "Hurry up Gracie yer as slow as cold molasses."

Gracie tears a piece of paper from a block of butter, and swipes it across the butter dish. She spreads it across the top of a loaf of bread as if she is painting a masterpiece. The melted butter glistens and turns the buns a deeper golden brown. She winks at me. "That's how you get a good crispy crust but the butter has to be soft, not hard."

"We lost some parts ta da game and I tossed her away, but Gracie wouldn't have no part of it. She dipped some toothpicks in food coloring rudder den give her up."

Gracie blushes, "Now, now, Arnold. No need to tell them that when they don't know what a cribbage board is s'posed to look like." I stare at the board wondering if they ever washed it. "Have a seat child. We never play cribbage without putting on a spread."

"Go on sit down. Eat."

Before I can pull my chair closer to the table, she has torn the bun away from the loaf and sliced it into four perfect slices.

It feels like I'm back at school in the cafeteria line. I have no idea what kind of casserole I'm eating. I only know it's warm and I finish before Sidney does.

A spoonful of casserole is hovering above my plate. I look up and shake my head, "No thanks. I'm full but that was so delicious. I have never tasted anything so good."

"Oh it's nothing. Just a little recipe I found on the back of a soup can. When it's cold out nothing like a hot soup. I use them as a base."

"What's a base?" I ask.

Gracie's slumped shoulders straighten. She glances at Arnold.

"It's like when ya makes beer and ya uses water as da base den ya adds da yeast and udder stuff."

Gracie slaps Arnold on his sleeve. "I doubt nary a one of them knows how to brew beer. Child, it's like when you make homemade soup and such. The—" She stops abruptly when I shake my head. "Did no one ever teach you to how to cook, child?"

I shake my head for the second time.

"Now Gracie ya knows yer going to have to fix dat."

———————

The next day I scan through the cupboard and find three soup cans. None of them have a single recipe on them.

Sidney taps my shoulder.

"Ready to go? I ordered oil so we can't be long and I need to cash my check to pay the driver, so let's hurry to the bank."

The bank is only two blocks away. And ten minutes later we have our first bank account and make out our first deposit slip. Sidney withdrawals half of it, and rushes back home to find the oil truck parked in the driveway. The driver saunters towards our car.

Sidney rolls down the window and asks, "How much cash do you need?"

"Lots. Probably more than you have."

"How much is the oil?" asks Sidney.

"I don't know. They'll send you the bill, I just pour it," he hops into his truck laughing.

"They bill us?"

"Yes Juanita. You heard him." Sidney's eyes are saying, shut up.

"They bill us? We froze for almost a week for nothing? You didn't phone them and ask?"

"No. Did you?"

"No but you're supposed to know better. You had a normal life, I didn't. Plus, you're older."

Sidney's eyes widen. He glares at me with a fake smile. "But sweetheart, I'm only older by a few months." I gulp. Lying about my age isn't going to be as easy as I thought. "Anyway, no need to get upset. I'll go light the furnace, and while the house is heating up we'll go get groceries." He opens the glove box and hands me a pen and a receipt. "Here make a list."

"I don't need a list. We need everything. All we have is three cans of tomato soup."

Sidney is back within seconds.

"That was fast."

"Lighting a match doesn't take long," Sidney grins as he backs out of the driveway.

At the grocery store the first end cap facing me is filled with cans of soup. I read the labels and toss a couple of them into the cart. Sidney stares at the cart.

"Why are you buying more cans of tomato soup? I'm sick of soup."

"So am I, but these have recipes on the back," I say. I pick one up and read it.

"For what? How to make tomato soup?"

"No, tomato soup cake."

"We have three cans at home, this will make five cans of tomato soup," he complains.

"The other one in the cart has a recipe for meatloaf," I say.

"I get meatloaf Juanita, but who makes tomato soup cake? It doesn't sound so good."

"But this cake recipe is on almost every single can, so it must be good."

Sidney picks up the other can and reads it, "We need some ground beef, some peas and some ketchup."

After we get home, I heat up the oven to bake the cake.

"What are you going to bake it in?"

"Oh my gosh. I forgot a pan. Can you go back and buy me a pan?"

"What kind of pan?"

"I don't know it says just says grease a cake pan."

"I'll go ask Gracie, I have to go pay them the rent anyway."

"Okay, but don't be long. I'm almost finished mixing it. Two hundred and thirty, two hundred and thirty-one—" I count silently as he kisses me. My arm is cramping by the time he gets back with two small square pans.

I sit by the oven and open the door every five minutes to check it. After an hour, it seems to be done. The cake weighs as much as a brick. By the time I get it cooled and frosted, we are famished.

"Wow it looks great," Sidney drools at the plate in front of him. I sit in the chair and scrutinize his mouth, as he chews and chews and chews and chews. I'd never seen Sidney chew so long. Maybe it just seems that long. Maybe I'm being impatient.

Impatience wins. "Well, how does it taste? Tell me the truth."

He works his mouth into a swallow, sips some water and swallows some more.

"It's, it's a, it's good," he gulps some more water.

I burst into tears, "You don't like it."

"I do, I do, it's just that it's, it's—"

"It's what, no good? You're lying. You're a liar. I can see it written all over your face. You hate it."

"Juanita, stop crying, I don't hate it."

"Tell me the truth? Tell me the truth or I'll never speak to you again."

"Fine. I'll tell you the truth. It's heavy. It felt like I was eating a sponge dripping with cement."

"I hate you," I sob and I run upstairs.

The next morning, we are laughing about it. "Please tell me you didn't pack any in my lunch."

"What lunch? I thought you'd be coming home for lunch."

"Not the first day. But I will after I get to know the routine."

"I have a great idea. Take the cake to school. If the students give you hard time, reward them with a piece of my cake."

Sidney is still laughing as he heads out the door. I follow him to the car and toss him a kiss goodbye.

Gracie is already up and hanging clothes on the line.

"My you're up early," she says. "Come in, child."

On the kitchen counter is a giant bowl with a cloth over it. I look at my stomach and back at the swollen rounded cloth.

"I don't know which of us looks more pregnant," I say.

"I'm making bread and the trick to getting the dough to rise is to keep it warm." She removes the cloth from the bowl and punches the swollen dough until it collapses to a third of the size. She punches it some more and then forms it into balls and puts it into bread pans and covers it with a cloth. "Now we keep it warm so it will rise up, then we bake it."

"Why not just stick it in the oven and let it rise while it bakes?"

She acts shocked. Her mouth opens but nothing comes out. "Let me guess. You've never seen someone make bread before." She punches at the dough. It sputters to half the size.

"So how did your cake turn out?"

"It didn't. He almost choked eating it. He said I'd discovered a new way to kill a man."

She chuckles. "Well you'll have to pick a different recipe next time. Didn't your mom teach you any good recipes?"

"No. My Mom is dead. She died when I was four."

"So what can you bake?"

"Nothing."

"What can you cook?"

"Toast and canned soup." I think about how many times I have scraped the black layer of the toast into the sink to make it edible and add, "maybe just soup. And I know how to make one slow cooker meal but I don't own a slow cooker."

"Oh you poor thing. Who's going to help you after the baby is born?"

"What do you mean help me after the baby is born?"

"Exactly what I said, child. A baby is a lot of work." She stops punching the dough. "An awful lot of work. What if you get postnatal blues, who's going to help you then?"

"What's postnatal blues?"

She wipes her hands on her apron, sits at the table and pats the chair to her left. "You best sit while I tell you what happened to poor Norma."

"Who's Norma? Your daughter?"

"Lord no! She's just a waif that lives . . . well use to live across the way." She slowly shakes her head.

"So what's postnatal blues?"

"Ah yes child. Back to that then. It's when you get depressed. It happens like clockwork after having a baby. Some folks don't get it at all but then there are those that get it so bad it turns into postnatal psychosis. That's what Norma Mullens had when she killed her kid. She went through all sorts of strange things. They say she got hallucinations and heard voices that weren't there but mind you, even if you did hear voices what soul would listen to them especially when it came to killing your offspring?"

A Stab in the Eye

I spend several mornings watching Gracie bake and today she's making another batch of bread. She pours some salt into the palm of her hand, "Wait!" I say. I grab a spoon from my pocket and scrape it from her palm into the spoon. It fills it halfway. "How many teaspoons are in a tablespoon? Two or three?" I pour the salt back into her out stretched palm.

"Where did you get that thing?" She tosses the salt into the bowl of flour, grabs my spoon and fires it into the garbage.

She reaches above the stove and pulls a big bowl from the cupboard. "Here, take it. It's the same size as the one I'm using." She shoves the sack of flour towards me. "Now fill the bowl half-full like I did."

I twist the sack around to read the weight.

"Child, what are you doing?"

"I'm reading how much flour is in here so I'll know how much half is."

"You fill the bowl like I did."

I spread my arm across the bowl.

"What are you doing now?"

"I'm measuring the bowl. I don't think I have a bowl this big."

"Do you want to learn how to bake or not?"

"I do."

"Good then stop trying to measure everything in my kitchen."

Somehow, my bowl looks like it's been used five times in a row, without being washed, and hers looks like she licked it clean.

After we wait for the bread to rise, I watch her make a cherry pie. When she's finished, she hands me a pie pan filled with a ball of raw dough and a can of cherry filling.

"What do you want me to do with this?"

"Take it home. Bake it and eat it." She winks at me. "He'll like it better than the tomato soup cake."

"What if I mess up?"

"Child, that's impossible to do?"

"The lattice looks hard." I grin. "I could mess that up."

She messes up my hair and sends me home with my head coated in flour.

The cherry pie is almost finished when Sidney gets home.

"Sit down," I say, "I have a surprise for you."

"Dare I guess? Another kitten? You saved another kitten."

"No." I laugh, "I baked you a surprise."

Sidney's smile disappears. He sniffs the air. He looks horrified.

"You know I am really full. I had snacks at school and someone brought in a giant pot of chili. I am so stuffed," he yawns.

I get a towel and hold it over the hot pie pan, and swirl around, "Tada!" I watch in horror as the pie slips and red goo oozes across the white linoleum floor. The only noise is the pan clattering to a stop.

I sit beside the oven and cry, "And you didn't get to see the lattice work."

Sidney massages my shoulders and kisses the back of my n.

"And I'm not cleaning that up. I'm leaving it there forever."

"You won't have to," Sidney's voice is muffled. "Yummy! Cherry pie is my favorite! Who cares about lattice work? Baked dough is baked dough, no matter how you shape it."

Stalked

I peek out from between my kneecaps. Sidney is lying on his belly scooping a fork across the pie. "Can you get me a spoon? I think a spoon would work better."

"Stop it. Don't do that just to make me feel better. Stop eating off the floor."

Sidney rises, opens a cupboard door, and reaches for a plate. I take the plate from him and scrape the pie into it. Then I dump it in the trash.

"What did you do that for?"

I frown at him. "What's wrong with you?" I kneel down and try to scrub the spill area. After two tries, it still looks stained. I sit back on my knees and cry, "How do I get this off the floor?"

"I don't know maybe someone wrote a book about it."

"What I need is a book on how to be a wife. I'm going crazy here."

He smiles at me and hold out his arms.

"It's not fair. Why can't men be the ones to get pregnant? Why do I have to be the one who can't do anything? I'm only sixteen and all I do is sit around and knit baby stuff."

"You can knit? Who taught you?"

"I watched Gracie. I was going to surprise you." I scoot over to the cupboard, pull out the needles and wool, and hold up the half-knit sweater.

"It's pink."

"So?"

"How come it isn't blue?"

"Because the blue wool wasn't on sale."

"A boy can't wear pink."

"You wore a pink jacket at our wedding."

"That's different. And it was mostly red and blue."

"Sidney I think we should start buying baby stuff."

"We can't afford it. Let's wait until it's born."

"Well if that's the case, you'll have to do it while I'm in hospital. Do you know anything about what babies need?"

"I'm only nineteen. How would I know any more than you would? Besides women are the ones who raise them. Not men." He's looking past me. His eyes are wide but blank. His fingernails tap against his teeth.

"What are you really thinking? Right now, at this very moment."

He bites at his forefinger.

"About bringing you to school . . . like back when we were dating. I know things are rough but I'll make it up to you. I promise. I'm thinking I can bring you to the school library. You could hang out and read about babies."

"I don't think that's a good idea. What if I'm not welcomed there? I mean won't it look weird?"

"How so?"

"Think about it. A pregnant girl among a bunch of students—your students."

"Are you forgetting I teach grade eleven? My students are older than you. I'm sure they've seen other teachers, or their wives, pregnant. I'll talk to Nancy today and see if it would be okay. I don't see why it would be a problem. I think the students only utilize it at lunch and after school. During lunch, I can drive you home or you go sit in the car. Think you can spend a few hours picking out some books? But don't check them out, I will because you need an id."

The next morning, I feel nervous and insecure. I'm afraid everyone will stare at me, and that's exactly what happens. It seems as if I'm on parade. Whispers follow our backs. I focus on the floor and count the tiles, while Sidney escorts me down the hall.

A chorus of "Good morning Mr. Sidney," echoes around us.

At the end of the hall are double doors to the gym. Sidney glances through the doors before opening a different one to our right. He points to a silver haired woman with hallow cheeks. She appears to be restocking books. "That's Mrs. Slaney. She can help you find anything you need. I have to rush. Class starts in two minutes," he whispers. He glances around, squeezes my hand, touches his heart, points at me, and leaves.

Stalked

A stack of forms rest in a plastic bin marked Library Card Applications. I pull one from the stack. I cringe when I read it Date of Birth. I leave the form blank and cough. "Excuse me?"

"Oh dear. I didn't hear anyone come in. You must be Sidney Simon's wife."

She frowns at me. I glance away. For some reason my throat feels too tight to speak. I look back at her and give a slight nod. Her eyes dart back and forth across my face.

"I'm Nancy Slaney and I hate to ask you this, but my husband has lung cancer." Her pale eyes blink rapidly. "He's at the hospital and they just called to say he's taken a turn for the worse. Is it possible you could take my place for an hour or so?"

I gulp. "I have no idea what to do. The last time I was in a library was at least eight months ago when—" I gasp. I almost said when I was in grade nine.

She looks at me expectantly.

"—when I broke my foot and couldn't work."

"Good! That means you know how the process works. The library is divided into four sections. The far corner area is where we shelf reference material—dictionaries and such. On the adjacent wall, over there, to the right is nonfiction. The fiction section is cross from those tables, and over in the last corner is the study area. Nonfiction is classified by subject such as religion and agriculture, whereas fiction is in alpha order." She opens a book and exposes the first page. "Accession number is here and the return date there." She holds up a black binder. "This is the accession register for recording new arrivals but no need to worry about this."

Thud.

"This is my Title Catalog and it's in alpha order by book title. That is the accession number and the F stands for fiction. Each of these index cards represent an in-stock book. I made this from a shoe box." A faint smile crosses her lips. Her chest heaves upward as she caresses the box. She pats it twice then wrings her hands. "Oh dear. What am I forgetting? Oh, that's it, yes. The students may only borrow one book at a time and that stamp is already set for the due date." Her eyes wander around the room and stop at her purse. "I guess I'll be needing this." Her gray skirt clings to her legs as she walks towards the door. She holds it open, turns and says, "Just one hour. I promise."

"Wait. Before you go can you tell me where the baby manuals are?"

She looks confused.

"Books about raising babies."

"In nonfiction. Under reference of course."

It takes me a while to find the books, they're in alpha order and I don't know any titles. Maybe it's under pediatrics. I find The Psychology of a Child by Jean Piaget. I put it back and select The Common Sense Book of Baby and Child Care and read it until the recess bell rings.

Surprisingly only a handful of students come in and they all leave within a minute or so. I breathe a sigh of relief. A minute later, a flurry of students, swarm in. They glance at me from the corners of their eyes. Every one of them picks out a book and waits in line.

I smile at the girl in front of me. Her bright blue nails match the book cover. "Good choice. This is a great novel." I open it, stamp the label and then I freeze.

She raises her eyebrows. I hold up my index finger and I open the drawers and find several packs of blank index cards.

I open another drawer. It's filled with paper clips and several boxes of paper. I notice two more boxes under the desk. One is another Title Catalog, while the other is empty.

I whisper to the girl, "Have you borrowed a book before?"

"No," she smiles. "It's my first time. I came to meet you. I'm Sara, Mr. Sidney's student."

I smile uncertain of an adequate response.

I stand up and address the room. "How many of you have been in here before?" Only six raise their hands. Sure enough, they are the same six students that came in earlier. "Could you six approach the counter and form a new line please."

Stalked

They rush towards me and jostle each other until a line is formed. I smile and say, "Which of you six have borrowed books before?"

They look at each other and shrug. One girl says, "Nobody borrows books during recess time. We just come here to hang out, you know, if it's bad weather outside. The real bookworms come in during lunch, and after school." The other five giggle.

Once their laughter wanes, I ask, "How many of you are here because you actually want to borrow a book?" Everyone raises their hands.

A grin sneaks across my face, knowing they won't read a single page, and they'll be back her tomorrow to return them.

I bite the edge of the plastic, rip the sleeve away from the index cards and grab a handful of pencils. "Excuse me everyone, but I need you to fill in these index cards. Please pass these to the students behind you."

A murmur fills the room. "On the side without lines, I need your full name, address and phone number. Open the book you are borrowing. and on the very first page you will see a number at the top right corner. That's the accession number for your book. On the side with lines, write down the accession number of your book. Those of you who have an identification card, move over behind these six girls. If you have no identification cards, you'll have to come back during your lunch break."

After a few groans. The crowd dwindles slightly.

I work my way through the line, collecting each card, matching the information with their books and IDs. Once recess ends, I count the cards for the second time. No wonder my face feels tight. In less than fifteen minutes, I smiled at least thirty-three times.

For an entire month, I fill in for Nancy. During that time, I get to know several of the teachers and most of the students.

The problem is they don't get to know me because I'm too fake and too busy trying to say the right things and act the right age.

"Mrs. Simon is it true this is your last day?"

"Where did you hear that?"

"Is it true Mrs. Slaney is coming back tomorrow?"

I smile at Bobby. "Yes but let that be our secret. I don't want everyone returning books all day today."

"They won't because school is closing at lunch. Are you going to the funeral?"

"I'm not sure. Probably not. Is Gracie—I mean are your parents going?"

"Everyone goes to wakes around here. All the adults get drunk and us kids get to eat all the food. They even have dancing and stuff. You should go."

"I'll think about it, but if I do, I won't be dancing or drinking."

The overhead speaker buzzes. I listen to the principal announce the funeral of Mr. Slaney. ". . . and I strongly encourage the staff and students to show up and pay their respect." I hear her rattle some papers before saying, "School is officially over at noon. Recess is now over. Please return to your classes."

Bobby snaps his fingers, "Told you. I know everything that goes on around here. See you at the wake."

When everyone leaves, I slump across the desk. So far this month I've had two false labors and now I feel like I'm heading for a third. I lean back in my chair and brace myself for a set of cramps. I wait a few minutes but nothing happens. Just a tight feeling.

I go over to the study tables to push the chairs in. I notice a book standing up on a chair across from me.

I flip through it, starting from the back. On the last page, after the epilogue, I see a penciled message. I read it twice. I can't believe my eyes.

Anna's pubic hair is black so you owe me five bucks.

I return to my desk, grab a pencil and erase the message. The pencil slips between my fingers and drops to the floor. I roll my chair away from the desk and bend to get it. Before I can straighten up, a severe cramp curls around my stomach. Without any warning, a warm fluid fills the seat of my chair. Warm water gushes down my legs. Fear grips its ugly fist around my throat. My heart is racing. The phone is shaking against my cheek.

"Do you need an outside line?"

"No I need a bucket and a mop. My water broke."

Five minutes later, I feel more embarrassed than fearful.

"Can she walk like this?" Sidney voice is an octave higher than normal.

The principal says, "Yes but bring your car to the entrance I'll wait here with her."

I close my eyes and cling to Sidney, "Don't leave me."

"I'll be right back. Don't move."

"Right like I'm going to run off. I can walk honest. Your car is just over—Oh my God this is real, this time it's real,"

Sidney sprints across the parking lot while I apologize for the umpteenth time. Another flood of contractions hit me just as I am trying to get in the front passenger door. Sidney seems to be in a state of shock.

"Help me."

The principal helps me into the back seat. Then he pushes Sidney behind the steering wheel. I pray for the contractions to stop and groan, "Dear God please don't let me give birth in the exact same place I was knocked up."

Sidney is ranting about the weather. "Of all days to have a snow storm. But snow is better than rain, or do you think rain is better?"

"Snow or rain, who cares? You know what's better? What's better is you and I never ever screw again." If I knew what these real pains were like, I would have known what false labor was. These pains have a built in timer. Each attack comes a minute too early and each lasts a minute longer than the one before it.

Sidney adjusts his mirror to see me. It reminds me of the first night I met him. "How are you doing? Are you okay?"

That's the same words he asked me the first night we met.

"No. I'm scared. I'm afraid something bad is going to happen."

"Like what? To you? To the baby?" It feels like the car is sliding off the road. My eyes jerk open.

Sidney hops out and pulls me to a sitting position. "I think I need to roll out of the car." I feel like a floundering whale but somehow we manage to make it to the nurse's desk.

Immediately my doctor appears and after a quick exam, I'm rolled into a delivery room.

Sidney rubs my hand and tries too sooth me.

"Stop. I'm okay," I gasp.

One minute later he asks, "How are you doing? Are you okay."

"YEE-EES."

After he asks me for the fifth time, I scream in pain, "NO! NO I'm NOT okay. STOP ASKING STUPID QUESTIONS. It's like someone is ripping my GUTS APART." I dig my fingernails deep into his arm.

By hour twenty, I have ripped through bed sheets with my teeth, swore at my doctor, cursed the day I got pregnant and promised to strangle Sidney several times.

"Oh my God I am sorry," I gasp. Another searing pain sets in and for a few minutes, I wonder if I have Tourette syndrome.

By hour thirty I'm certain Jekyll and Hyde reside inside of me.

Every now and then, the doctor disappears and returns.

"She's still seven centimeters, call me when she's eight," Dr. Collingwood says.

I plead for him to stay but he promises he isn't going anywhere.

I pull on his sleeve. The nurse pries my hand away.

"What does that even mean? He just left! What if the baby pops out now?"

The nurse assures me he hasn't left the hospital all week except to go on some emergency house calls.

"Where's he gone?"

"Not far. He's close by checking on other patients."

Sidney asks, "Where does he sleep? Here?"

The nurse frowns and whispers, "He doesn't sleep."

"Who cares where he SLEEEEEEEPS!" I scream, as an earthquake erupts and rips my stomach to shreds.

"Pant, pant, pant!" Sidney and the nurse are both holding my hand panting like overheated dogs. I feel like punching both of them in the face. I swing at Sidney and get his shoulder.

"What's that for."

Stalked

"FOR GETTING ME KNOCKED UP! You two can have this baby, I'm NOT having it. I don't want to be in labor anymore. It feels like I'm dying."

Dr. Collingwood returns and pokes his head under the sheet. He wiggles in closer. "The birth canal is too small. I'm going to give her an episiotomy and I'm going to have to use biceps."

"I don't care if you use a pick-axe. Get this thing OUT OF ME!" I bite my teeth into the sheet and swing my head back and forth. Strands of loose threads dangle across my face.

"Here," Sidney doubles his red sweater around his hand.

"Bite down. Bite me." Sidney jerks his hand away. His screams accompany mine.

By hour forty-nine, I hear a smack followed by a, "Wah, a-wah, wah."

A mucus-covered alien with an arrow shaped head suddenly becomes deadly quiet. I strain my head to get a better look. My throat is hoarse, "Is its head supposed to look like a huge tear drop?"

"Oh that will round out after you turn the baby for a bit," the nurse assures me. "Just put a rolled up towel between his skull and the headboard of the crib."

Turn the baby? It wasn't in any of the books. I didn't read anything about turning a baby.

"Congratulations," the doctor smiles at me. "You did it without drugs and you made a handsome little fellow. He's a boy. Seven pounds and nine ounces."

"Did you count his toes and fingers? How many toes and fingers does he have?"

The doctor slowly leans back and turns his head sideways. He lowers his mask revealing his salt and pepper unshaven chin. "Sidney would you like to do the honors." His voice sounds tired, but amused.

Sidney smiles, "He has eight—"

"Eight? Not ten!" I panic.

"Sweetie, he's normal. He's perfect. He has eight fingers and two thumbs," Sidney says. "And all ten toes."

167

My glare turns into a smile. "Good. I'm so glad. Whew! I'm so happy this is over. I'm never ever doing this again."

"I don't care how many fingers he has, I GOT A BOY!"

"Would you like to hold him?"

Sidney lifts his elbow and awkwardly cradles him.

He shakes his head. "We made this. We made this miracle. We have a son! Juanita we did it!"

"What would you have done if it was a girl?" I ask.

"What would you have done if it didn't have ten toes?" Sidney replies.

Two days later, I head down the hall towards Ward B looking for Dr. Collingwood. They have Little Sidney in an incubator and I want to see when we can leave and go home. I pass a frail man in the hall. He looks like he's about to fall out of his wheelchair. He is bent forward, struggling to breathe. I kneel beside him. He pats my shoulder and puts my hand on his seatbelt to show me he's strapped in. He pats me again still struggling for breath. I look into his worn eyes. He tries to smile and feebly waves me away.

"How are we today Mr. Turpin?"

"Do you need to push him back into his chair?"

"No honey, that's the only way he can breathe . . . thanks to Altann and its damn mine," her voice sounds bitter.

His rhythmic rasping fills the long cold hall. His eyes look hauntingly familiar. My mind flashes back to an earlier time . . . back to when I was eight. Those were the dull eyes in the mirror, filled with devastation when they saw my shaved head and bruised face. The only difference between those eyes and his sunken ones were his didn't hold any flickers of fear. I shiver as I look back into his eyes. His face floods with pain. His wheezing body lurches forward. Suddenly what I went through seems insignificant.

"You okay?" A finger taps my arm.

I shake as I take a deep breath. I can feel my nose burn. My eyes turn into broken facets. I turn my back.

Stalked

"I know," says the nurse, wiping her nose, "never in all my years has there been anything harder to see. After all these years you would think I'd be able to take it in stride."

"Years?" I ask. "How can someone who can't breathe live so long?"

"Sheer determination, I imagine. Doctor Collingwood mentioned you were a foster child. I heard lots about those foster homes and orphanages. You were never in St. Anthony's were you?"

"Yes. Actually once my father went salmon fishing there."

"I meant the orphanage. So your father died—or did he give you up?"

"Sort of. The courts took me away from him, after a hearing."

"Oh I see."

Her eyes drift down past my torso.

"No not that. It was his girlfriend. She did horrible things to us, but not that."

"We all have our cross to bear now don't we? I see you had your baby. Years ago, we had such a lovely maternity ward but after the miners all turned ill, we got rid of it. More people dying than being born these days. Now the best we can do is isolate the men from the women. But enough about that dark stuff. You need to think about good things, like raising that newborn. Shall I walk you to your ward?"

Sidney! Please don't be gone! "I have to go wave goodbye to my husband," I say. I tear down the hall, towards the Ward B window.

Out of breath, I scan the parking lot. A hint of yellow sparkles out from underneath a snowy mound. A movement to the left catches my eye. It's him! He backs up until he is knee-deep in a snow bank. I wave frantically. He pulls his hood over his head and looks up. My reserved husband dances around in circles. I have never seen him act so happy. I rub my eyes to show him I'm sad he's leaving.

He raises his arms waving wildly to me oblivious to anything but his joy. He points to his eye, makes a heart, points to me, cradles an imaginary baby and drops to his knees.

I smile. Someone behind me make a cooing sound.

169

His black gloved finger draws a huge heart into the snow. He stands and points to it. He bends over and adds some x's and o's.

I laugh.

He points at me, falls backwards and makes a snow angel.

A young nurse presses her noses against the window and giggles.

An older nurse presses her hands into her hips and murmurs, "That's what we could use in here, a few angels, but no angel in his right mind would want to hang around a dreary place like this."

"Well, well look who's here. My favorite little fighter and good fight it was."

Dr. Collingwood's voice sounds loud and boisterous. His Irish accent is stronger than normal and his words are heavily slurred.

"This girl is such a brave child. Hiccup. I don't know one woman here who could do what she did at sixteen, just a wee—" Dr. Collingwood staggers to the middle of the ward, "—wee child having a child."

I recoil out of the ward, back to my room and hop into bed. My heart is pounding. He stumbles into the ward and points at me. "There you are. I'm so proud of this little lassie."

He rocks back and forth as he bellows, "Sixteen. Look at her she's just a baby herself while you," he points to the overweight woman in the bed across from me, "you act like a spoiled child day in and day out. Moaning and groaning over nothing but a bit of pent up gas."

I stare at him as a black heavy shroud swirls beside me. It's one of the nuns helping a nurse navigate him out of the room. "Only sixteen! No parents and coming to this place and having to put up with . . ." his voice fades down the hall.

I cringe into a ball, cover my head under the blanket and cry.

"Sweetie. Are you okay? What happened? I knew something was wrong when you disappeared without a wave goodbye. I know it's not the baby because that's the first place I checked?"

He peels the blanket from my head.

Should I tell him what just happened? He'll die if he finds out. After all of this time walking on splinters, hiding my age—now we're liars.

I ask him to close the door. Instead, he reaches up and pulls the curtain around my bed and whispers, "What's going on?"

"He's loaded drunk and . . ."

"And what?" Sidney's eyes pierce mine.

"He announced my age to the entire hospital." I hold my breath and wait.

"Who?"

"Dr. Collingwood?"

He raises his eyebrows.

"Are you sure?"

"Are you deaf? You must have heard him somewhere along the way."

"That was him? I thought it was some drunk in the next elevator."

"The worst part is he went on and on about it. And his voice was so loud."

He releases a heavy sigh of relief. "Don't worry about it. It's not like he came to school and announced—"

The curtain is yanked open. The head nurse avoids my eyes. She reorganizes a few items on my bed tray. "Dr. Collingwood got called away. He will be back to see you in a while. He performed six surgeries during your labor. He spent his lunch hour making a house call and he hasn't slept a wink since I don't know when. He's a good man but he's lost a few this week."

I blow my nose.

"He meant no harm child. The doctor is friends with most of his patients and this morning alone he lost two more. It's hard for any of us to take. They're dying and there's nothing we can do to fix them." The nurse wrings her hands together. Her frown shortens her chin.

Sidney smiles at the nurse and asks her to thank the doctor for doing such a great job on the delivery. "I want to stay, but I have exams to correct. Will you be okay if I leave?"

"If you're okay, I'm okay."

Throughout the night, nurses wheel their cart around the halls. Every few hours they take my blood pressure. I find it impossible to sleep. Every time I doze off, the woman across from me lets out long loud farts.

I glance at the clock. It's eight. The last time I looked, it was 6.45. I must have drifted off for an hour or so.

A nun is standing at the foot of my bed. She's holding a breakfast tray. "Nothing like hot oatmeal on a cold blustery morning." She glances at the clock. "Dr. Collingwood should be in shortly."

I pull the bed table over my lap. She places the tray on it and brushes her hands together. "Dr. Collingwood undoubtedly is the best doctor around these parts but unfortunately the man attends more wakes than births. Lately he has been going nonstop. Forty-eight hours in labor is the most I've seen to date. Probably because you aren't fully developed. Well the good news is you get to go home today. If Dr. Collingwood's marathon of triple shifts doesn't soon end, we'll need that bed for him." She picks up my chart and glances at it. "I don't know how St. Lawrence would survive without him—you know, if there was a complaint or anything."

I swallow hard. "I don't see why anyone would complain about him."

"Bless you, child. It looks like Dr. Collingwood should be in within the next hour."

It seems like hours but only forty-five minutes pass before Dr. Collingwood shows up.

"Thank you," I say, "thank you for helping me."

His eyes are red, yet he appears to be dead sober. He pats my hand longer than normal. "I came here as a chest surgeon but as of late I've been covering all the bases. This isn't a normal hospital but that's no excuse, and I'm not about to make any excuses. I'm truly sorry if I upset you."

"It's just it looks bad for Sidney with him being a teacher. He's nineteen and I'm only sixteen."

"Well obviously you don't know how it is in this community. Sure, there is gossip but the people here accept outsiders as if they were family. When I treat a miner, I counsel the entire family. The people here don't expect anyone to be perfect. They just expect us to do our best. And yesterday was far from my best. Frankly, there is no adequate excuse. I truly am genuinely sorry," his Irish accent is easier to follow today. He pats my hand again.

"I know it's unforgiveable but I'm hoping you'll show me some mercy and come back and see me in two weeks. You have a few stitches down there but it could have been worse. For a while I thought I was going to have to C-Section you. It was rewarding to bring a life into the world. You had me worried for a while."

"Are you serious?" I can't believe he thinks what I put him through was rewarding.

"When every odd day, men are dropping like flies, and your hands are tied, it wears on you. As a doctor, all I can do is make them as comfortable as possible, while I fight the powers that be for justice, not just for them, but for the families. Down the hall, I have a father and son suffering side by side, in the same room, dying together. That's the kind of widows we make here and I don't have enough fingers to count how many times I've ate at their tables."

"What made you come here? You're Irish, right?"

"Yes. My parents owned a hotel best known for its bar. I wanted no part of it. I wanted this life instead. Do you know I earned my degree the year you were born?"

"Really."

"Yes and that's not the only date we have in common. When I reviewed your medical chart all the dates on it coincided with my life altering moments."

"Like what?" I sit up higher in the bed.

"Well for starters we are both from islands. Yours is a quarter bigger than Ireland. Let us see . . . 1960, the year I came here to St. Lawrence was the year your mother died. Like you I came here from St. John's. It was there I first encountered these fluorspar miners but the disease they were suffering from was unknown at the time. I bet you don't know that St. Lawrence has more widows per person, than any other place in this country."

He dabs the corners of his eyes. A missed tear, falls on my sheet.

"Some of them are so far gone, beyond helping but they hang on and fight anyway. Most of them believe in God but they don't pray like us. Most of them pray to die faster." He inhales a deep sigh, "I don't drink at wakes but with Christmas coming up in ten days, I made the mistake of indulging."

Sidney knocks as he enters the room.

"Hi Doc, good to see you." Sidney shakes his hand and gives me a hug. "Good to see you too, young lad." He shakes Sidney's hand again and walks away with his shoulders slumped.

We wait anxiously for the baby to be brought to the room. As soon as he arrives, we dress him in a bunting suit, carry him away from the stale air, and walk into a gusty breeze.

The air smells so fresh. I never realized how stale the hospital air was until now.

The ride home is quiet. I put my finger in the baby's hand. He instinctively grabs tighter yet he seems to be fast asleep. I crawl over the seat and smell his soft hair. He smells so good. He stirs a little and settles back down. It still feels magical to have him stirring beside me instead of inside of me. Sidney opens the door and lifts the baby up and frowns at the pink bunting bag.

"A teacher at school gave me a bag of used baby clothes but after Daddy gets paid he's going to buy you lots of boy things for Christmas. Oh! I called Mother and told her she had a grandson."

"What did she say?"

"She said she would send us some baby clothes. I told her we only wanted blue items."

"Did anyone ask you anything about my age?"

He turns towards me.

"Keep your eyes on the road and stop looking at me like that."

"Like what?"

"Like I have three heads. I'm serious. Answer me. Did you hear any rumors about my age?"

Sidney grins, "What did you expect? Protesters marching down the hospital halls?"

"So what age do I say I am now?"

"Eighteen."

Sidney balances the baby in one arm and turns the doorknob with the other. "If there are any rumors, I'll be the last to hear them."

"Congratulations!" Gracie greets us at the door. Sidney passes her the baby and pushes me towards the living room. A huge crowd yells, "Congratulations!"

My body jerks. I drop the baby bag. There are two thousand people in St. Lawrence and two percent of them are here. Introductions go in one ear and out the other. Teachers, their spouses and relatives or friends of Gracie each take turns looking at the baby.

Sidney smiles, "Gracie planned it."

Dr. Collingwood was absolutely right. These people do treat outsiders like family.

By the end of the afternoon, the female teachers and teacher's wives, decide to form a basketball team and compete against the community in a fund raising game.

One of Gracie's relatives, a coach for the community basketball team, promises to have a date set by Christmas Eve. Sidney knows I played basketball in school so he volunteers on my behalf.

"But the baby."

"It will be after school or on weekends so that's not an issue."

I cave under the peer pressure.

Nine days later, when Christmas Eve arrives, I get the best gift possible. Sidney tells me that the basketball game is postponed. Thankfully, nobody can agree on a date, which suits me just fine. My hands are full, between the baby and helping Sidney correct his students' exams. With Sidney spending afternoons and weekends playing floor hockey with the students, it's either he corrects the tests, or spends time with the baby, and both of those things need to happen.

He does help make formula, and he helps with the feedings every night. Still, despite all his help, I'm too exhausted to move. At first, I had the energy to do fifty sit-ups. I read it would accelerate me fitting into my old clothes. Now I don't have the energy to walk upstairs to the bedroom. Neither does Sidney. Some nights we'll sleep on the sofa because it's closer to the kitchen.

Today, I can't make it past the couch. I have the baby sleeping on top of the coffee table, in a drawer. Every two minutes, my chin hits my chest. I wake up briefly, scan for the baby and fight to keep my heavy eyes open. They are barely shut, when the sound of somebody kicking at the door, jolts me wide awake

It sounds urgent. I force myself to get up and answer it. Nothing greets me but a swift cold breeze. The only thing standing outside is our broken-down car, buried in a bank of snow. I kick some stray snow back where it belongs and swing the door shut. It hurtles open. A kid dashes up the steps and into the house. "Close the door! Quick!" He pulls back his hood, unzips his jacket and pulls out a kitten. "I had to run around the house, they were chasing me."

"Who?" I ask.

"The Heckell boys. They had the cat pinned to the clothes line and they were firing snowballs at it, so I stole it and they're chasing me to get it back."

"Oh Bobby, it's just a baby."

"I heard you save kittens."

Sidney walks towards us. He takes one look at the kitten and says, "I told you not to pay that Willard boy for saving the drowning kitten. I told you we'd have every cat in the neighborhood on our doorstep."

"Ignore him. He's upset because he's on Santa's naughty list."

I reach for the ball of fur. It curls up its lips, reveals it tiny goblin teeth, and makes a soundless hiss. "I'm calling you Snowball or Tattered." I cradle it like a baby and say, "Bobby, you did the right thing. You're a good boy for saving this kitten." I hold out my hand to Sidney. Reluctantly he puts a dollar in it. "Take it Bobby. Go buy yourself a candy bar."

"I didn't do it to get paid."

"I know you didn't but bravery deserves to be rewarded."

Bobby protests. I close the door gently on his hand until it wiggles outside the door, offer Sidney my best evil eye, and say, "It should have taken you less than a split second to say yes."

"You do realize they grow up to be cats."

"Look how cute she is. You're a teacher. What kind of example would you set if you made any other choice?" I cuddle the kitten for a minute and hand it to Sidney. He turns his head sideways and holds it a foot away.

"How do you know it's a she?"

"Because she looks like the other three. I think they might be sisters."

"No more, agreed?"

I say nothing.

"Promise me."

The doorbell rings. It's Bobby. "Here. I don't want it." He hands me the money back. "Keep it for milk for the kitten. If I see more people killing kittens can I bring them here?"

"NO."

"You sure can," I say. "This house is way too big for three people."

"Juanita no." Sidney lurches from the couch, stomps towards the door, glares at Bobby and ask, "What exactly do you intend to be when you grow up? Animal Patrol?"

"No sir! A vet!" Bobby grins, wipes a frosty mitten across his brow and races away. Sidney pushes the door with his foot. It bounces back filling the door jamb with snow.

"I don't suppose we own a shovel?"

"No," I grin, "but we own a big soup spoon."

He barely has reached the couch when the doorbell rings again. "See what you started?" He swings the door open. "Make yourself useful. Go get a shovel and dig out the drive—" I hear different sounds of laughter.

"That's not a nice way to greet your best friend!"

"Angel it's Harold. You remember Harold. Harold, our best man."

"It's so great to see you!" Puzzled I give him a big hug.

"You look absolutely stunning. Where's my godchild?"

"Godchild?"

"Cute kitten." He pauses and scratches her under the ear.

"You can have it if you want."

Harold throws his arms up in the air. "I'm not the fatherly type."

"I thought you were teaching in St. John's? What brings you here?"

"After Sidney invited me down for the christening, obviously without consulting you, I figured, I'm on Christmas break so why not drop down a week early—or is that a problem?"

"It's no problem at all is it Juanita." It's not hard to tell when Sidney is nervous. The only time he calls me Juanita, instead of Angel, is when things aren't cohesive.

Harold turns to Sidney. "Expecting someone to shovel out your car? Too lazy to do it yourself?"

"The car died the day we got home from the hospital. Sidney can't figure out what's wrong with it."

"Let's go look at it. We can catch up while we shovel."

"Don't waste your time. I've shoveled that thing out twice and it was snowed back in within an hour. It's got a fair amount of mileage. Probably needs a new engine."

"Hey kid got an extra shovel?"

Bobby runs over to Harold and says, "What for?" Follows Harold's eyes to the car and says, "Here. I'll go get more."

It only takes ten minutes for the four of us to clear the car. Harold listens as he turns the engine. "Hear that?"

Sidney says, "I don't hear anything."

"Exactly. I think it's a dead battery."

"No. The car would make a ticking sound if it were the battery. It's not the battery."

"When did you become mechanically inclined? I'll boost it."

Sidney gives him a condescending look. "There is no way I am wasting any more time trying to fix that car. And I am not shoveling out yours for nothing either."

Harold turns. Booby says, "Oops." And runs off with the shovels. Harold dangles the keys in his face. "It won't kill you to hold these. I'm just going to clear the hood and look under it."

"I'm going in. It's freezing out here. I'll make you guys some hot chocolate."

"I'll come help you watch the baby."

Sidney follows me to the kitchen. "I forgot how stubborn he is," he groans. "I'm almost sorry I called him about the baby's baptism."

"You mean the baby's christening," I say.

"No. I mean baptism. It's not a naming ceremony. Anyway, I asked Harold to be the baby's Godfather. Is there anyone you want to be his Godmother?"

"Do we need one?" I ask.

Harold flings the door open and puts Sidney in a headlock. Grinning from ear to ear, he drags him to the door. "Listen." He sits in the car and revs the engine.

We stand in the doorway in awe. Harold shuts off the car, kicks his boots on the door jam and says, "Back in high school, I told you to take shop."

"What the heck did you shut it off for," Sidney slumps against the door. "Now it'll never start again."

Harold grabs Sidney's coat off the chair and shoves it at Sidney, "Get your ass outside. I can boost it again, but we have to shovel the rest of it out. The muffler's packed with snow."

I glare at Sidney, "A boost, a boost? I've had to walk to the hospital and back, carrying a baby, to get my stitches out and this whole time all it needed was a boost."

He shrugs, "I thought it was the motor."

When they come back in, I'm sitting at the kitchen table scoring papers.

Harold grabs one and says, "You let her correct your exams?"

"Sure. I help with the baby and she helps me correct papers. She's good at it."

"She marks them?" Harold is staring at me. "What grade did you leave high school?"

"I didn't get to high school. I had to quit during grade nine."

"Jesus Sidney, that's not right."

"Your right, maybe I shouldn't let her correct them considering her lack of education."

I glare at them both. "It's not like I'm making up the answers. You wrote them down." I force my voice lower. "Just in case either of you forgot—I can read."

"No. No. I didn't mean that it was wrong for you to help Sidney. But he should be doing it himself, like I do."

Sidney playfully jabs Harold's shoulder. "That's because you don't have a good wife."

"Hey," Harold cups my chin. "I meant it's wrong for you to help Sidney. We get paid to do that. It's our job. I think you're brilliant and could have easily been a teacher like us." His eyes switch to Sidney. "Why don't you sign her up for her GED? She can do that by correspondence."

"Hello." I wave at them. "I'm sitting right here. And for the record, have zero interest in being a teacher. If someone told me I had to go to school for the rest of my life, I'd shoot myself." I give Sidney my best glare. "And the next time you infer I'm stupid, I will do something really stupid . . . to you."

"I did not infer any such thing did I Harold."

"I don't think he meant what you heard."

My glare switches to Harold. "If you have a grain of intelligence you will stay out of this." Harold makes the motion of zipping his mouth and crosses his eyes.

I laugh.

Sidney tosses his arm across my shoulder. "You don't need an education for everything. She does gives great haircuts."

Harold eyes widen. I know what he's thinking. Sidney's hair always looks the same. He's stuck on one style, because he hates frizzy curls. Instead of looking cut, it looks like it never grows.

I push him away and stalk out of the room, "Next time cut it yourself. And you might want to take advantage of Harold, and get an education on how to boost a car."

"I didn't study mechanics I studied EDUCATION," he yells after me.

After an awkward dinner Harold breaks the silence. "I know what I'm getting Sidney for Christmas."

"What a battery charger?" I make a face at Sidney.

"No. Some silver polish. His tongue seems a little tarnished."

I burst out laughing.

Later that night Sidney and I make an oath to avoid petty arguments during Harold's visit.

Even though Harold's stay is short, once he leaves, all those petty pent up fights, break free and we argue about everything, every day. The problem is I think I'm the one to blame. According to my doctor it's normal because my hormones are jacked up and I'm exhausted. Maybe if I didn't treat the baby like he was a fragile piece of glass I wouldn't be so edgy. According to my doctor, at sixteen I'm doing better than some mothers in their twenties. Apparently, some of them have depression and others reject their babies. Either way, after six weeks, we all go back to normal and stabilize. My six weeks will be up in three days, but my emotions are still wreaking havoc.

"The doctor mentioned birth control pills. When he comes back in, remind me to ask him if they make women moody."

"Don't bother. I already know they do."

"How would you know anything about birth control pills?"

"Deborah was absolutely insufferable before she got her tubes tied. Ask Harold. He refused to come near the house if she was visiting."

"You miss him don't you."

"Yes. but not as much as he misses me. I have you to fill all the gaps. He has nobody."

"I can't believe he fixed the car for us. Imagine walking all the way to the doctor's office, and back, in this weather? Especially with the baby."

"I'm surprised it's even working. It's barely chugging along. I still think the engine's going out."

"Well if it does, we'll invite Harold down for spring break," I grin.

The door makes a tapping sound. And Dr. Collingwood steps inside with folded arms. "Couldn't wait could you?"

"Pardon?"

"I told you to wait six weeks before you had sex. You were supposed to wait until I cleared you."

"Cleared me from what."

"I warned you that your womb needed a chance to heal."

"How far in is your womb?" I ask.

Sidney coughs and blushes.

"Had you listened to me you wouldn't be sitting here pregnant all over again, now would you?" His Irish accent sounds irritated.

"Pregnant? Me?"

"Of course you. Who else in this room would I be referring to. How do you feel about being pregnant so soon?" His eyes dart from Sidney, to me, then back to Sidney.

"I . . . uh . . . don't know . . . I need a moment for it to sink in. I'm shocked but maybe it's good. I don't know."

Sidney's face turns from worried to excited. "Actually I think it's great news. Little Sidney will have a baby sister—or brother to keep him company. I'm good with it."

Two of them look at me.

"I-I-I want Sidney to have a brother or sister but—"

"But what?" Sidney asks.

"Labor. I just can do the birth thing— I can't do that part again."

Doctor Collingwood pats my shoulder. "Well unfortunately we haven't yet invented an alternative to giving birth."

"I want the baby. I just don't want the labor."

He lifts a pen from his pocket and writes a prescription. "There may be a better way for you. What you think about me fixing that?"

"Really? How?"

"Let me worry about that when the time comes."

He hands me the prescription. "You just take care of yourself for the next eight months and we'll do just fine. I promise."

Sidney and I hug each other. I wrap my arms around his neck and look up into his eyes. I can tell he isn't faking it. He's genuinely happy about having another baby. I just wish I felt as excited as him.

I sit back on the edge of the bed and study my fingernails. My hands are trembling. The doctor reaches for my wrist, turns the heart charm on my bracelet, and reads it aloud.

"Sweet Sixteen. Half a century ago, when I was sixteen the only things my lips touched was a beer. Sweet sixteen . . . that's the problem we're facing."

"What problem?" Sidney stands up.

"The problem is your wife is not fully developed, and on top of that she didn't allow time for her womb to heal, which increases the risk of not reaching full-term."

I gasp. "What does that mean? A premature baby?"

"A higher probability is a miscarriage. But, maybe neither if you take it easy."

The sound of crunching snow is getting on my nerves. I stop in front of the stadium. Sidney swings around. His dark blue vinyl jacket makes his shoulders look bigger than they are.

"Sidney, let's not. Maybe this isn't such a good idea after all."

"Oh no you don't. The doctor said this would be good to do."

"Fine. Then have him do this. I don't want to. I have a bad feeling about it."

"That's because you're depressed."

"No I'm not."

"Yes you are. You have been depressed since you had the miscarriage. You know I lost a baby too. It wasn't just you."

"Yeah but you get to go to work and forget about it. I don't. I stay home, and think about it every time I scrub a diaper."

"We'll buy disposables."

"We can't afford it. And it's still a diaper."

Sidney holds my face between his hands. "I think of it too. Every time I change the baby or look at the baby, but you have to think of something else. That's why you're going to go in there and enjoy yourself for a change."

"Maybe I just need to stop doing what everyone else wants."

"Please . . . for me. It'll be good for you."

"I'm too worn out from walking to watch basketball, never mind play it. What if nobody pays to watch us? And even if some people do come, what good can the little bit of money we raise do? What difference will I make?" I ask.

"All the difference. Everything counts. Especially you."

Sidney squeezes my hand and pushes me inside the door.

Twenty minutes later, my lungs give out before my legs do. My daily sit-ups did absolutely nothing for my stamina.

I glance up at my husband in the top bleacher. He throws me a kiss and cheers me on. Some woman with long striped nails is going for a fast break. I come at her, from behind, and steal the ball. I twist and dribble in the opposite direction. She's tall, lanky, and twice as agile as I am. She jostles me for the ball. I twist and turn away from her. She dives in to scoop it.

A piercing stab shoots to the back of my head. I scream and drop to my knees, clutching my eye.

I roll back and forth, making sounds I've never heard before.

Sidney is yelling. He holds me tight. I open one eye and see a blurry crowd. Both my eyes are watering profusely. Someone is asking me to open my eye. I can't. I refuse to remove my hand.

I hear Doctor Collingwood's voice before I see his face. He and Sidney propel me to his car. Minutes later, he pulls in front of the emergency doors.

"Open your eye."

"I can't. The light hurts it."

I am flat on a gurney. Dr. Collingwood is trying to pry my eyelid open.

"Try to open it enough so I can get two drops in."

My eye rolls up in my head, hiding from the light.

"This is going to sting, but only for a few seconds, after that, your eye will go numb."

Sidney holds my hand. I sound like a wounded cat. Finally, the pain lessens to a dull ache.

"It's not good news. I can't treat this. If she stays, she risks losing the eye. To save it she needs to get to St. John's."

I touch the bandage.

"Keep your hands off that. You'll be wearing a patch for a while and if you don't keep your hands away from it, you'll be wearing it a lot longer than you think."

"For how long?" I ask.

"I don't know. The specialist will tell you more."

"Can't you help her," Sidney asks, "We have no car to get her to St. John's."

"The hospital will transport her there," Dr. Collingwood says.

"When will I be back?"

"Wait. Can't we just send her there every two weeks or something?"

"I can't leave Sidney. I don't want to. I'm not leaving."

Sidney taps the back of his index finger against his teeth.

"Stop. You sound like a woodpecker." I slip my hand into his. "I think it's getting better already."

Doctor Collingwood smiles at me. "It's the drops."

Sidney shrugs. "She's stubborn. I can't force her to leave."

"Yes you can, and yes you will. This is a very serious situation. She requires daily monitoring and treatment by an ophthalmology specialist. Let's hope she doesn't lose her eye."

His Nervous Breakdown

The thought of brain damage crosses my mind, as a drool slides down Sidney. The dryer is vibrating so bad I stop it and rearrange the laundry. Sidney opens his eyes, and cries at the top of his lungs. The second I turn the dryer on, he stops. It was Mr. Simon who suggested it. He said Sidney enjoyed the same thing when he was a baby.

I plunk the baby, chair and all, on top of the fresh laundry and carry the load to our room. Narrow striped wallpaper fades into a purplish-blue paint. Everything else in the room is a different shade of blue, except the crib. I put Little Sidney in it, grab a stack of sleepers, and catch my reflection in the mirror. This eye patch makes me look like a cyborg. According to the doctor, in four weeks, I'll be back to normal but until then, I'm tied to my mother-in-law's apron strings. I try to avoid her as much as I can but it's impossible because she's the one who changes my gauze. Once the doctor found out she was a nurse, he elected her for the daily task of caring for my eye. Now I only have to see him twice a week.

Stalked

Ting-a-ling. Ting-a-ling. I race for the phone and wait for the tap on the door.

"It's for you."

"Hi . . . I miss you too. I wasn't expecting you to call until tomorrow. Was your mom mad that you called?"

"No. I'm at school. I cancelled the phone service. One less bill to pay. I really miss you so much. I miss you both. I don't know if I can last much longer. I'm lost without you. At my wits end."

"I miss you too—But it's not all that great here either. The baby is really good . . . but—"

"Is everybody treating you okay?"

"Yeah but it's not the same it's like . . . like a long visit that never ends."

"Is it still going to take until the summer?"

"No. He thinks I'll be healed in four weeks."

"Juanita that's great! That means you'll get here by the beginning of May. Right in time for Mother's Day. I can't wait!"

"Did you get the car fixed yet?"

"No. It really is the motor this time. I was going to mail you money but Mother says she will buy what the baby needs and I can pay her back every month. I just paid her back for the crib she bought and I just sent you a letter, along with twenty dollars, in case you need some personal things."

"So what have you been doing since I've been gone? Anything different? Are you still going to the card games?"

"The teachers and spouses still get together once a week to play cards but I missed the last game."

"Why?"

"Because I started an afterschool hockey team. We actually travel by bus, stay in a motel and play other schools."

"Who pays for that?" I feel a little envious. "What's a motel like?"

"The school does and when you get back, in May, you can see one first hand. How about I book one for May 13th, Mother's Day?"

"I think Sidney is cutting his first tooth."

"Really? Already?"

"Yes. He's turned into a drool monster."

"Juanita, I asked you when you were coming back."

"Do you want me to send you a picture of him smiling?"

"You're not coming back are you?" His voice is low. "Is this because you lost the baby?"

"Pardon?"

Silence.

"Juanita I can't do this without you."

"Yes you can. As a matter of fact, it sounds as if you're doing better than when I was there. And I think you'll keep doing a better job, without having to worry about me, and the baby."

"Please come back. Please."

"I can't. You can come here when school finishes in June. What's one extra month. You should be getting a full eight hours of sleep because you're the one with a job to lose and me staying here would help you get that."

"Did my mother have anything to do with this? Did she suggest this?"

"She thinks it's a good idea that you focus on teaching and that Little Sidney get to know his grandparents. I think, she thinks, I'm too young to raise him."

"I don't care what she thinks, I want you back and I expect to help with the baby. He's my responsibility too. It won't be like before, it'll be fun. This place looks way better now that it's spring."

"Spring won't change people dying or sick as a dog. It feels like the entire town is one big funeral home."

"It is about losing the baby, isn't it?"

"When you finish the year out, maybe you can apply for a job somewhere else. Anywhere, just not there."

"I will. I promise. You won't have to spend another year here."

"I know I won't because I'm not coming back. It's not the best environment for a child. I want a better life for my son."

"I don't think I can survive here without you . . ." Sidney's voice trails off.

"You love teaching and you love hockey, besides if I move back, you wouldn't get to go off gallivanting all over the peninsula every weekend."

"I'm only gallivanting all over the peninsula every weekend, because you're not here."

"It's not fair to ask me to come back. You have a life there I don't."

"What are you doing at Mother's that you couldn't do here? Tell me."

I think for a minute, "Nothing."

"Exactly my point."

"But I can do things here, that I can't do there."

"You name one thing you can do there that you can't do here, and, I'll accept you waiting there for me until June."

"I can study for a GED and not have to hide my books when your students or the other teachers visit. I won't have to lie about my age anymore. My mind is made up. Please don't make me feel worse than I do. You have no idea of how bad I want to be with you. Or how much I miss you. I'm doing this because I love you."

"Fine, you win." Sidney voice sounds tired, "Is Mother treating you decent?"

"She seems to like me a little better since I started doing her hair with rollers."

"How about Father?"

"I like your dad. He's nice—really quiet though. He doesn't say much."

"He's given up on trying to get a word in edgewise," Sidney chuckles. "Hear that? There's a huge storm blasting against the windows. On nights like this the main thought I focus on, is you're better off there. I just wish my heart could agree."

I'll always hate snowstorms. They remind me too much of my past, sitting outside, looking in the windows, trying to see what time it was, wondering if I'd survive before she unlocked the door. "I'm really sorry about not coming back. Something about St. Lawrence reminds me of my past. It's so bleak. It's like wearing handcuffs while watching rabbits get caught in a snare. I felt trapped."

"Juanita you're living in one room with a baby, at my mother's house. Doesn't that make you feel more trapped? You had the whole house here."

"Sidney winters are worse there, and everything is so hopeless, like God lost track of that part of the world. I can't forget that chilling wind, or the haunting sound of it whistling and howling. Day after day trying to bring life back to my fingers."

"Are you talking about you're past or here."

"Both. I have to go the baby is crying."

Sidney's mother has spent the last few weeks brainwashing me about it being best if I stay here and let him finish out the year. At first it seemed like a bad idea, but now it seems like the best thing to do. Why move back and risk getting pregnant for the sake of a few weeks?

Four days later, an hour before everyone is getting ready to call it a night, there's a banging noise coming from the porch area.

"I haven't seen a storm like this in twenty years. It must have blown the screen door ajar. Must have forgot to lock it." Mr. Simon groans. His knees crack as leans ahead, trying to rise from the chair.

"It's okay. I'll go lock it. I have to get up and go check on the baby anyway."

The wind howls as I pull the door shut. A hand grabs the bottom of it. I scream.

He lifts his frozen hood from his face and exposes a frosty white beard.

I scream again. "It's Sidney!" I yell. "Oh my God it's Sidney!"

Mr. Simon and Mrs. Simon drag a staggering Sidney into the house while I stand with my hands across my mouth. My entire body starts to vibrate.

"Strip him down naked," she orders. "But be gentle. Stop massaging him. He could go into cardiac arrest." Mr. Simon balances him upright. Sidney's clothes are stiff as a board. I unzip his jacket and pull his arm out. Ice particles crumble to the floor.

"His pants too? They're froze solid."

Mr. Simon nods. His lean furrowed face is grim.

"His shirt too. In case it's damp. And his socks." Mrs. Simon is kneeling beside me with a laundry basket of hot clothes and a blanket from my bed. She hands me a pair of bright red wool socks and a pair of furry blue slippers.

She wraps the blanket around Sidney, and says, "Make sure his head stays covered. Take off his shirt, and his underwear and put these on him."

"His teeth are chattering like crazy."

"That's okay, it means his brain is contracting his skeletal muscles to keep him warm. The shivering will help increase his body heat."

We drape a second blanket around Sidney and move him to the living room. Mrs. Simon and I have one foot each, helping him walk, while Mr. Simon balances his upper body. We lower him to the floor, next to the fire.

"Turn it down dear, too much heat can cause the heart to stop." Mrs. Simon wraps a third blanket around him. It's then I notice her hands are trembling as much as mine. We lock eyes, and for the first time we connect. We both share a something in common.

Sidney tries to talk but all he can manage is a stutter. Mr. Simon starts to panic, "Grab the brandy, Dora. Get a shot of brandy in him."

His melting beard drips onto the blanket and his black eyebrows are covers with tiny beads of water. Mrs. Simon returns with the brandy and another blanket, removes the damp one from his head and rewraps him.

I hold my hands close to the fire. When I can't stand the heat anymore, I press them against his cold face. Mr. Simon props him up and Mrs. Simon feeds him small sips of brandy. "Give him another sip and make them bigger."

"He doesn't drink. I don't want to make him sick, and alcohol isn't what he needs right now."

After a dozen or more sips of brandy and six sets of warm blankets, Sidney becomes more coherent. That's when I stop holding my breath.

"I left three days ago," he says.

"How did you get here? What happened? Why are you here?"

"I hitchhiked, and walked. I walked for the past twenty miles. The roads were closed. Nothing open. No phones."

"My God Sidney, have you lost your mind? How the heck do you plan to get back?"

Sidney looks at his confused mother, "I don't. I quit."

"You what?" she says. "Have you lost your mind?"

"Dora, stop, the boys in shock, talk about it tomorrow."

I wrap my arms around Sidney and rock him. "You could have died out there. Froze to death. Are you warm enough?"

He pulls his arms from the blanket and hugs me back. He and I cry like babies. No matter how hard I try, I can't swallow the lump in my throat. "You're okay. You're okay right?"

"Of course he's not okay. Can't you see he's not okay?"

"Dora, hush now. Let it go. We can talk about this tomorrow. Let the boy warm up and get his senses back." Mr. Simon pats Sidney's shoulder. "It'll be okay son . . . it'll be okay."

"How's it going to be okay? He just quit his job."

"Dora, can't you see he's exhausted? Let the boy get some rest. Here. Have another shot of brandy."

Sidney refuses. "I just need some sleep."

I stay awake half the night listening to Sidney breathe. I lay my head on his chest to listen to his heart beating. I hear a wheezy, rattling sound. I move my head up to his shoulder and sleep better than I have in a long time.

Two days later, he is diagnosed with pneumonia and bedridden for weeks.

Over the next month, Sidney loses interest in everything. Nothing snaps him out of it. Not even the baby.

"Here change your son."

"Why? What do you have to do?"

"I have to listen to you tell me what the heck is going on inside of that brain of yours. That's what!"

He reluctantly removes Little Sidney's soggy diaper, balls it up and tosses it on the floor. I lean over and kiss the baby, then him. He turns his head away. "Listen, I'm sorry I got hurt. We both know that's the real reason you quit. If I hadn't gotten hurt, we would have stayed."

"I regret quitting, but I had no choice. I couldn't live without you." He sprinkles powder on Little Sidney's butt. "But it's not your fault. I'm the failure, not you."

"Your mother would disagree with that."

"It doesn't matter what she thinks about it?"

"Really? Since when?"

"The school sent me my final check."

"You got a check?"

"And an apartment. Mother works with a nurse who owns the house across the road and the basement apartment is vacant."

"Are you sure you want to move across the road?"

"No. But it's all we can afford. Oh my god. TAKE. HIM TAKE HIM."

I stare at the yellow spout aimed at Sidney's eyes. I laugh so hard tears roll down my face.

Sidney runs for the bathroom.

"He did that on purpose. He planned it. He was laughing."

I change Sidney and put him in his crib.

"Well are you ready to pack?"

"Pack? Now? The baby is sleeping."

Sidney rubs the towel across his head and tosses it on top of the diaper. "Good thing we put a plastic cover on that mattress."

"What is wrong with you. Since when did you throw towels on the floor."

"I learned it from you," he says and walks out of the room.

I put the towel in the laundry basket and drop the diaper in the trash. Sidney waves a pair of scissors at me and mutters, "Here you go."

"Here what?"

"Cut my hair."

"No. You need to go to a barber."

"I'm not in the mood to listen to a barber tell me his life story."

"No. Your mother will have a fit if I use her sewing scissors to cut your hair."

"Will you cut it when we move to the apartment?"

"Yes I'll cut it after we move."

"Then let's pack."

"Now?"

"Why not? The place is vacant."

"What about boxes?"

"Father has heavy duty construction bags."

"Shouldn't we wait until your mother gets off work?"

"No. It will be too dark by then."

"What about the bedding? Does the apartment have a washer? Because I for one am not sleeping in piss tonight."

"I doubt it. Use Mother's—or I can ask Father for a sleeping bag."

There isn't much to move but Mr. Simon insists on Sidney taking his old bedroom furniture.

"But what if you have company?"

"Then they can borrow the sleeping bag. Son you left everything behind when in St. Lawrence. Starting fresh is hard."

"He left everything because it belonged to the house . . . well maybe not the toaster." I glance around the room. The only thing here that reminds me of St. Lawrence is Sid's white plush toy rabbit. It reminds me of the kittens. Sidney gave the kittens back to Bobby and told him if he kept them he could have the yellow Camaro.

Over the next few days, we get offered towels, dishes and a few pots and pans. I swallow my pride and humbly accept everything offered.

It takes less than an hour to move across the road. But it takes me a week to sort and organize the baby's things, and during that time, we ended up back at his mother's for meals. I haven't used the stove once. I twist the knobs and hover my hand above the burners. Then I try the oven.

"What are you cooking? Tomato soup cake?" Sidney shuts the door and tosses a newspaper on the table.

"That's not funny."

"I got a job." Sidney voice is quiet. His smile is forced. His jaw is tight.

"That's great!" I say.

"Well I wouldn't call plucking chickens for a living great, but it's better than nothing. You know what this means don't you?"

"What? We get to eat here for a change?"

"No. It means you get to change all the shitty diapers."

"Not on your life. I get off when you get off and then we take turns!"

"You actually think your job is as hard as mine?" Sidney asks.

"Fine. I'll go pluck chickens and you play Mr. Mom."

"You can't. They wouldn't hire you."

"Why not?"

"Because the job called for grade eleven or higher."

"Are you serious?"

"Yes I'm serious. They said they were shocked to find out I had a degree."

"What did you say?"

"I told them not as shocked as I was to be wasting it on plucking chickens."

I don't say I'm sorry. I have said that too many times already and he made me promise to never say it again.

"Stop it."

"Stop what?"

"I can read your eyes. Stop it. Juanita did you ever see the movie love story?"

"No. The only movies I have seen are the couple you took me to."

"Well it's how I feel about you. The story is about two people in love and it's all about how love means never having to say you're sorry. So stop saying it."

"I didn't say it."

"Your eyes did."

After plucking several hundred chickens, Sidney decides to look for a second job. The baby is growing out of his clothes and it's impossible to scrape by on a minimum wage. With each passing day, Sidney becomes more and more withdrawn. His dislike for his job turns to hatred. He despises chicken and refers to his boss as a filthy pig.

He shoves away the toast and eggs. "I'm not hungry. These," he stabs the eggs, "remind me of work." He kisses the baby on the forehead and leans back against the door.

Little Sidney squirms in his lounge chair tipping it to the right.

"We have to get him a highchair," I say.

"Already. So soon?" He tilts forward and hits his forehead against the door. "With what?"

I clear the dishes from the table and stand at the sink. "Maybe I could get a job and—"

The lounge chair tilts forward. I am only a few feet away. I scream, lurch toward the baby, and try to slide under the lounge chair. I'm still screaming when I grab the upside down chair from the floor. Sidney picks Little Sidney up. His mouth is open but nothing is coming out. His face is blood red. He shakes him until a blood-curdling squeal is followed by a torrent of deafening screams. "Call your mom, call your mom," I yell. "He's bleeding like crazy. Do we hold him up? Down? What?"

Sidney with the phone against his ear. Runs a cloth under water and wrings it out. "We have no ice and—she hung up on me!"

"Stop. You're smothering him! Give him to me."

"Mother said keep pressure on the wound," he yells back.

"I don't care what she said get that cloth off his nose."

The door flies open and Mrs. Simon's grabs the baby, washes his face, and applies pressure with a cloth. I stay out of the way, crying like an idiot.

After the bleeding stops he has a slightly swollen lip and that's it.

She puts the baby in his crib. "He'll be fine," she says and puts a soother in his mouth. At first he whines a little then he suckles it at top speed.

"The child needs a high chair," she says.

"I know Mother but I can't afford one yet."

"You would be able to if you hadn't quit your job."

"Please Mother. Not that again."

Stalked

"Everyday someone at work asks me how my son likes teaching. I say he loves it. I am dreading the day someone says I heard your son is plucking chickens. Do you know what a disgrace you are to this family?"

She belittles Sidney while he says nothing. He just slumps to the floor with his back against the cupboards.

"Don't you talk to him like that."

"He's my son. I'll talk to him whatever way I want."

"Well he's my husband and this is my house and you will not!"

Mrs. Simon glares at me, "You would not have this place if it wasn't for me and it is your fault he has such a worthless job."

"That's not true. I didn't ask to get stabbed in the eye," I glare back.

"I didn't ask for you to get knocked up and ruin my son's life, look at that child, he could have died. You're not even fit to be a mother."

Pressure pumps to my head. My face feels like an overinflated tire about to have a blowout. "You! You, you're nothing but a hypocrite. You have your nerve calling someone an unfit mother. What kind of mother calls her son a loser when he's half dead with pneumonia and frozen stiff? All you care about is prestige and money. You don't care about how people feel. All you care about is bragging to the rest of your prestigious friends."

She yells back, "I regret the day he met you. You're just welfare trash and my son deserves better."

"Get out!" I scream, "Get out of my house or I'll call the police."

"Stop it now. Stop it or I'll kill myself," shrieks Sidney. "Stop blaming each other. It's my entire fault." He rolls back and forth on the floor in a fetal position.

His mother glares at me, and in a deadly voice hisses, "Now look what you've done."

"Me? Get out! Just get out," I shriek at her.

He puts his hands over his ears and whimpers more. I try to hug him. He winces. I try consoling him. He doesn't respond. His mother kneels beside me trying to calm him down. He recoils.

"Dr. Reilly? It's Dora Simon. It's an emergency. It's my son again, the one that had pneumonia . . . He's acting insane . . . No not at my house—across the road from it . . . Yes, in the basement level."

I have Sidney's head on my lap but he's ignoring me, scrunched up, crying and moaning.

"He's here," her voice is barely audible.

Doctor Reilly kneels beside Sidney, opens his satchel and pulls out a syringe. Mrs. Simon rolls up Sidney's sleeve, while the doctor swabs his arm and injects him with a clear liquid.

Within minutes Sidney relaxes.

"He's had a nervous breakdown," Dr. Reilly says while writing on a pad. "Get this filled and give him one every four hours."

A Second Chance

All day I pace back and forth. I even pace while feeding the baby. I stare at the clock and pace some more. I walk in circles wondering how to approach this without triggering him into a relapse. I crawl under the bed and pull out the toaster and the electric frying pan, and place them as far apart as possible on the counter. By the time Sidney gets home I'm dehydrated and my heels are blistered.

"Is something wrong with the baby?"

"No. He's been a good boy. He's sleeping now."

"Slow down. Why are you talking so fast? Did Mother come over here?"

"No-o." My voice cracks.

He walks past me. No hello, no kiss, goes over to the baby, watches him stir and looks relieved. "What's wrong with you?"

"I think I need some water. I feel faint."

The water spills out of the top of the glass and rolls over his wrist watch. Sidney turns pale. "That looks like the toaster we had in St. Lawrence."

"It kind of does, doesn't it?"

"And that electric frying pan—Juanita what's going on?"

"Maybe you should turn off the water and sit down." His entire body is shaking worse than mine. The chair scrapes, as I scoot across from him. My swallows sound like water gurgling down a sink.

Last month your father received a bunch of boxes from St. Lawrence. Gracie sent them. I've been unpacking them while you're at work. I didn't want you to be upset by them.

He looks relieved. "Geez for a minute I thought I was losing it again. Hallucinating or something."

"So-o-o-o, you're okay seeing those things?"

His smile widens, "Of course sweetie, get over here."

"Okay. So I'm not finished. I found some job positions and applied for them."

"I told you it makes no sense for you to work. Your entire check would be handed to a sitter."

"Not for me—for you."

"For me?"

"Teaching jobs. I found some."

"You did what?"

"In one of the boxes I found your resume and," I swallow hard and talk faster than I ever have before, "I copied it forged your name and sent it to different school boards."

He grips the edge of the table. "YOU DID WHAT?"

"I knew you missed teaching and I wanted to make it up to—"

"ARE YOU CRAZY!"

"Sidney you—"

"No Juanita. It's humiliating. I'm probably the joke of the school district."

"Well one isn't laughing at you, they're hiring you."

"What?" His mouth hangs open.

"I took the torn up newspapers out of the trash, ironed them and taped them together and sent off some applications."

"One of them offered me a job? When? How do you know?".

Stalked

"I read the mail."

"You read my mail?"

"Someone had to. It's been sitting there for over a week. Besides it's my mail. I wrote them. It's me they're writing back—"

Sidney grabs the letter that I'm waving at him. It rips in half. A look of terror sweeps across his face.

"Don't worry, I'll tape it back together. I'm good at it."

I'm as dizzy as a dog by the time Sidney stops twirling me around the room. He's dancing with the baby, dancing with me, laughing and smiling. It reminds me of that day outside the hospital. The day Dr. Collingwood told everyone my age.

I tape the letter back together and then I tape it to the table.

"What did you do that for?"

"Because last time you got one of these you lost it and freaked out." I tape the bottom edge. "See. Now it's safe."

"What's wrong?"

"What do you mean what's wrong."

"Your face. Your smile is gone."

I chew at my lip. "I am just wondering if this place will be worse or better than St. Lawrence."

Sidney smile narrows.

"No. No. I promise you we'll stick it out for the entire year no matter what and we won't play any basketball this time."

He is sitting in the chair, twirling the baby above his head chanting, "Daddy is a teacher again. Your daddy is a teacher again." A thick trail of vomit spews out of the baby's mouth and covers the letter.

Sidney and I lock eyes. With the baby suspended midair, he asks, "Do you remember the school name?"

"No, don't you?"

He drops the baby in the playpen.

We try washing the letter but all we succeed in doing is grossing ourselves out. The only parts readable are where I taped it.

I watch Sidney's mood crash to the floor.

"Please try to remember something. Anything?" he pleads. "That district has fifty-four schools."

I dive underneath the dresser and pull out a bunch of letters. "I made copies and I kept the ads—you bath the baby and I'll find them."

We narrow it down to two ads. We hardly sleep a wink, and when eight o'clock arrives we start calling.

Three calls later, Sidney confirms the school, grins at me, and holds up eight fingers and a thumb.

He barely has the phone hung up when I ask, "Is it thumbs up and grade eight or grade nine?"

"Grade nine. Juanita we're leaving tomorrow."

"What about your job."

"Who cares? They can kiss my white ass."

I gasp. "Sidney!"

He grins.

"How do we get there?"

"It's going to involve making up with Mother."

"Why?"

"Because someone has to cosign for a used car loan."

"Well she hates me so sucking up to her is your job, not mine."

"Juanita please, I need you to do this with me. You owe me."

"So you did think it was my fault you quit."

"No. This is your fault. And if I don't show up after accepting this position it will definitely, beyond a shadow of a doubt, be your fault!"

"Your mother told me not to dare set foot inside her house, ever again."

"She didn't mean it. She has too much pride to be the first to apologize."

"Go tell her I'm sorry and I'm too ashamed to tell her in person."

"If she invites you over will you come?"

"Sure." I say, knowing she won't. "Take the baby with you. Maybe she'll have a kinder heart."

Sidney is gone for an hour. I feel like I am waiting for someone to have a baby. Another hour passes. I hear a car rev in the driveway. It's a bright purple Javelin with white stripes.

Sidney sticks his head out the window. "It's ours."

I look inside. The black leather smells new. "What do you mean ours? I can't drive. Hey, where's the baby?"

"Mother wanted to have him overnight because it's the last time she'll see him for ten months. Father is coming over with more boxes. He's going to store everything in his basement. All we're taking is our clothes and the baby's playpen."

"Why not the crib?"

"The playpen folds up smaller and it only has a pad not a mattress. We will get him a bigger crib later—or a bed—at first he'll sleep with us."

"Where will we live?"

"Someone in Harbour Breton is going to rent us a room, just until we get a place."

Two days later, we're on the road, but the drive to Harbour Breton is worse than the drive to St. Lawrence. Once we leave the highway, it is miles and miles of bumpy gravel along a winding road. My stomach rolls as we drive down the arm of the sea between borders of steep cliffs.

"It's hard to believe this road is only two years old," Sidney laughs. "Up until two years ago you had to swim here. It was totally isolated until they linked it to the highway by road." The car is vibrating so much I almost throw up twice. The journey seems endless. After we reach pavement, the turn reveals an unnerving sign.

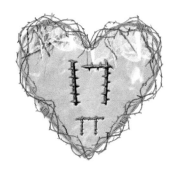

The Town with no Undertaker

"Is this a joke?"

"No," Sidney slowly shakes his head. "I don't think it is."

The sign is large and daunting.

"Can you back up? Maybe we read it wrong."

Sidney glances at his watch and throws the car in reverse. "Why would a mayor put up a sign like that? Certainly not to attract tourists."

"Maybe they don't like outsiders," I say and read the sign out loud. "Welcome to Harbour Breton. Population 500. Drive with Care We Have No Undertaker." I squirm. "What do they do with the dead? Pickle them?"

Sidney drives past the sign, but he's watching it from his side mirror. He shakes his head and grimaces. "Even if this town is worse than St. Lawrence we have to stick out, for the entire year, agreed?"

I point towards the coast line, and say, "Maybe this town doesn't have any builders either."

He looks to my right, "What the heck have you gotten us into?". A large barge, towing a house, floats out of view, across the harbor.

"Maybe it's their idea of a house boat. Or maybe they don't have taxis."

"Well, this town better have a cook, and serve food in that bar," he nods to his right, slows down and pulls in to the parking. "Because I'm starving."

We sit at the bar, drinking non-alcoholic drinks and eating some food. The bartender talks a mile a minute.

"You folks here to get photos of the landslide?"

"What landslide?" Sidney asks.

"It was all over the news. Where've you been? Under a rock?"

I watch Sidney's face turn blood red. I can't believe there is something he doesn't know. "You really did stop reading the newspaper!"

He nods.

"The landslide was huge—massive. The hill just gave away. A bunch of families woke up staring at a moon and mud. And some of them houses had more than one family in them." The bartender leans forward. "One of them homes took four children and buried them alive. But the baby just floated up above the mud and that one was saved. Now the government is building a bunch of houses, so they can have somewhere safe to live. You know it's bad, but some good always comes out of the bad. People got new jobs and all the construction workers, and mainlanders, are here spending money left right and center. Every boarding room is full and most days, so is this bar. So, are you comin' or goin'?"

"Coming. The sign says, the population is—" says Sidney.

"Don't mind that sign. It's old as the hills. Thanks to the relocation plan were countin' two thousand now."

"What's the relocation plan for?" I ask.

"Well years and years ago all kinds of people were scattered everywhere. No electricity, no schools and no jobs. The government relocated them all here. The last family that they moved here was from a small island, twenty or so miles off the coast. Only five people moved off the island and four of them are married to each other. Wink, wink, nudge, nudge. The year they moved here is the year we had that landslide. Some people think they jinxed us."

"So how many people live here now?" Sidney asks.

"Oh we're up to near two thousand and six hundred and not one of them is an undertaker. We're still waiting for one of those to be shipped in. You're not one are you?"

"No. I'm a teacher." Sidney takes a piece of paper from his pocket. "Would you happen to know the directions to this place?"

The bartender looks up and says, "Oh that's easy. It's over on the other side. Follow the road around the harbor and you'll find yourself smack in the middle of the Anglican side."

"The Anglican side?"

"Yes. You'll know your there when the house colors change to bright. You'll be looking for Linda's place. The two-story pink house with lime trim."

"Do you mean Anglican as in religion."

"Yep."

"You have a Catholic side too?"

"Yes but you wouldn't want to live there they'll shoot you. No Anglicans on the Catholic side and no Catholics allowed over with the Anglicans."

I tug at Sidney's arm. "It's almost dinnertime, we really should go."

The right side of town looks like a muddy ski slope. Debris is scattered everywhere. Roof tops are growing out of mountains of mud. Standing in the middle of the road, staring at the mess is a tall gaunt man. Sidney swerves to avoid him and blows the horn. He doesn't move.

"Maybe he has dementia or Alzheimer's," I say. "Maybe we should stop to help him. He looks like he is in shock."

Sidney stops the car, "Stay here."

I'm about to get out but the man limps away.

"What's wrong with him?" I ask.

"He didn't make any sense." Sidney pulls back out onto the road. "I asked him if he needed help and he muttered something about it being too late to help and he left."

Once we reach the other side of the harbor the houses look like a field of flowers. The pink house is halfway over on the Anglican side. Sidney and

I gape at each other. Finally, he speaks. "It's so far from the border. You don't like guns, is that typical for Anglicans?"

"Why did they put us here? Don't they know you're Catholic?"

"Guess not. Maybe we can stay here because you're Anglican."

"If we're here because of you and you're Catholic this doesn't make any sense whatsoever. Neither does two religions worshipping the same God fighting about division."

"Ssshhh!" Sidney rolls down his window. A slender woman looks inside. Her short hair looks like blades of grass, then it flattens as the wind subsides.

"Youse can sit here and gawk at the house all day or youse can come in and have some tea."

We follow her into the house down a hall into a room at the far end. It's furnished with a double bed, one dresser and a crib.

"When I heard youse had a baby I got the old crib out of the attic and cleaned it up for youse."

"You shouldn't have," I say.

"If youse have your own, or don't like it, I can move it back up."

"No. I love it and we left ours behind . . . I just meant I didn't want to trouble you."

"Oh 'twas no trouble at all. Go on, settle in and I'll make some tea."

The table has cold cuts, cheese, golden fresh baked bread and an apple pie. Small glass bowls of mustard covered pickles, red beets and olives are over to the side. In front of us is a plate with a banana loaf and a knife stuck down the middle.

I look at the knife wondering if they would use it if they found out Sidney was Catholic. I glance at Sidney. His eyes follow mine and I know he's thinking the same thoughts.

The next morning, at breakfast, when Sidney asks for directions to the elementary school the shit hits the fan. Every face around the table looks like they swallowed a mouthful of crap. Everyone hastily excuses themselves from the table but us. I get up slowly and pick up the baby while I pull on Sidney's collar. He grabs a napkin and wraps the egg in it. We retreat to our room and huddled together.

"Move your legs," I say, and tug on the suitcase.

"What are you doing?"

"Packing."

"Noooooo," Sidney groans. "Not again? You're leaving already?"

"We're leaving."

"To where?"

"I don't know."

"We can't leave."

"Well one thing's for damn sure we can't stay here, now can we?"

"Just wait."

"Wait for what."

"I don't know."

I shove the suitcase under the bed and lie down beside the baby.

For the rest of the morning we stay in the room, waiting.

At noon, a tap sounds from the door. I answer it. Linda's face is tense. Her thin lips are drawn downwards. "It's not me it's my husband. He says you have to leave."

"Leave to where?" I ask. "We have nowhere to go."

"Over to the Catholic side," she says. "They'll make room for you over there."

"But I'm Anglican," I say.

"You're what?" she gasps.

"I'm Anglican so I can't go over there."

"You married a Catholic?"

Sidney groans a weird noise. It sounds like a noise he made the day he had the nervous breakdown. I let go of his arm and start counting in my head. I walk around the room back and forth.

"What are you doing?" Sidney asks. "Stop you're driving me nuts."

"I'm counting my footsteps."

"Why?" Sidney sounds impatient.

"I don't know. I guess it helps me pass time," I say.

"Ssshhh, listen," he says.

The floorboards creak outside the door. I hear a cough then a knock.

"I made you lunch?" she says looking at me.

I wasn't sure why it was a question or what the answer should be. I nod a few times in case she's asking if I'm hungry.

"I'm not sure what Catholics eat so I hope it's okay."

I glance at Sidney, "He eats whatever I feed him so I'm sure anything at all is fine."

She looks slightly relieved.

At the table is the same spread that was there the day we arrived. Steam is rising from the bread.

As we sit at the table Linda prays silently. While she has her eyes closed Sidney quickly crosses his chest.

She ends her prayer out loud, saying, "And dear lord please show them favor at the town meeting. Amen."

"What do you mean show us favor at the town meeting?" Visions of a lynching mob and dangling ropes sway in my mind as I wait for her answer.

She speaks slowly, "There is going to be an emergency town meeting."

"Who is going?"

"Everyone."

"The Anglicans and the Catholics?"

"Yes."

"Are we going?" I ask while Sidney chokes on his bread.

"No. It's best if you don't. It might upset too many folks."

This evening is the quietest evening I have ever heard. The baby sleeps more than usual. Probably because he was awake the entire night before. Finally, I hear footsteps. Muffled voices sound closer.

Linda knocks on the open door. "The priest is coming. He'll be here any minute."

"Here? I thought you didn't allow Catholics over here or in your house?" Maybe this is a huge joke, I think, maybe all the teachers are in on this. Maybe it's an initiation for new comers.

"Not so child. He's a man of God even if he's wearing the wrong cloth."

The priest looms over the door. He looks like a wrestler wearing a priest costume. He softly says, "Excuse me Linda," and closes the door. "This town hasn't had so much excitement since 1963 when electricity came."

"You were here? Before electricity?"

"No and I thank God for that. I heard about it though. Do you know what the biggest problem was? Fighting over which side got it first. That's probably why it took so long to get here."

He sighs deeply and says, "I've got good news and I've got bad news. The good news is the meeting is over. The bad news is neither side wants you. The good news is the Anglican side will take Juanita and the Catholic side will take you if you were willing to live separate lives for the next year."

"No!" I say. Then I remember the promise I made myself. I promised no matter what happened I would stick out the entire year so Sidney could have his dream. "I mean no I don't like it but it's up to Sidney." I look at him. "If you want I can."

A tear falls down Sidney's face. "That's what happened last time. I had to q—"

I press my fingers into Sidney's back. "He had to quit living with me because last year I got an eye injury and had to go to St. John's for emergency care. We can't do that again, and I don't think the school board lets people fire someone just because they married an Anglican."

The priest looks at me, "You have a point. So I guess that settles it. You'll have to come and live with me until we figure out something different."

Living with the priest is different than I ever could have imagined. He actually has a maid and a cook, and only appears for meals. Eventually I become friends with all the nuns and find they are the most open minded people in the community. They laugh when I tell them I used to want to be a nun when I was a kid.

The housekeeper does all the chores so for once I don't have to scrub floors. The priest's cook makes the greatest gourmet food I have ever seen, but it isn't until she makes hot wings that I beg her to let me watch her cook. After that I spend the better part of my day in the kitchen watching her.

I watch her make meatloaf but vow to never make it. Too many onions, plus it looks like dog food with ketchup sauce. She reads my face and smiles, "Juanita your lips are curling down, but this will be delicious I promise you."

"I love your wings, when will you make them again?"

"Tuesday."

"Not until Tuesday? Why not tomorrow?"

"Because Friday is fish and Tuesdays is wings unless you can convince the priest otherwise. Go try. You can leave the child here."

I find Father Peddle next door sitting on the church steps. The house is higher into the cliff but the church is nestled near to the road. "Excuse me, Father Peddle?"

He pats the step beside him, and says, "I was just thinking about you and your husband. As a matter of fact, that's what I think about most of the time lately. I'm trying to figure out a way to get you into a house."

"What are they doing with those houses?"

"They're relocating them to a safer part of the harbor. They were too close to the landslide."

"What happened during that landslide?"

The priest twists and stares for a moment, his eyes fill with tears. "This August, a week ago, in the middle of the night all you could hear was a roar like the gates of hell had opened up. People dug for days on end trying to find survivors. Found twenty, and lost four they did, just wee children four to eight years old. All from the same parents."

"Oh my God, they lost all their children?" I look at the slope he points to. I feel dazed.

"No, two girls survived. The father found the first one on top of a collapsed roof. And he searched and searched. He had nails and splinters digging into his feet, but he wouldn't quit. When he couldn't walk anymore, he crawled through the mud and broken glass, looking for his children. The first person he found was alive, a neighbor, buried up to her neck in mud. He saved her but could never save the other four he owned."

I turn my head and wipe my eyes.

"We prayed for a miracle and got one. People came and dug for hours. It didn't matter what religion they were. They heard a muffled whimpering coming from just below the roof, that one over there, barely sticking out of the mud. It was a baby girl, just a year older than your boy, in its crib, surrounded by mud."

"Alive?"

"Yes! By the mercy of God."

"Under the mud?"

"The crib rose above the mud and up into the attic. Somehow the child was still afloat. People used chain saws to get through the roof."

"When we came into town we saw a man staring at the slope. He was hobbling."

"That would be the father."

"Still looking for his children?"

"No. He had to identify their remains just the other week. He's probably trying to figure out what happened. It's hard to wake up and find your house off the foundation, sliding into the beach. Imagine trying to run through the mud, outside for help, only to see the same thing is happening to all of your neighbors." He takes a deep breath and looks into my teary eyes.

I say nothing. I feel a little numb and my chest feels like someone just hit me with a tree trunk.

"Now it makes sense," I say. "Now I see why everyone left the table. It wasn't us, it was about the landslide. The children went to Sidney's school didn't they?"

"Yes all except the four-year-old and of course the infant."

The darkness of the conversation is killing me. I need to hear something good.

"How about survivors?"

"Twenty. The worst one was Beatrice Hunt. Pinned behind a cast iron stove. Everybody lost precious things that day but the Hickeys they lost the most precious things of all. Their sons and daughters . . . how do I help them make peace with God after that?"

I try to think of an answer until I realize he isn't expecting one.

He clears his throat, "See that barge down there, the one carting away the debris? Too much of a risk right now, but come spring, early summer, the barge is going to move every one of those remaining houses off the slope and relocate the houses to another spot."

"People still live there?"

He nods and picks a blade of grass using it like dental floss. "It only happened a few weeks ago, had the same slide in the exact same spot twenty years ago, but there were no houses on it yet. With fall and winter coming it's going to be too risky to move any of them."

"I can't believe people still live there. Aren't they afraid?"

"I suppose so, but they believe God spared them for a reason and it isn't their time yet."

He points over to the left. "See over there? See those prefab houses coming in on the trailers?" I follow his finger. "They're bringing in four houses to replace the ones that got destroyed in the landslide and over there they're putting nine more for people who have been living with their in-laws forever."

"How can they afford this when they've lost everything?"

"The government. The Newfoundland and Labrador Housing Corporation is paying for all of it."

"The government? I can't believe it's actually doing something decent."

"I can see you've had a bad experience with the government?" Father Peddle looks at me with kind wet eyes.

"Yes. But I'm glad to see them doing something so nice for a change."

"Oh, the government can do all kinds of nice things. It just depends on which department is in charge."

Juanita Ray

On Christmas Eve we move in to a furnished home. When the priest told us eighty-two-year-old Mrs. Reilly fell and broke her hip I felt awful for her. But now after living here for a month I know she's much better off in the nursing home than she was here.

"Sidney. We need another pot." I pull off the shirt Little Sidney spit up on, throw it in the washer, grab a blanket from the rocking chair and wrap it around me. "Are you as cold as I am?"

"Juanita you have a kettle and three pots on the stove already. If you had another pot, there would be nowhere to put it—How did Mrs. Reilly manage to raise a family of six in a one-bedroom house, with no tub, no shower and no hot water?"

"Do you know what it's like to boil water to wash clothes? Do you know what it's like to not have any water because the pipes are frozen solid?"

"As a matter of fact I do. Who do you think thaws them out? I'm the one with the flashlight and blowtorch, squeezing under a two-foot crawlspace, trying to locate them. If they built this on a glacier it wouldn't be any worse."

Stomach cramps, buckle me in half. I can barely stand. I stumble to the bathroom and pull the curtain shut.

"Are you okay?"

"Actually, I'm not. I used all the hot water and I just started my period." I wash my hands in icy water, yank open the plastic curtain, grab a fork from the drawer and scratch my back until it's raw. "Why am I itching like a pig?"

Sidney examines my rash, "Can you get chickenpox twice?"

"Do I look like a doctor to you?"

He takes off his jacket and picks up the phone. "What are you doing?"

"I am calling in sick and getting you to a doctor."

I sit in the chair and hold my hands together.

"Are you praying?"

"No I'm trying to keep from scratching. What did the doctor say?"

"You can't get chicken pox twice, it's most likely an allergy but he wants to see you, just in case—let's go."

214

"Just in case of what?"

"Just in case it's shingles."

An hour later, I have two dozen tiny prick marks in my left arm. He picks up a tray of vials and drops different solutions on each mark. Three of them look like mosquito bites and the other two look like hives.

"Young lady you are allergic to wool, dust, ragweed, cats and pollen. Is the lotion helping?"

"Yes. Do you have extra?"

"No, but you can buy it over the counter. It's calamine lotion and this," he hands me a prescription, "is for a supplement."

"Doc, what's the supplement for," Sidney asks.

"It's something all expectant mothers take."

I almost faint at the thought, "Oh I'm not expectant. As a matter of fact, I am on my period right now."

"It's called a final washout. It should only last a day or two. You are expectant all right. Could be six or eight weeks, but either way you are very, very, pregnant."

The Games Nuns Play

"Should I turn Catholic?"

"What do you mean?"

"Well we agreed to raise our children as Catholics and you're Catholic, and with all the fuss about where we live . . .?"

"Like now?"

"No. Not here. When we go back to St. John's for the summer. You said you were going back to summer school right?"

"Yes. But only for the summer until school reopens." His eyes avoid mine. "It might work out better if you were Catholic. Mother would like you more and we wouldn't have this problem in the future. Plenty of other places have the Anglicans and Catholics living on separate sides of the harbor, just like here."

"Do you know what the difference is between the two religions?" I ask.

"Holy communion, that's about it."

"Also confession," I say. "We confess our sins to God and you confess them to a priest."

"That's not so different."

I raise my eyebrows at Sidney. "A priest is just a man."

Sidney yawns. "I need another coffee."

He stands over the stove looking for the kettle, "Juanita, five pots of potatoes? What army are you planning to feed?"

"God's army."

He opens the oven, "Where's the meat?"

"There is no meat."

"No meat? How are you going to make gravy?"

"I'm not. I am making four different potato salads. A beet salad, a peas and carrots salad, an egg salad and a pickled mustard salad."

"Just make a beet salad."

"No I'm making four, that way I know they'll like one of them."

"They?"

"Our guests."

Sidney's eyes are bugging out. "Guests?"

"Hmm-mm. Is there a rule about what people eat on St. Georges Day?"

"What are you talking about?"

"Food. Appropriate food."

By the time the guests arrive I have the table set and the food prepared. Sidney sits with the same mystified look he's had on his face all day. It reminds me of the time I made him a tomato soup cake. The only difference is he hasn't touched a morsel of food yet.

I pass him a bowl.

"Oh . . . no . . . uh . . . um . . . our guests should go first."

One by one I watch the ladies compliment me on my food. I wonder how they can swallow anything at all. They look like choking chickens in their white coifs and black tunics.

"Are you ever allowed to take off your uniforms?" I ask.

"These are called habits," says Sister Beatrice. "The Vatican doesn't require every order to wear them but our order chooses to and the Bishop prefers we keep them on at all times."

I wonder what they sleep in?

Sister Beatrice says, "Juanita you are Anglican. Correct?"

"Yes," I say. "Father Peddle told you?"

"No . . . no. It's just that your salads are so . . . so . . . colorful."

During dinner we talk about the landslide. After I clear the table they talk about St. Lawrence. Sidney cringes when I tell them that in St. Lawrence, after dinner, we played cards for money.

"I know gambling is against the Catholic beliefs but I'm racking my brains for a safe game we can play. Does anyone want to play darts?"

Sidney coughs profusely and says, "Can you excuse us for a minute, I think I hear the baby crying. Juanita and I will be right back."

I open my mouth but before I can utter a word he says, "We need to check on the baby now."

"Together?"

"Yes after all you are pregnant and he does weigh a ton."

In the bedroom he hisses, "You're are being unbelievably rude. You should know better than to ask nuns to play darts. They aren't allowed to have fun."

"Rude? I bet they think you're rude. They know you're whispering behind their back. We live in a three-room doll house, no bigger than an average living room. Baby crying? Do you think their habits make them half deaf?"

Sidney ignores me and walks back to the kitchen.

He pulls his chair towards the table and says, "Congratulations on St. Joseph's Convent celebrating its 100th Anniversary last year."

I hand everyone a bowl of green and yellow Jell-O cubes, covered with whipped cream.

Each nun takes a mouth full of desert and slowly squishes it between their teeth. A few of them nod at Sidney.

"Sidney told me that you're not allowed to play darts, so maybe we can play a game of charades instead." Sidney chokes and sputters. A second later he gropes for his glass of water. He gulps it down and reaches for mine.

Sister Theresa smiles apologetically and says, "I don't see the harm in playing darts, but I suspect our inept abilities would cause undue suffering to you both."

"Maybe we should try charades," says Sister Madeline. She looks to be not much older than I am.

"Maybe we can do both," I laugh.

After a round of charades and two games of darts, I learn that although the nuns dress identical they are quite different from each other. They tell me they are not the same as Catholic sisters who live in the community and have simple vows. Yet these nuns are quite likable, fun and no different from most women.

After two hours, they thank us and file outside. Sister Madeline turns and says, "We had so much fun I so hope we can do this again."

"Come along Sister Madeline," Sister Beatrice chimes from the road.

I wave as they walk up the hill.

"Juanita close the door it's getting cold in here."

"Sidney I think they're on foot. It's freezing out, maybe you should drive them."

"No, they're not walking. They probably have a van. How do you think they deliver food to the poor? Trudge through the community with hot pots of soup?"

"What if you're wrong?"

"If I'm wrong, which I never am, what do you expect me to do?"

"What do you mean?"

"Should I pile some on the roof, or stuff some in the trunk? Smarten up. It only has four seats."

"Don't you dare call me stupid."

"I didn't call you stupid, I said smarten up."

"Would you tell someone you thought was smart to smarten up?" I turn my back to him. "And just for your information, you could make more than one trip!"

"What's that on your legs?"

"What?"

"Look there's something on your legs."

I look and see nothing.

"It's on the back of your legs. It looks like ketchup."

"Shut up lying. We don't have any ketchup. Why would k—" I freeze.

I slowly turn around and lower myself into a chair.

"Don't move," Sidney points at me, "Don't move, I'm just going to grab the baby!"

As we drive to the hospital a thousand thoughts go through my mind, including if I am hospitalized, who looks after Little Sidney?

Inside I have to wait my turn. I whisper, "The last doctor said there's a final wash out. Can you have two of those?"

Sidney whispers back, "How the heck would I know? It might be normal. I heard Mother talk about people having periods while they were pregnant . . . so I guess you can."

As I wait in the chair, the doctor returns. "It isn't abnormal for women to continue menstruating while pregnant and your pregnancy test is still positive. I suggest you go home and relax. Everything is fine. It wouldn't hurt to take it a little easy though."

Sidney spends the day at home playing with Little Sidney and pampering me. While I spend it scared shitless.

That night he whispers in my ear, "I want this baby so much. I hope it is a girl, but a brother for Sidney would be good too. Let's pick out a baby's name."

"If it's a girl, I choose Nakita," I say.

"If it's a girl I would rather name her Shilo."

"Is that even a name?" I ask.

"Sure it is. It was the name of an old Neil Diamond song. It's on the oldies station."

"How come you like all those old songs so much?"

"I don't know. I just do. I want to start collecting old records."

"Like old vinyl albums?"

"No the old forty-five—singles—not albums."

I fall asleep listening to him hum a Neil Diamond song.

Stalked

For the next several days, I spot on and off, and by Friday afternoon, it increases. I put the baby in the playpen and lie on the bed. Sidney should have been home an hour ago. Finally, I hear his car outside.

He whistles, walks in the door, calls my name but I am afraid to yell back. He yells my name again and bursts into the bedroom.

"You scared the living crap out of me. Is the baby okay? Are you okay?"

I cry and shake my head no. Sidney pulls at my slacks.

I shake my head again.

"I have to look. I have to see how bad you're bleeding."

He looks. His voice is hoarse, "I'm calling the doctor."

"It's bad isn't it?"

"Yes. I mean no. It isn't that bad. Relax. I just want to be on the safe side. Okay?"

Sidney is stretching the phone cord. He yanks on it while trying to get closer to me.

"I don't know maybe an ounce or so, maybe more, maybe half a cup, could be a quart. I just got home." He twists the cord around his finger, untwists it and twists it back. "She's calm." Now he is twirling the cord like a skipping rope while he listens. "I see . . . I see . . . I see . . ." He stops twirling the cord. "And then what?" He stares blankly at me batting his eyes. His voice trembles. "I see." He hangs up.

"The doctor's office is just closing. It won't be open until Monday. They said that the best thing is total bed rest. If you hemorrhage, I have to rush you to the hospital, but right now, there is nothing they can do for you. It's in God's hands."

Sidney and I exchange stares.

"They said it's in God's hands?"

"No they said wait until Monday you should be fine until then. Can I get you anything?"

"Maybe some tissues and a new pillowcase. This one is soaking wet."

All night, I lie still, afraid to go to the washroom. By morning, I have to pee so badly yet I am afraid to get up. I am afraid gravity will make me lose the baby. Gravity or not I cannot stand it anymore. I hold my legs tightly together and waddle to the bathroom.

When I am finished, I think that wasn't so bad and flush the toilet. I see a huge red mass with trails of blood seeping from it swirling in the toilet. I watch horrified, as the toilet bowl gets redder.

A blood-curdling scream is still coming from my mouth as Sidney holds me in his arms.

"I think the baby's in the toilet. Oh my God it's in the toilet. Oh my God, what do we do?" I cry hysterically over his shoulder.

I twist to turn. An intense cramp shudders through my body.

"Don't look. Let's go."

"Where?"

"The hospital."

"Why? What good can they do now?"

"What if we can still save it?" He grabs Little Sidney, "Let's go."

He gets the keys and rushes me out the door. He yells at people who can't hear him, honking at them to move. He races through an empty intersection, past a stop sign. I close my eyes and think, this can't be happening again.

At the hospital they transfer me to a gurney. They won't let Sidney come with us, not unless he leaves the baby.

I hear him call out, "Does anyone here have a student in my class? I'm Mr. Simon, a teacher. Do any of you know me?"

I am lying on a gurney calling the doctor a murderer, when Sidney rushes to my side. His face matches my pillow.

"I left Little Sidney with one of my students." He squeezes my hand. "Everything is going to be okay, right Doc?"

"She needs a D and C."

"Sidney, don't sign that," I yell, "He's trying to take away the baby. He's trying to murder the baby!" I yank at the pen in his hand.

An injection stings my arm. Sidney is holding me down. Sidney tries to stay brave but he fails. "You heard him, Juanita," he sobs, "the baby is still inside you, but it's . . . it's not alive. It's dead."

Stalked

"You're wrong, you're wrong, YOU'RE BOTH LIARS. I hate you both," Sidney bursts into tears. I put the pillow over my face and scream murderer into it until my screams sounds like they are in a faraway tunnel. Then all I hear is a windy sound.

Three days disappear. And for the next two all I remember is a dismal fog. Today, everything is quiet. The sky is full of gray clouds.

Sidney and I cling to each other inside of the car. I don't know where Little Sidney is and I don't ask. A man, carrying pink roses and a bunch of pink balloons, smiles from ear to ear.

We sit in the car and stare blankly at the balloons.

"A girl," he yells. He lurches towards the car, sticks a bubble gum cigar under our wiper and whistles away.

Sidney and I weep like babies.

"Are you okay?" he asks.

"Yes," I lie and blow my nose. "Are you?"

"Yes," he arches his back. "Actually no I'm not and neither are you. You didn't even notice Little Sidney was missing."

"I noticed. Where is he," I ask, disinterested.

"At the neighbors, I just need a moment to get myself together and then I'll go get him and come right back, okay?"

I nod. I don't want to hold him right now anyway.

"You know the doctor said the reason you miscarried so far into your pregnancy is because the baby was probably not normal."

"He's an idiot. Who's he to decide whether it was normal or not. What kind of doctor sends you home when you're bleeding? Doctor Collingwood would never do that. This place is worse than St. Lawrence ever could be."

I go inside, sit at the table, and stare at my hands. I hear a yelling outside. Through the window I see Sidney stomping up and down on the bubble gum cigar. He yells up at the sky. My mind flips back to him jumping up and down outside the hospital back in St. Lawrence, with tears falling from his face, as he yelled upwards to the sky. How can two same actions mean something so different?

I know I should console him but I don't bother to try. I can't even console myself.

I spend the next few weeks alone, in a deep dark crevice. I go through the motions of feeding Sidney and doing chores but it's always a blur. Never a distraction.

I sit staring blankly at Little Sidney and I in the mirror. I wipe a tear from my face. He makes a sob sound and wipes a tear from his face. I squint my eyes. He squints his. I draw a frown face on the mirror in lipstick. He struggles for the lipstick. I won't let him have it. He grabs my wrist and squirms to reach the mirror and forces my hand to draw.

An electric bolt jump starts my heart. He is mimicking everything I do. He is what he sees!

Through the mirror I see piles of clothes, dirty dishes, two pails of shitty diapers and wonder how this place got that way. The sun is too bright— hurting my eyes. I close the curtains and shut out a beautiful spring day.

With the baby on one hip, I light the stove, fill four pot with water and wait for them to boil. First I bath the baby. Who looked after you all this time? Your hair looks like it belongs to a little girl.

Now it's my turn. No matter how much soap I use or how many times I refill the sink to wash and rinse, I don't feel clean.

Little Sidney's baby curls flutter to the floor, until I can see his neck. I'm almost finished cutting his hair, when the doorbell rings.

A young stranger, with round blue eyes and v-shaped bangs, held in place with silver clips, says. "Well can I come in or not?"

Little Sidney's wraps his arms around my knees. I keep the door half open and block him as he tries to squirm past me.

"Who are you? Are you related to the owner of this house?"

"No. I'm Shawna Tibbo."

"I think you're at the wrong house."

"I'm in your husband's class. You're Mrs. Simon right?"

"Ri-iii-ght," I hesitate, "and . . . you . . . want?"

"I heard you lost the other baby and I thought I could come and help you with this one." She points to Little Sidney. "Like babysit or something."

"Did Sidney send you?"

"No Mr. Simon doesn't know I'm here."

"How do you know I lost a baby?"

She points to Little Sidney. "I watched him at the hospital, when they rushed you in. I was there because of my Grandma." She chews her gum and smiles at my son. "Cute baby, looks like you." She removes her backpack, "So where do I start?"

"Start what?"

"Start helping." She walks towards the washer. "It's stopped. I can hang these out on the clothes line if you want."

I pick up her backpack, "Look I don't mean to be rude but you should leave. I can't afford to pay for help right now."

"I'm not doing it to get paid. I'm doing it cuz I'm bored out of my skull. There's dick all to do around here."

"Are you sure you're in my husband's class? I mean how old are you? Fifteen?"

"Nope. Seventeen. You?"

I am amazed she's my age. I ignore her question.

She sits on the counter. "I'll be eighteen in July. You?"

I can't believe she's older than I am. "Twenty," I lie, "and the truth is I can't afford to pay you."

"Truth is I don't want any money." She points to the scissors, "You cut hair?"

"Just his."

"Anybody else's?"

"His father's."

"You cut Mr. Simon's hair? Man I think he has the coolest haircut in the world."

"Thanks." I hold out her backpack. She takes it, smirks, and tosses it on the table.

The chair scrapes as she pulls it out and sits down. "Cut mine."

"Say what?"

"I'm sick of it, and the barber always gives me a hack job."

What is this girl up to?

"Anyway, instead of paying him I can pay you. Then you can pay me the money back for helping you."

I look at the pile of dishes. "What do you charge?"

"Whatever you charge to cut hair."

The scissors remind me of Irma. "What if I ruin it? What if I accidentally give you a bald spot or something?"

She laughs, "That would be so cool. I love weird!"

I cut her hair an inch shorter.

"It's okay she says," as she looks in the mirror. "But I want it shorter so next time I come, cut a few inches off, okay?"

By the end of the school year, I am cutting hair for half the students at Harbour Breton, and most of them pay me back by helping us pack for our summer move to St. John's.

I look in the rearview mirror and wave my arm out the window.

"Did you see that? Half of those kids were Anglicans. Both religions side by side!"

"Who knew one haircut could lead to that? But don't think for one minute that's going to get you out of driving. You are going to drive part of the way, right?"

"No way. Not until you get a standard."

"I still remember the principal being late for school because of your driving."

"What? That's not true!" I lean back and check the car seat.

"Why do you insist on strapping him backwards?"

"If we have an accident I want the baby to be against something soft and if the seat belt breaks the back of the chair, not his face, hits the back of our seat."

"What if he chokes on something? There's more of a chance of that than an accident. I'll drive slow. Turn him around so I can see him."

At the edge of town, Sidney stops at the lounge. "Let's grab some bags of chips and some snacks for the road."

Bernie Bishop is behind the bar.

"I sure am going to miss you guys coming to my watering hole." It was no secret Bernie Bishop still lived at home. The bar belonged to his father but he considered everything his father owned to be his anyway.

He takes the baby seat from Sidney and sits it on the bar. He looks at me and brushes his hand across his short spiked hair. "But I am not going to miss waiting at the bottom of the hill while you keep trying to make it past the stop sign." He pours half a shot of Baileys and pushes it towards me. Then he pours Sidney and himself a shot of whiskey. He leans back and grins.

"Anytime I saw that purple Javelin on the road during school hours, I knew it had to be you driving, and sure enough it was. More than a few times, I was right behind you, trying to reverse backwards, while you rolled towards me."

He laughs and clinks Sidney's shot glass with his. "It didn't take me long to smarten up and stay at the bottom of the hill. Most times, it took her three or four tries. People used to hang out at the bottom just to watch her. Some of us would bet on how many tries it would take."

Sidney and Bernie are laughing. I push my Baileys away and wonder when did Sidney start drinking whiskey? I thought he only drank the odd beer.

"I never told a soul your real age. Did she ever tell you she almost killed my cousin when she took her for her driving test? She plowed down a stop sign," he slaps the bar and laughs loudly, "and he said she—"

Little Sidney wakes up crying. Bernie grimaces and apologizes for startling the baby.

Sidney leaves half of the shot untouched and moves to a bar stool below Little Sidney. He tries to rock him but it's obvious he wants no part of being in the car seat.

"Thanks Bernie. We'd better go. He's getting antsy. I'll see you in a few months." He shakes Bernie's hand.

Bernie walks us out to the car and gives me a hug while Sidney positions the baby in the car face foreword. "If he cries I want to see what's wrong."

"You better keep your eyes on the road, and not the baby, especially driving back through that fiord. If he cries, I'll handle it. Maybe I should sit in back with him," I say.

"He'll be fine. Don't sit back there unless he cries."

I wonder if the bumpy road is hurting the baby's brain cells because it's giving me a huge headache. Half a mile from the paved highway, I ask, "Isn't this where you got snowed in? With that teacher?"

Sidney groans. "Not this again."

"I still don't believe you," I say.

I told you it was innocent. We only held each other to stay warm. My God we were trapped in the middle of the road in a snowstorm."

"The point is you lied."

"I lied because you would have had a fit if I told you I was driving three hundred miles to a four day teachers' conference with a female teacher."

"Of course I would have. What woman in her right mind lets her husband and a female coworker drive away on a Sunday and return together the next Saturday."

"It wasn't like that."

"Bull droppings! She has a license and a car. She could have driven herself."

"Juanita she was scared to drive alone in the winter. Besides we went halves on the gas."

"Why didn't you strike up that deal with a male teacher? Speaking of male teachers, Doug Parsons is single why didn't she beg him for a ride?" I try to shut up but I can't. "How do you think I feel when every teacher in the community is back the day before you and her? It was the talk of the town."

"Juanita, you need to drop it, before it ruins our relationship."

"It already has. You lied to me. I asked you if you were driving with anyone and you looked me straight in the eye and said no. When I mentioned carpooling, I said only with a male teacher and you told me, you were driving solo, but if you didn't, it would never be a female passenger. Those were your exact words."

"I didn't tell you because it was a last minute thing and I knew you would be upset and try to keep me from going."

"Then why didn't you tell me when you got back. No you had to lie three times."

"I was afraid you would leave me alone. Like you did in St. Lawrence."

"You have your nerve! I didn't just leave. I was forced to leave or lose my eye. You need to stop milking that and twisting it around. I'm sick of it. Every time you want to get your way or get out of a lie, you shove that in my face and expect me to act like a martyr. I'm sick of it."

"So am I."

"Good. Maybe we're even. Maybe I don't owe you anything else. Maybe I owe me a new life, one where you can't keep making feeble excuse to get away with stupid stuff."

"Go ahead. Leave if that's what will make you happier."

"Oh I'll leave all right, but not in the middle of nowhere." I hop into the back seat and hang out with the baby.

Sidney twists the mirror. The more I change positions the more he twists it. "Stop spying on me."

"I'm not spying. I'm admiring how beautiful you are. Doesn't this remind you of the night we met?"

"No. It's not winter and our son is sitting beside me, not Frankie or Denise, so stop staring."

"I wasn't staring. I was admiring. Trust me. I'd never cheat on you. I love you more than the world . . . I'll stop staring if you sit beside me."

I grin, slap his arm and climb back into the front seat.

"See, I am the silver tongued devil." He lifts my hand to his lips and murmurs, "If I can change your mind, I can talk anyone into anything."

"I'm not so sure that's something to be so proud of. And I want you to know, that I know, that silver tongue hasn't told the whole truth about what happened on that trip."

"Let's make a deal. I'll stop spying on you, if you drop that subject."

Poisoned by Weed

Our basement apartment feels like a palace compared to the house in Harbour Breton. I sit at the kitchen table across from Sidney and crank my neck to scan the front and back page of his newspaper. He tosses the paper on a chair, points at the ceiling and says, "What are they doing, beating up the place?"

"Probably," I laugh.

Gillian was ecstatic to find out I had a boy her son's age. Her thirteen-year-old son, George, had outgrown playing with his hyper brother Matthew. Little Sidney is two months older, and two inches shorter than Matthew. Their favorite pastime is racing each other to the end of the hall.

"Gillian offered to babysit every day for free just so Matthew could have a playmate. That way I can get a job and we can keep all the money."

"No way. You need to stay home and raise Sidney. If I wasn't taking university classes, I'd be with him all the time. You don't realize how lucky you are."

"I'm sick of having to scrounge around under the couch looking for change to buy milk. Besides you're so busy reading the newspaper and watching TV, you don't even notice him, or me anymore. How can you read the newspaper and watch the news on TV at the same time anyway? Who does that?"

"Got to run." He stretches the upper half of his body towards me, brushes his lips against mine and says, "For my birthday I want two sets of earplugs."

I pick up the newspaper, flip to the employment section and browse through the ads.

Against Sidney's wishes, I get an interview with the Dairy Scene. When the manager hands me a red apron, I know I've been hired on the spot. For the first hour I mop the floors and wash dishes. Every employee is working hard at gossiping about favoritism or griping about scheduling.

Maybe I'm unemployable, I think, as I look solemnly at the dripping cone machine. I have cleaned it three times and if she makes me clean it once more I'm out of here.

My boss scrutinizes the machine and says, "That will do. Think you might be adequate at making soft cones?" Is that a trick question? I told her on my interview that I was inexperienced with ice cream. She answers for me, "My guess is no . . . it's so hard to find decent staff these days."

She pulls the knob, twirls the cone, contorting her wrist until it looks deformed, and twists the ice cream, until it matches the height of the cone.

"Now you try it."

I feel nervous for some reason. Maybe it's because of her scowl. I mimic what she did and end up with a cone that looks identical to hers. I feel proud. She sets mine on a scale and tells me it weighs an eighth of an ounce too heavy. She lifts it off the scale, and lectures me, while the customer's ice cream melts away and drips down the side. "Have at it. Welcome to your station."

How can so many people all want ice cream? I weigh every single cone for no apparent reason other than to give her an excuse to lecture me over and over again for being slightly over or under.

"I can't babysit you all day. You have to get this right."

"Which weighs more half frozen ice cream or half melted ice cream?"

"Don't be a smart ass."

"I just don't understand why it's slightly under when I put more in it than the last one and the last one was over."

"Well did you weigh it?" she chides.

"Of course I weighed it. That's how I know it's under. I'm just asking what to do about it? Maybe you need a new set of scales."

She writes me up for insubordination.

"Why do we weigh them? I mean what for?" I ask on day three.

"Because they are supposed to be exactly this weight." She makes a few cones but none of them are the right weight.

"Yours didn't weigh the same and you've been here a long time."

"Striiiiike two, insubordination," she hisses, wagging her finger at me. "How dare you insinuate I don't know my job. Strike three and you are out! Hear me, fired! I will fire you just like I fired all the rest."

I look at her harsh eyes as she wags her finger at me. I try to pass by her. She crosses her arms and blocks my path.

"Where do you think you're going? I'm not finished with you."

"I suggest you stick those scales up your ass. There. That's insubordination. Now I feel like I got fired for something!" I walk partway through the door and realize I still have my apron on. "Oh, here's your apron, you can shove that up your ass too."

I walk to the car, turn the music up and pull out of the parking lot.

When I get home I pour myself a hot bath.

"Juanita, where are you?"

"Hi Sidney, I'm in here."

"Where?"

"In the bathroom."

"Is everything okay? I thought you went to work today?"

"Yes. Everything is perfect. Gillian is going to babysit while we go out dancing tonight. We're celebrating."

"Celebrating what? You got a raise already didn't you?"

Stalked

"Yes. I did." I nod, "Yep. I got a good raise."

Sidney examines his sideburns in the mirror, "How much?"

"Oh about half an inch or so."

"That's gr—" he turns towards me, "What does that mean?"

"That's about how high her eyebrows raised when I told her to shove the scales up her ass."

"You told your boss what?"

I get out of the tub and dry off. "I told her—"

"I know what you said but Juanita I just can't believe you said something like that."

"I know," I giggle. I unpin my hair and let it fall around my face.

"It's not funny. You can't burn bridges like that."

"Sure I can. I just did."

"Did she fire you?"

"I don't know. I think she would have when she got her wits back. She threatened to, before I said it. I don't know. What do you think? Do you think I got fired or quit?"

Sidney grinned. "I think that constitutes a quit."

"Good. So when I look for my next job I'll say I quit."

"If and when you look for another job I wouldn't even mention this one."

I slip into fresh underwear and slide a red dress over my head.

"Okay I won't."

"Won't what? Look for a job or mention it?"

"The latter," I grin back. I slip into my shoes. "Let's go."

"Juanita I can't. I have to study." He settles onto the couch, flips open the newspaper, hits the TV remote and switches to the news.

"Your birthday is coming up soon. We'll go out and celebrate then."

He leans forward towards the TV. "Did you see that?"

"See what?" I head to the bathroom to change into sweats.

"You should stop taking a purse when you go out to get groceries. A bunch of kids are hiding between cars and robbing purses."

I sit beside him and kiss his ear.

"Where will I put my lipstick?"

"In your pocket."

"What if I don't have a pocket?"

"I don't know, in your bra."

"What if I'm not wearing a bra?"

He ignores me.

"Guess what else I did today?"

He buries his nose further in the paper and continues to read.

I shake his arm.

He holds the paper higher up over his face. "I heard you. I'm waiting for you to tell me."

"I also got a new job today but I can't start until next week because I have to be eighteen to work there."

Sidney drops his paper. He gives me a chilling look. "What kind of job." His words are slow. "Where? Doing what?"

"I'll be working as a clerk in a gas station. They sell beer so I have to be eighteen. To work there."

"No. That is far more dangerous than a grocery store. What will you do if someone half-drunk makes a pass at you?"

I get up from the couch, move a few feet away, say, "That depends on how cute they are," and bolt for the bedroom.

The hardest job is keeping the cooler filled with cases of beer. I count the pimples on the manager's face as he tells me the history of beer, which brands go in front, and how much of it we sell.

I'm at thirty-seven pimples when he pulls my hair away from my neck and tells me how he got married too young. I jerk away.

"You had hair in your mouth," he apologizes. "It wasn't a pass. Not unless you want it to be, then it could be a pass." He lifts his eyebrows up and down. "We can continue this conversion after that customer leaves."

A man wearing all white, covered in multi-colored paint droplets, saunters to the counter throws a case of Schillers Lite on the counter, a crumpled ten-dollar bill on top of the carton and holds out his paint splattered hand and counts his change.

"You shorted me a buck."

"No. I distinctly remember you gave me a ten."

"Yeah but you charged me a buck more than the sign says."

The manage folds his arms. "What's seems to be the problem?"

"Problem is your girl can't read or else she can't count. The sign says beer should be a buck less than she charged me."

The manager pokes his head out the door, and says, "Oh shit! I forgot to change the sign back. That was yesterday's special. Juanita do this void, while I go change the sign."

"I don't know how to do a void."

He gives my waist a pinch and winks, "How about I teach you that and a few other things, but first go change that sign." He turns to the customer and winks. "She's new, but I'll fix you up." He strokes my palm as he hands me a black magic marker. "Change it from $7.99 back to $8.99."

I slip on my jacket and go outside. My keys rattle in my pocket. The more they rattle the more I want to drive away. I walk over to the A frame sign and take out the black marker. I change the 7.99 to 2.99, walk to the car, and drive home.

I sit in the car and listen to the music. For some strange reason I don't want to turn off the radio and go inside. I see the curtains move. One minute later Sidney walks towards the car and sits in the passenger seat.

"You forgot your purse," says Sidney.

"No. I decided to use my pockets like you said. Where's Little Sidney?"

"He's gone to a birthday party."

"You're home early . . . how did you do?"

I shrug.

"Juanita it's obvious something is wrong. Spit it out."

"I don't want to talk about it."

"Did that pimple faced pervert try something?" He points to my face. "That's it! It's written all over your face. He did something disgusting didn't he?"

"He suggested something I didn't like, so I quit."

"He didn't lay a finger on you, did he?"

I shudder as I think about his hand squeezing my waist. "No he didn't lay one finger on me. He's too weird for my liking. And half of the customers smell like booze. I'd rather wash dishes for a living."

"Juanita why don't you just stay home and wash dishes here?"

"I just might do that."

"Really?" He wraps his arms around me.

"Really. At least until I get my GED."

His arms drop to his sides. "What GED?"

"On the way home I went to the community college and applied for a GED."

"Juanita why would you do that? There's no way we can afford for you to get an education. We can't just hire a sitter while you to go to school."

"The receptionist said I can take it at night or—"

"Night? I have to study at night. After I finish these courses, my check goes up a tier. I can't entertain Little Sidney and study at the same time."

"He likes TV. If you can manage to read a newspaper while you listen to the television, you should have no problem reading a text book while it's on."

"Little Sidney doesn't like the news so—"

"—or, as I was saying earlier, before you rudely interrupted me, I can study at home and just go in to write the exam which is what I opted to do."

"Juanita you won't pass. You can't just get a high school diploma like that." He snaps his fingers. "You have to take some classes to bring yourself up to a higher level of education first."

"Don't tell me what I won't or will do. I am sick of you inferring you have superior intelligence to mankind and especially to me."

"I do have superior intelligence Juanita. I am smarter than most people—not just you."

"Sidney I don't know how you can keep your head up on your neck. I'm surprised it doesn't just fall to one side, between the weight of your brain and the weight of your tongue."

"What do you mean my tongue?"

"Silver? Heavy?"

"Oh that," he laughs. "Speaking of my silver tongue, look what I got for you. Cover your eyes." He leads me into the apartment and sits me on the couch.

"Happy Birthday! You're eighteen!" I open one eye, then both pop open. A brand new TV sits on a shiny wood cabinet. On the coffee table, a birthday cake with eighteen candles.

"My birthday isn't today. It was Friday."

"I know."

"How did you buy this? Where did you get the money?"

"I charged it. I get forty percent off and free delivery and a hundred dollars off the stand and we still have enough credit approval to buy another one. Ha! Told you. I'm the silver tongue devil."

"What is with the devil part?"

"Haven't you heard the song, Silver tongue Devil by Kris Kristofferson?"

"No, but let me guess it's on the oldies but goodies show."

"Not show, station," he says as he flips on the TV.

"What did you do with the old TV?"

"I put it in the bedroom."

"Look at this pic—," he taps his finger across his teeth and mutters, "I could do that. Now that's a job I'd quit teaching for."

"What?"

"They're advertising for a news anchor."

"Where would you have to live if you got the job?"

"Here."

"So apply for it."

"No I probably wouldn't get it."

"A minute ago, you said you would get it."

"I said I could do it."

Dust falls onto my cake. The ceiling sounds like it's going to cave in any second. Loud, fast footsteps race back and forth. "They sound like a bunch of wild Indians, I'll run upstairs and get him." Before he can get up, Luke is at the door with Little Sidney.

"Want to watch TV with Daddy?"

I shake my head, grin at Luke, and say, "I swear that man breathes, eats and sleeps just so he can watch TV. If he notices I'm gone tell him I'm upstairs with your wife."

I bump into Gillian at the top of the stairs. "Perfect timing. I was just going to get you, for a chit-chat. Where are the men?"

"Downstairs, watching TV."

"Must be something good on."

"Yeah, my birthday present."

"What?"

"He charged a TV for my birthday. It was for him, not me. That's all he does, watch TV and read the newspaper."

"All men do that," Gillian grins.

"At the same time?"

She shakes her head and laughs.

"It's like we're living in two different worlds."

She shuffles closer and whispers, "Luke used to be so cheap and tight. Too serious and worried about everything. One day I told him it was over. He thought I was kidding until he saw my bags packed."

"What did you do?" I ask.

Luke yawns, arches his back and slumps into a recliner. "Sidney told me to tell you, your son is in bed, and to take your time."

"Maybe he's planning another surprise for you. Luke what did he say to you? Anything about a surprise?"

"No. He asked if I wanted to sit and watch the news. And why are you talking to her about something that happened years ago?"

Gillian jerks her head at me and puts her thumb upside down.

"Oh-oh," Luke says, "trouble at the O.K. Coral. Want to know how to make a marriage better?"

I nod.

"Weed."

"What?"

"Weed. Marijuana. We smoked some pot and all of a sudden I saw the truth."

I look at him and laugh but Gillian's expression is stoic. She isn't amused. "Listen to him. He's telling the truth. Sharing a joint saved our marriage. It was magical. We talked everything out and the lights went on. Better than any counselor, and we've had plenty, I kid you not."

Are they on drugs now?

Gillian reads my mind and assures me they no longer use weed. She says, "You should try it just once. It will help both of you."

"Yes," agreed Luke, "I can get you some, consider it a birthday present."

I venture downstairs. Little Sidney is asleep in his room.

I sprawl in an armchair and tell Sidney about the conversation I had with Gillian and Luke. He doesn't look like he's listening. "What do you think? I'm not sure it's a good idea at all. Should we do it?"

"Sure. Sounds good. Look they are still looking for that news anchor person. Look at that list. Look at that." He gets up and touches each line on the screen. "That's me, and that's me—that's me." His eyes gleam. "I tell you I could do that."

"Then go apply for it. Phone them. There's a number on the screen."

"No. I'm not phoning them."

"Here," I hand him a cloth.

"What?"

"If you're not going to take the time to apply for the job you can at least take the time to wipe your finger prints off my present. I'm going to bed. If Luke comes down with the weed wake me up."

"Weed? What weed? Why would Luke bring us weed?"

I look at him and shake my head.

"It's my birthday p—"

Luke and Gillian are peering in the door window knocking and giggling.

"Come in," I say.

Luke pulls out a snack bag, of something that looks like dried herbs mixed with short grass clippings. He rolls it up in a paper, lights it and takes a long deep puff. The smell is disgusting.

Sidney and I exchange looks.

"It'll save your marriage man," Luke grins. He holds the smoke in his mouth until he turns blue.

"I have a great wife. Our marriage is fine, right?" Sidney takes my hand.

"I disagree," I say.

"Juanita, it's perfect."

"Yeah, it's perfect for you. I give you massages, I cut your hair, I cook all the meals, tiptoe around when you're studying and I do all the cleaning. You buy me presents you like and never ask what I want. We don't talk anymore and whenever I try to have a decent conversation with you, you tell me I'm a dreamer. To grow up." I take a deep breath. "You hate my cooking, you criticize my ideas and you think the world—"

"Stop!" He grabs the smoke from Luke and shoves it in my mouth.

I hand it back, "No, you first."

"How do I do this?"

"Man I just showed you twice. She's got a point. You do seem self-focused, and drown out others around you. You need to chill."

"I hear just fine." I roll my eyes at him.

"You need to drown out your heart, and open your ears."

"Jesus, she doesn't even do drugs and she already sounds like you. What's this going to do to her . . . to us?"

"Nothing. Maybe give you the munchies. If this weed doesn't loosen you up, you are officially un-chill-a-ble."

"This rolled cigarette reminds me of Paul Chafe," I say.

"It's called a joint," Luke says in a weird voice. He gasps and blows out a flume of smoke.

Sidney inhales, gags, coughs and chokes.

Luke's jabs the joint at me. "Take a deep breath, like this."

Gillian pokes her husband. "She's a woman with a kid. She knows how to take a deep breath or two."

"Seems they have the general hang of it." Luke sucks on the joint and lays it across the lid of a soda can. "Come on Gill, time to split."

Sidney doesn't say thank you or goodbye. He's too enthralled with the newspaper. He scrutinizes every square inch of it.

Occasionally his eyes drift to the TV then back to reading the news.

I crawl across the floor and flick the paper. He flicks at the air. I flick the paper again.

"Juanita there's a fly out here. Get the swatter."

I snatch at the paper, "Buzz, buzz, buzzzzzzzzzzzzzzz."

He pries the paper from my hands and smooth it out. I sit back on the floor hypnotized by the smoke furling from the burning joint. A half inch of ash topples down the side of the can and scatters onto the table.

"I think you need to smoke some more before it burns away. You don't feel anything, do you? Maybe we should stuff a pillowcase full and get you to smoke that." I laugh hysterically.

His eyes peer at me over the paper. He looks like Scrooge.

I bust out laughing. His nose is exactly like Scrooge's nose. "If I died your hair gray—" I roll on the floor laughing.

He lowers the newspaper, tilts his head and asks, "What's so funny?"

"I don't know? I never realized how big your nose was. Ha-ha. Haahahahahah."

Suddenly things are not so funny. A weird sensation creeps across the back of my neck. Within seconds it intensifies to full on paranoia. It crawls up my skull. I can't outpace it. I'm freaking out.

"I feel weird," I whimper. "I'm really freaking out." My heart is pounding so loud . . . I can hear the blood gushing through my veins.

I crawl back up on the couch and squish into the corner. I reach out over and pull on Sidney's arm. He seems a million miles away. The couch looks the length of a stretch limo. After he brushes me off, I curl back into my corner. His eyes are glued to the screen. He lifts the newspaper closer to his face.

"Arghhh. I hate this feeling."

I try harder to get his attention and finally I do. He drops his newspaper down below his eyes, and says, "Stop bugging me. You're acting like a child."

I hyperventilate and pace back and forth in the living room.

"What are you doing? If you're trying to drive me nuts—it's working."

"I'm trying to walk it off."

"Walk what off?"

"THIS! Don't you feel anything weird or strange?"

"No . . . Not unless you call annoyed strange. If you can't sit still, can't you at least go do something constructive?"

I go into the bedroom and pace around the bed. Did someone put poison in the weed? I drop to my knees and pray, "Dear God please get me back to normal. I promise never ever to smoke weed again and I'll start reading the bible tomorrow."

After several hours of feeling incredibly anxious it is blatantly clear my bribery fell on deaf ears. Maybe I should go to the ER. What if his mother is the on duty nurse? I switch the shower to cold and hop in. The ice-cold water is worse than a slap in the face. For a few minutes my mind is distracted. I switch it off and shiver while I count to three hundred. I do it three more times and each time after I catch my breath I yelp.

"WHAT ARE YOU DOING?"

"Ten—LEAVING—eleven—YOU—twelve—GO AWAY!"

Finally, an hour and two more showers later, the anxious weird creepy feeling dissipates and a sleepy numbness takes its place.

The first thing I smell, when I wake up, is sulfur mixed with skunk. It's worse in the hall but near the kitchen, the scent mingles with coffee. The summer sun is beaming in through the kitchen window reflecting off Sidney's glasses. He's leaning forward with his elbows on the table and his head tilted down at the newspaper. Little Sidney's in his high chair crushing Cheerios with his fist.

I reach past him, yank the window open, reach into the cabinet, and find the only clean mug left. It's a black mug covered in a cold winter scene. I cover five teaspoons of sugar, with two inches of creamer, top it with coffee, and sit across from Sidney.

Little Sidney stretches forward and gropes for the handle.

"NO. HOT!" I take a sip but the coffee is only lukewarm. His bottom lip curls up as I place the mug out of his reach.

"Eat some banana and I'll make you peanut butter toast."

"Want to head out to a garage sale?" Sidney is sitting at the table circling ads in the newspaper. "This guy is selling a bunch of hockey gear."

"Hockey gear? It's only August."

"Now is the time to buy it. It'll be cheaper. We can drive around and check out a few other garage sales. There's a bunch in here."

"Maybe we'll find some mugs."

"What's wrong with the ones we have?"

"It's not Christmas."

"What's that suppose mean."

I shove the mug against his elbow. "Take a guess."

With his eyes peeled on the newspaper, he lifts the mug to his lips and takes a big gulp. He hurtles from the chair and dives for the kitchen sink. He sucks his lips against the faucet, gargles and spits. "Did you use one or two bowls of sugar?" He gargles and spits again.

"That's gross. You realize your son is watching you."

"How can you drink that? It tastes like syrup." He grabs the coffee pot and chugs down the rest of the black brew.

"Feel up to hitting some garage sales? Yes, or no?"

"Not really. Go without me but if you find a guitar buy me one."

"A guitar?"

"Yeah. I want to learn to play like Don Felder—and if you had bothered to ask, that's what I really wanted for my birthday." I make a face and leave the room.

I spend the day outside pushing Little Sidney around in the stroller. When I return Gillian opens her door and asks, "How did it go?"

"What go?"

"Oh that? It didn't. We're as different as chalk and cheese. Well talk later."

She lifts her thumb and index fingers towards her face and whispers, "Call me," and wiggles the finger by her mouth.

Sidney is behind me with an armload of hockey sticks. He throws them on the floor, rushes outside and returns with a six-string guitar. Then he grins, leaves and returns with a box.

"What's in the box?"

"I don't know. They're mostly oldies. Only ten bucks for this whole box of records. Check it out."

I flip through the box while he peels the old electric tape off the worn hockey sticks. At the very bottom is a brown paper bag covered with hand drawn hearts. Inside I find the latest release from The Eagles.

Sidney smiles, "Happy now?"

I lie down by the stereo, and with Little Sidney nestled against my ribs, close my eyes and listen to Hotel California.

Once he's asleep in my arms, I take off the headphones and whistle at his father. Sidney lifts him up and carries him to his bed. I pick up a sock that falls to the floor. I pull off the other one, that dangles from his toes. He fidgets. Sidney taps me and shakes his head.

"Should I undress him?"

"No," he whispers back. "He might wake up." He grabs my hand and pulls me out of the room. Back in the living room, he fondles his hockey gear and straddles the hockey stick across his lap and pulls out the electric tape.

"Want to do something?"

"I am doing something," he says, and reaches for another stick.

"But I'm bored."

"Go play some guitar."

"I don't know how yet."

"Well go write a song for after you learn." He overlaps the electrical tape until the wood blade completely disappears.

"I don't write songs."

"You write poems, it's the same difference. Just throw in a chorus, between some versus and repeat it a few times." He reaches for some wax and says, "It's that—"

Sidney bolts forward and turns up the volume.

"You're going to wake up the baby. I'm getting sick and tired of you salivating over this ad and doing nothing but gripe about it."

He stares at me, "Don't you agree they are describing me? I think I would make a great newscaster."

"I'm done with listening to that ad—you rant and rave about it day and night. I told you before, if you think you're that good, apply for it so they can hire you. How are you going to deal with it when they stop running the stupid thing?"

"What's that mean?"

"The ad will be filled one day BY SOMEONE ELSE."

"Why are you getting so upset."

"Because you refuse to apply for it but you won't DROP IT."

"I think they want someone with experience."

"It didn't say one thing about experience. You're driving me freaking crazy. They should hire me but they won't. Of course they won't hire you, BECAUSE THEY CAN'T UNLESS YOU APPLY FOR THE JOB. OH MY GOD!"

Sidney folds his arms, "What if they say no? What if I lose the job?"

"Sidney. Why are you acting so dumb? The answer is already no. You have nothing to lose because you don't have the job and you never will, unless you apply for it. Don't you get it? If they say no, nothing changes. You lose nothing. Personally, I think you're too much of a chicken shit to apply—if you think you're so good, why wouldn't you? You have everything to gain and nothing to lose because if you DO NOT HAVE a job you CANNOT LOSE IT! Cripes! I swear to God if you don't apply for that job I will divorce you." I grab the phone, dial the 800 number and shove it against his ear.

He grabs it, hangs up and hands it back to me. "Juanita what if they say no?"

"Sidney it's just a job you don't need. Are you forgetting you have one, back in Harbour Breton? Their no won't ruin your life."

"Maybe it would." He stares at the TV tapping his teeth.

"I can't take this anymore. The only thing about to ruin your life is me. Listen. You eat, sleep and live for the news. If you're not reading it, you're watching it. They want someone aware of current events. They are describing you—I don't get how you can want something so bad and just sit and watch it, instead of going for it. But why am I surprised? You did that with me." I grit my teeth, pick up the phone and redial the number.

"Talk to them or I'm divorcing you."

"You're faking right? The number is gone from the screen—how can you remember that number?" Sidney looks horrified.

"1-800-THE-NEWS? That's a tough one Sidney—here, it's ringing."

He refuses to take the phone and hisses, "Hang up."

"Just a moment please, here Sidney it's for you." I drop the phone down his shirt.

He pulls the cord up past his head and retrieves the phone, "Hello?"

I watch as he twists the cord around his neck like a noose. He swirls the phone above his head and says, "My name is Sidney Simon and I'd like to apply for a position advertised at your station." His voice sounds two octaves lower than normal. The more I listen the more I have to agree that he does have a silver tongue. Minutes later he is jumping up and down. "I've got an interview. In one hour! What should I wear?"

"Whatever the other newscaster wears. You watch them enough—you should know."

"What should I say?"

"Talk about whatever is in the news. Pretend you're an actor and impersonate that famous guy who does the prime time show."

"Can you drive, so I can focus on the interview."

For the entire trip I listen to multiple versions of, good evening, this is Sidney Simon bringing you late night news.

Two hours later I'm still waiting in the parking lot with Little Sidney. I have fed him an entire box of animal crackers and recited five versions of

The Three Little Pigs. I rummage around in the glove box. Nothing but cassette tapes. I put one in the player. Instead of music, I'm listening to The Late Night News Show. I wave the cassette at Little Sidney and show him how to pull the tape from the holder.

Three tapes later Sidney appears, grinning from ear to ear. He casually slips slowly into the passenger seat of the car.

"Hit it," he says.

"Why are you talking from the side of your mouth?"

"They have cameras on the parking lot."

"I'm not going anywhere until you tell me if you got the job or not."

"I don't know how, but I did it! I start tomorrow."

I yelp and lean over to kiss him.

He pushes me away. "No not here. I want to look professional."

"But we're in the car."

"Journalism has a code of ethics. The network frowns upon public displays of affection."

My Celebrity Husband

I am not sure what the phone bill will be this month but Sidney doesn't seem to care. The school board, doesn't want to take no for an answer, and neither do the principal or the priest. On top of that he received several offers by mail. Apparently, calling to decline these, is my job not his, because I'm the one who sent off a truckload of applications, last year.

The phone rings just as I hang up from my sixth and last call. My hello sounds angry.

"Hi it's me, I'm on lunch. I miss you."

"I miss you too."

"Can you pay the car insurance? I forgot to do it."

"I'm not your secretary," I grumble.

"No. That's true. But it's a gorgeous day to go for a drive."

"You took the car remember."

"Oh . . . right. I did didn't I."

"I have to cram for my GED test this evening. Do you have any idea when you will be home from work? I'll need a ride there."

"Well we have to cover an event tonight." His voice sounds normal again. "I'll be home late so don't wait up."

"How can you not know a time frame? And how can an event be more important than my education or me?"

Silence.

"Well?"

He whispers, "Look I'm making good money and this is on top of my vacation pay. Just hire a taxi or postpone the GED test."

"Postpone the test? Why?"

"You know you can't just study a book for a month and expect to pass on this first try. If everyone could do that we wouldn't need teachers."

A deep sigh slips from my mouth. "I'll ask Gillian to drive me."

"Do you want me to call Mother to babysit?"

"No. Gillian will—he'll have more fun there. But I want to give her some money, for gas and buy her something for all the babysitting she's done for free."

"I have to go," his voice sounds strained.

"What happened to, I love you Angel?"

"Juanita I'm at work," he whispers.

"Well . . . I love you, have fun," I say.

"Me too." He coughs, and hangs up.

I shake my head at the phone.

It rings again. I know it's him. I answer it grinning from ear to ear, "Yes?" I say in my most seductive voice.

"Can you turn on the TV and critique me. I'll be on in five minutes." Then I hear nothing but a dial tone.

I sit through the newscast scrutinizing Sidney. His voice is different than the one I hear all the time. It's lower—deeper and lacks some of the emotion. He uses the same tone for the good news and bad news. His eyes look like he's reading and he's not looking up enough. I make a few more notes until the weather man appears on the screen.

I climb up the counter and reach into the cupboard above the fridge for the money jar. I dump it on the counter. Some slips of paper remain crammed inside it. I pull them out and flip through them. The larger one is a receipt for the TV. I gape at the others. Bar tabs? Restaurant receipts?

I look at the date. It's from this spring when we lived in Harbour Breton. I feel stunned. Numb. I grab the critique notes from the coffee table, rip them up and flush them down the toilet.

I take every cent in the jar and bring it and Little Sidney to Gillian. She stares at the money and refuses to take it. I slump in a chair and shove it back towards her, crying.

"Oh my gosh, what is wrong? Did you and Sidney have another fight?"

"I think it's over. We're done."

I tell her about St. Lawrence and Harbour Breton. "It's eating my guts out. He lied to me. I knew he was lying and after I confronted him, he still lied."

"Christ! Thank God I don't smoke up in front of the kids or I'd get stoned out of my mind right now."

"That's it?" I sob. "No advice?"

"I didn't know you needed advice. I thought you made a decision. I can hold onto the money in case you leave him, if you want. But I can't just take it."

"I was saving the money for his birthday and for Christmas but I want you to take it. When I pass my GED I want to go to a university and get an education. I thought maybe you could babysit full time if I pay you."

"I would do it for free, besides I have a built in free sitter myself, George is thirteen. But I have to pee I'll be right back."

"That's okay, I need to go wash the dishes and study for my GED. I'll see you later."

I lean over the sink. Bubbles burst into nothingness exposing the submerged dirty dishes. The water is lukewarm. I roll up my sleeve and pull out the plug. My tears splatter onto the plates. I rinse them with hot water and refill the sink.

"Mommy I'm not little. I'm big!"

I kneel down beside him, "You are! You're getting real big."

"Mommy why are you sad?" he wipes my face.

"I'm not sad sweetie," I smile. "The water splattered in my face. I flick my hands at him. Like that."

He giggles, then frowns and asks, "But why are your eyes wet?"

I brush my cheek against his curls. "Do you remember that time we got soap in your eyes?"

His eyes are as big as saucers, "It hurt. I don't like shampoo."

"Well Mommy just got soap in her eyes and now I don't like dish soap."

"Come on Little Sidney," George yanks on his hand.

"Stop calling me that. I'm NOT LITTLE," he pouts and stomps his foot.

"Tell you what George, because he is getting so big, how about we call him Sid from now on. Would you like that, Sid?"

He nods excitedly, hugs me, nods again and runs off.

"That's exactly why you and Sidney have to work it out." Gillian is leaning in the doorway with her arms up in the air. "Kids. They'll do it to you every time."

"Why don't you get a job just to have something interesting to talk about with Sidney?"

"Sidney doesn't want me to work. Besides you don't work and your marriage seems fine."

"My husband isn't aloof or selfish. Maybe if he doesn't know what you're doing all day he might think about you once or twice."

I bite my lip.

"I'm not you and Luke is not Sidney," she hugs me and whispers, "but every now and then, we all get bored. I think you should start thinking about your needs a little more because the new job is going to be his priority, not you." She pushes me out the door, "I want you to bring Little Sidney— I mean Sid—up every day, even if you don't go anywhere?"

"Why?"

"Because eventually you will. Good luck with your exam." She hands me the money jar, her car keys, and gently closes the door in my face.

It's hard to focus on the test. I have no clue what Pi is. I read the questions and four options twice. They are talking about a circle and one

251

answer has the word circumference and ratio in it, and check that. Some of the terms, I vaguely remember from crashing university classes with Sidney, others I recognize from some of the exams I corrected, back in St. Lawrence. A few I know. The rest, I guess, by eliminating the senseless possibilities and choosing from the most logical of the left over options.

There's just a few that absolutely sump me. I tap my pencil and watch the second hand rotate around the clock. The arm of the examiner catches my eye. She points to her pencil and shakes her head. I stop tapping, erase a dot, and skip ahead. Later, I see a similar question and only one answer is a duplicate of the one I skipped earlier. I flip back a page and check the same answer.

I glance over the questions a second time but the buzzer rings, halfway through. I hand in the test and find Gillian in the parking lot waiting.

"Thanks for offering me the car, but I was too nervous to drive. So I really appreciate this."

"How did you do?"

"Who knows? All I can do is wait."

Three months later I'm still waiting but at least I've stopped biting my nails raw. Gillian was right. Getting a job was the best thing I could have done but she was wrong about it stopping the boredom. A month ago, I quit a very pathetic job only to land another one just like it and I'm beginning to think I'm unemployable. Maybe if my GED results would come, I'd get better opportunities. My coworkers seem content just to have a job. Maybe I'm the problem. Maybe I expect too much. Or maybe all jobs are equally boring.

Drizzle is streaking down the window of the Discount Arcade and I'm inside folding towels. The Discount Arcade is a large department store located on Main Street in the heart of downtown St. Johns. It's what some might call a bargain shop.

This area of Main Street is littered with homeless people. Some look like prostitutes, others look like war vets. Somehow, I have managed to keep this job for almost two weeks. My job is to refold the clothing bins after people ransack them. The entire storefront is glass windows. Even the doors are glass. For the pass five minutes I have been watching a mentally challenged homeless woman, lift her dress at every passing car.

"I wonder what that does for business," I whisper at Kelly as I tackle the bin of wrinkled towels. I dip my chin in the center and fold the terry cloth into quarters.

"She's over sixty. Too bad she isn't younger. If she was, we might have more men in here." Her twinkling eyes becomes serious. She points at the bin behind me. "Women are pigs. Absolute pigs."

I laugh but her crow's feet don't budge. Her face looks like crumpled paper and her mouth is twisted into a scowl.

"It isn't funny. Watch and see. This bin will be trashed again in one or two hours. You'll see. You were just transferred to this department yesterday. Me—I've been a supervisor of bath and bedding for fifteen years now, and even though the sign says the sizes, the shoppers shake out the towels to see how big they are. You would think they would know the difference between a hand towel, a bath towel and a face cloth when they've used them all their lives."

We finish the towels and move onto the bedding rack. Her wrinkled hands meet mine when we fold the sheets. Is she an epitome of my life? Will I be folding fabrics until I retire?

"May I ask how much you make as a supervisor?"

"I've been working here thirty years and the golden rule is: Don't Discuss Wages but you don't learn that until you're here awhile." She cautiously looks behind her and whispers. "I started at the minimum wage cleaning the restrooms and look at me now. Right now, I am making twenty cents above the minimum wage. They say some others are still only making the minimum. Is that what the Arcade paid you to start?"

I nod. I don't have the heart to tell her I am making thirty cents an hour more than her. The more towels I fold the guiltier I feel about my lie. I picture myself working here, lying about my wages until the day she retires.

"What's retirement age around here?"

"Oh that's the good part. After you retire, if you want to work part days they will hire you back."

My eyes flutter shut.

"Isn't that great?"

"I quit."

"Was it something I said?"

"No."

"Oh dear," she fidgets with some pillowcases, "what am I supposed to do? They didn't train me for this. This hasn't happened here before."

"I can't stay here, I just can't. It'll kill me."

"Oh dear." Her hands won't stop trembling.

I cup her hand, under mine, and say. "Wait until I leave. Just tell them the truth. Tell them exactly what I said."

"What did you say," she asks bewildered. I notice a couple of supervisors are eavesdropping nearby.

I raise my voice so they can clearly hear me. "Kelly, I just can't see me staying her folding towels for the rest of my life while they pay me only fifty cents above the minimum wage. I'm quitting and don't try to stop me." I walk out as the words, "fifty cents above the minimum wage," echo across the Discount Arcade.

On the bus ride home I notice everyone looks worn out, except the business people. They don't look tired or haggard. They look confident and calm. That's what I need, a career, not a job

I find Sidney asleep on the couch.

"Sidney, Sidney," I shake his shoulder, "It's important. I need to talk to you! Please!"

"What?"

"Did you do anything with my test results?"

"What test results?"

"It's been three months."

"I don't know. So how do you think you did?" Sidney asks.

"I don't have a clue. I'm sort of nervous . . . and worried."

"That's good." I look at Sidney as his eyes are pinned to the TV. It's not even the news! He's watching talk show hosts!

I muster up the dirtiest look imaginable. "Talk show hosts?"

"You said my voice sounded flat and you were right. I'm studying voice fluctuation."

"Tonight you're studying The Three Bears and putting your son to bed. Oh, and by the way, everyone, but you, calls him Sid."

"Hmm-mmm."

"Did you hear me? You don't even know your son's name!"

Finally, I have his attention. "Have you lost your mind? Of course I know his name."

"Really, then what is it?"

"It's Little Sidney."

"Why don't you go tell him that?"

I stalk to the bedroom and slam the door. In case it wasn't hard enough, I open it and slam it again. I jam a chair against the knob, sit on the bed, and play guitar. I ignore the bangs on the door and wait until my bladder is about to burst, before I remove the chair.

For the next several days, I try to ignore Sidney as much as I can. Why waste my breath talking to him, when he never listens? When he's home, I stay in the bedroom, strumming the guitar. And that's what I'm doing, the day he grabs it, and kicks it into the chair.

I keep my eyes on the broken strings and the giant hole in the body. I scowl at him. "Did that make you feel like a man?"

I run into the back yard, lie on the grass and stare up at the sky. Anger fades and a sad stark naked truth stares backs at me from the stars. It's a big world out there, with lots of men in it, and I've chosen the wrong one.

"What's so interesting up there?"

"Sidney did you ever think that maybe somewhere out there at this very moment someone could be doing what we're doing right now?"

"What missing TV?"

I smack his arm.

"I'm joking," he laughs.

"Well I'm not. I mean the universe is such a huge place, I bet there's somebody out there right now, looking at the stars, thinking the exact same thing as I am."

"So what are you thinking?"

"I just told you."

"I don't get it."

"Sidney don't you see we are going down a road and we're at a fork . . . and you're going down one way and I am going down the other?"

"That's called growing. We're still going in the same direction."

"Yes but the further we go the greater the distance between us. Do you think, maybe, we got married too young?"

"Maybe . . . but I do love you."

"I know but it's like loving a best friend."

"You are my best friend. You're the one that told me I was looking down too much—to look at the camera more. You're the one who got me the job at the station."

"No you got the job," I say.

"Oh," he bolts upright. "I almost forgot. We need to find you a dress. We're having our annual party at the station and I want you to sit by my boss."

"Say what? I'm not siting by your boss."

"He said he's looking forward to meeting you, so you have to go. It will only be for a little while."

"Looking forward to meeting your wife, is just a cordial expression. Anyway, what kind of dress?"

"Something fancy. A formal. I'll ask Mother. She's been to a couple of black tie events."

Sidney's mother is fully back into our lives now. After he recently refused several teaching positions, he became the son she had always wanted. The son that had choices.

"Mother. it's Sidney. Juanita needs a gown for a gala event and I have no clue where to shop."

The store she recommends has dresses that cost more than our monthly living budget.

"Sidney why don't I buy a cheaper dress and sit somewhere else?"

"Because I need him to see that you can handle any situation. Apparently he has met every single wife but you."

"You've been to all those after work gala events, so why don't you pick out something that looks appropriate."

Sidney is smitten by a tight black satin jumpsuit-dress combination. The sheer black organza tunic has slits on the sides and is covered with fine gold embroidered flowers. The small diamond shaped gems shimmer, as I parade up and down the aisle. The clerk gushes over the gown while her younger assistant gushes over Sidney. I wait until he signs her autograph book. "Well?"

"I'm up for a raise," he says to the clerk. "Think my boss will like it?"

"Everyone will love it."

On our walk back to the car, he winks, and says, "If my boss doesn't like you, and I don't get that raise, I plan to return you and the dress."

"What do I have to do with you getting a raise?"

"Lots. Everything. He believes behind every powerful man is an even more powerful woman."

I reach out to hold his hand. He withdraws his. I stop walking and poke him in the ribs.

"Now what? Are you too good to hold my hand?"

"Juanita please, we're in public."

"Don't make a scene because we're in public or don't hold your hand because you're in public."

"Both."

"Here," I slam the shopping bag against his chest. "Carry this before your precious public realizes what an inconsiderate asshole you are."

Sidney looks around nervously smiles, waving at some people we don't even know.

I stand by the car door. He walks towards me. "Who do you feel like when you wave like that, the Queen or the Pope? And who exactly are you waving at?"

"The public."

"What public?"

"Excuse me, excuse me," a person is sprinting towards us. "I watch you on TV all the time. I've been practicing my voice, want to hear it?"

Sidney tosses me a smug look. "Sure. Fire away."

The kid clears his throat. "Good Evening, I'm Sidney Simon and this is the ten o'clock news." In a higher pitched voice, he asks, "How did I do?"

"Great. Fantastic. Keep up the good work kid!"

"Can I get your autograph? For my sister? She loves you."

"Sure, what's her name?"

"She doesn't need her name on it."

Sidney smirks at me, writes a couple of sentences and signs it.

I get in the car while Sidney chats with the guy. A couple of other people come over for his autograph. One takes a photo.

He slides into the car and smirks, "That's the public."

"I still don't see why you can't hold your wife's hand. It's not like I expect a kiss in public anymore."

On the way home Sidney, and I have the strangest conversation. Of all the things we could be discussing he chooses to talk about drugs. He informs me that drug use and abuse are too different things and that most marijuana smokers are recreational users but even some of those can become addicted depending on usage and cravings.

"Did you know that hashish is made from the flowers of a marijuana plant whereas marijuana is made from the plant itself? Kids are spending their lunch money on Hash instead of food. And the homeless they spend their life addicted to alcohol or drugs. Maybe you could talk about drugs at the party tonight."

My mind flashes back to the homeless people, downtown.

"When I worked at Stoolworths and I was—"

"When did you work at Stoolworths?"

"Right before I got the Discount Arcade job, anyway—"

"When was that?"

"Stop interrupting me. Right after I took my GED I was—"

"How come I didn't know that?"

"Oh I don't know probably for the same reason you'll never know what I'm trying to tell you now! You never listen."

"Go ahead. I'm listening."

I watch nothing from the window.

He turns the knob of the radio. "But hang on, I have to hear this news story first."

I reflect on my first day of work at Stoolworths. By noon I had made over five dollars in tips from serving soup and sandwiches in the cafe. All morning, a disheveled man with torn clothes kept coming into the lobby. Within seconds, he was repeatedly escorted outside. He finally gave up and slumped down against a light pole. I asked the boss why he couldn't come in considering the place was empty.

"He has no money. He's here to beg not buy. He's nothing but a filthy bum."

Every now and then when I was clearing tables, I would look out the window and see him looking in. Each time he would quickly glance away. While my boss was out back accepting a delivery, I knocked on the window. The homeless man shifted further away and nodded. He was so use to rejection he thought I was telling him to move. I knocked again and I motioned for him to come in. He looked around in amazement as if he had seen a miracle. He pointed his finger at his chest. I nodded yes at him. His caved in toothless mouth smiled as I mouthed, hurry.

He was fearful and cautious. He kept looking behind him. I asked him to sit down. He insisted he wasn't allowed. I informed him he was now. He refused and backed away saying he had no money. I emptied my pockets onto the table and told him, you do now, sit down. He was still afraid but he sat.

I asked him to wait while I got him some soup. I lathered some dressing on bread and piled some sliced turkey on it and wrapped it in plastic. I put the soup in a takeout cup and gave him a plastic spoon. I advised him to hide the sandwich in his pocket in case the boss came back and kicked him out. I counted the money he would need to pay for the food and put it at the corner of the table. I shoved the rest his way and told him to pocket it.

"Well what were you going to tell me?" Sidney asks. "There I turned off the radio."

I tell him my story.

"So the boss is still in the delivery area and has no clue this guy's sitting at the table eating food? Did the homeless guy get kicked out?"

"I'm not there yet. You'll never believe what he said to me next."

"Thank you?"

I ignore Sidney's smirk.

"He told me that standing on your feet all day could make them really itchy and he said warm water with baking soda and a bit of peroxide would fix that."

"A homeless bum doesn't soak his feet in warm soda water." He glances at me with a frown, "How would he know that?"

"That's exactly what I asked and he told me he used to be a doctor. Can you believe that?"

"No. He probably lied."

"I believed him then and I believe it now."

"Juanita you are so gullible. Anyway finish your story."

"That's it, I'm finished."

"Did the boss come back or what?"

"She was livid at me. Tried to kick him out and accused him of stealing the food."

"What happened did the police come?"

"No. I told her he had the money for it. She called security and told him to keep his filthy money."

"What did you do then?"

"I called her a heartless bitch and quit."

"Thank God."

"Thank God for what?"

"That there were no police involved because we get faxed copies of all the police reports and I wouldn't want you in one."

"That's all you care about? Why all this talk about homeless people and drugs if you don't give a crap."

Stalked

"The party is tonight, you'll be sitting by my boss and he likes to talk about drugs, legalization and homeless people."

"That's it? That's what it's all about?"

"No he likes to talk about current events too."

The Fart Platform

I cling to Sidney's arm. "I feel too spruced up." Sidney assures me I'm not, and I'll fit in just fine providing I hold my head up higher. He pauses to introduce me to some of the camera crew, leads me to a head table, and it's evident I am definitely not overdressed. We pass a few empty seats, and squeeze behind eleven that are occupied.

A distinguished man stands as we approach, and shakes my hand while Sidney introduces him, "Juanita, this is Jim Swirling and Mr. Swirling this is my wife, Juanita." I see there are no seats beside him and feel relieved, knowing I get to sit at the other end of the table. While we exchange pleasantries, everyone is eyeballing me. I can't get out of there quick enough. I turn to leave.

His arm gently loops through mine, "Stay awhile. We are one big family around here and I like to get to know new members." He clangs a fork on his wine glass until the crowd turns quiet. Now everyone is looking at him, and I, linked at the arm. "I need two chairs everyone on my right move down two spaces."

262

As the evening wears on Sidney disappears. I wait for him to rescue me but he never does. He shows up at the end of the event.

The ride home is quiet. He loosens his tie and places his shoes exactly one inch apart. "I got to sit with a main news anchor." He taps his teeth and glances my way. "Why are you so mad at me?"

"You're with the wrong wife. You need to go buy a life sized Barbie doll. One with a string that talks on demand."

"What are you so upset about?"

"He wants to come to the house. That's what."

"What? Why?"

"He invited himself to your birthday party."

"What birthday party?"

"I told him I was having a surprise birthday party for you and wanted to know if you had made friends with anyone special. He wrote a list of names. See." I take the napkin out of my purse and throw it at him.

Sidney gapes as he reads the napkin. He grabs our photo album from the shelf.

"What are you doing it's not a photo!"

"No," he says as he inserts it. "But this is a keepsake. This is Jim Swirling's autograph. Juanita the man is a legend in the broadcasting industry. See he wrote his name on it. This guest list is the best present you could get me." His smile fades. He taps his teeth. "You know what this means don't you?"

"Yes. I have to scour this place and put on a proper spread."

"No guess again."

"You plan to forge his name one day? I don't know. You get the promotion?"

"Who cares about the promotion, Jim Swirling is coming to my house. Juanita we have to move."

"What happened to our house?"

"This place isn't good enough, we need a better place!" He picks up the phone and dials 411. "Yes operator, I need the number to Home Built."

He hangs up and dials the number. "You know they're closed right?"

"Of course," he snaps. "Thanks a lot. I missed the recording." As he redials he glares at me, "This time be quiet so I can hear what time they open . . . good, tomorrow morning first thing before I go to work I'll grab some boxes. While I am at work you can pack."

"But we haven't found a place. What if we can't find one in time?"

Sidney puts the photo album back up on the shelf, grabs a pile of envelopes and flips through them. "What's this?" He opens the manila envelope and pulls out a letter and a certificate. "Congratulations on passing your GED. Your above average score qualifies you for—Juanita do you know who Clifford Penney is?"

"No who?"

"The minister of education wrote you a hand written response."

"Good, stick in the photo album next to your napkin, in case they know each other."

"You know what this means don't you?"

"That you want him at the party too?"

"No. According to him you are in the top percentage of graduating high school seniors. You could further your education," he opens the photo album and puts the certificate in between some pages. "But you don't need to because entertaining is a job in itself."

"What do you mean?"

"You're a natural at entertaining. Look at how well you did when I was a teacher."

"Really? Nuns and newscasters are a different breed."

"The point is you don't need to work. You can quit your job."

A honking horn blares from across the road. Sidney kisses me on the forehead, and quietly tiptoes away. I maneuver around the open boxes and am halfway down the hall when the door flies open, and half of his head appears. He looks surprised to see me. "I was going to leave you a note. I've got a ride, and Sid. I'll drop him at the sitters. Don't forget to pick up some more packing tape. The keys are on the table."

"Sidney, I can take him." I rush towards the door. It slams in my face. I open it in time to see Sidney leave in a white car. I squint my eyes. I must be seeing things. I could swear that was a woman behind the wheel. I shake the thought out of my head. It was probably just one of the camera crew. Some of them have long hair.

Out in the car, I adjust the rearview mirror but barely see over the stack of flattened cardboard boxes. Past an industrial section, I notice a sign for the Unemployment Insurance office.

The tape can wait. I swerve into the lot.

Inside the lobby, the first thing that catches my eye is a large bulletin board with job postings. I read a few but none of them are suitable for me. A few people look bored. One person in work boots and jeans is nodding off. To his left, an old man in a suit looks preoccupied with worry. I sit beside him and watch his thumbs twirl in circles around the breast button of his suit jacket. His eyes look like a still life painting.

"I wouldn't do that if I were you," I say.

He jerks an inch out of his seat, "Do what?"

I nod toward his button, "That. You'll snap the threads. I'm an expert at snapping buttons, especially if you give me a wringer washer."

"Those things went obsolete years ago."

"Maybe here," I say, "but on the outskirts of this island they are alive and popping buttons as we speak."

"You on unemployment?"

"No. I'm looking for a career."

"You're in the wrong department."

"Oh?" I look at his shoes. He looks like a professional, "What kind of job are you here for."

"I'm just waiting for five o'clock." He leans towards me and whispers, "My wife thinks I'm at work. I'm here every day until five." His face is twisted in a sad grimace.

"Well you must know the place pretty good, so do you know where I'm supposed to go?" I ask.

"I only know this bench and the name of this department." He smiles and points at the security guard.

After forty-five minutes, I settle into a chair opposite a counselor, only to find I don't qualify for retraining or any job placement programs. He asks me to fill out a form.

"Why? If you can't help me, then you can't help me."

His East Indian accent is very thick. "It's the policy." He hands me a card and says to call him next week.

"What for?"

"Something might come up by then." He points to the card, "That's me, Mr. Khalid."

He leads me to a large corkboard. "Daily we post new jobs here. Maybe tomorrow will bring you better luck."

Every day for the next week, after I drop Sidney to work, I visit the unemployment office and check in with Mr. Khalid. An hour or two later, I drive home, pick up Sid up from Gillian, pack all day, sleep, and head back to corkboard and Mr. Khalid's desk.

"Why do you keep coming here every single day when I tell you to phone me once a week? Do you know how much paperwork you are creating for me?"

"Do you still have to fill out all those forms if I phone—instead of coming in person?"

"I do, but why come here when all I do is tell you there is nothing here for you? If you have a problem with my English I can transfer you to another counselor, yes?"

"No, I like you, and I understand you just fine."

"Then if you like me why do you torture me every day?"

"Fine I'll phone. I have to spend more time packing anyway."

His eyes light up. "If you are moving then maybe I can look up an office closer to your new home."

"We're only moving a block away, so you're stuck with me. Did you find any new programs I qualify for?"

"Oh dear," he sighs.

Each day I pack for two hours before phoning Mr. Khalid. After we move, I unpack for two hours and check in even though he told me not to call him for a month.

I sit on a box with the phone cradled in my neck.

"I think, I have something, but it is conditional."

I squeal with excitement, "What is it?"

"Promise me if you get hired. You will never bother me again."

"I promise, now what is it?"

"Can you come down here?"

"I thought you didn't want to see me again."

"I have to according to policy."

Sidney's still in the bathroom when I slip out the door. His recent promotion caused his schedule to change. He won't need the car for several hours, and knowing him he won't notice I'm missing. I stop at the donut shop and buy two coffees, half a dozen donuts and a newspaper.

I say hello to my friend in the suit. He told me his name once but I forgot it and I don't have the nerve to ask him again but he does remember mine.

"Juanita, where have you been the past few days? I missed you." I sit beside him in the wooden chair. "Mr. Khalid has a job for me, it's a new program, just out. Maybe he can help you. But wait until I go and don't say I told you about it." He squeezes my hand and kisses it. I pass him the paper. "Here, I bought you a coffee and a couple of donuts but I have to run, before he changes his mind."

Mr. Khalid is beaming. Not because I bought him coffee and donuts but because he's finally getting rid of me.

He shows me a row of index cards. "We don't even have the board made yet, but I thought of you first thing and for the first time I didn't dread talking to you." He seems more excited than I am. I pick three jobs. Apparently, the government pays half of the wages in lieu of on the job, work training. Mr. Khalid scrutinizes my face as I read them.

"Nothing you like? No worry, I have more to sort."

He pulls out a box, "How about an architect. Do you like drawing?"

I nod.

He thanks God for the miracle, and sets up the interview.

Sidney isn't too excited about the fact I'm going to train as an architect. He sighs, "At least it's better than working at that Chinese restaurant mopping floors. Don't ever tell anyone you were a waitress."

"Sidney that was three years ago and it was only for a month."

"Just don't mention it, especially at the party." His straight lips turn upwards. He switches on the TV, turns to me and asks, "What did you get me for my birthday?"

"The party," I say.

He disappears into the kitchen and comes back smirking.

"You know you still have time to shop," he smiles. "Oh and I asked Mother to take Sid for a day, but when I told her you were training as an architect on Monday, and this weekend, we had unpacking to do along with a work party to plan, she decided to take him for the entire weekend."

I look around. The only thing left to unpack are two boxes filled with teaching supplies, which he vowed to never use again.

He throws them in the laundry room and says, "It's party planning time. Follow me."

On the kitchen table is a stack of old albums.

"Where did these come from?"

No answer.

I carry the pile over to the stereo cabinet and open the door. It's hanging by one hinge. The battered cabinet was our first garage sale purchase. I cram the albums in the cubbyhole

I hear Sidney in the shower singing, "Happy Birthday to me. Happy Birthday to me . . ."

That's it!

I poke my head in the bathroom and say, "Sidney I'm heading out."

"Where are you going?"

"Shopping."

Stalked

I put the money jar in my pocket and back out, drive one block, pull over to the curb and pull the TV receipt from my bra. I drive straight to the electronics store and ask for the name on the receipt.

A wiry geeky looking boy, about my age smiles from ear to ear.

"You want to buy a stereo?"

"Yes."

"What kind do you want?"

"One that sounds good— one that's under our credit limit." I hand him the TV receipt.

"How long will it take to deliver it?"

He points to a couch and says, "How long before your show is over?" A blue plaid arm lifts up five fingers. "He'll be ready before you. Let me check your credit first . . . Okay, you seem to have two payments left, but the next one isn't due until three weeks' time."

"Can I afford a stand and a stereo?"

Fifteen minutes later, I'm back in the car, trying to make it home before the delivery driver does.

That weekend I spend every spare moment, lying in front of the new stereo. Sidney is standing in the door laughing his face off.

"You're singing off key and you're missing half the words."

"That's because I don't know them."

"Well you can squawk all you want." He dangles a new set of headphones in my face.

"For me?"

"No. It's my birthday. These are for the TV. I know you hate listening to the news. This way you can sing all you want and it won't bother me. I can block you out anytime I want."

"But the TV was my birthday present, so doesn't that make the headphones mine?"

––––––––––

At eleven, Monday morning I'm back in front of Mr. Khalid.

Panic sweeps across his eyes.

269

"Why aren't you at work? Don't tell me dey fired you already."

"No. I told him there was a mix-up, a paperwork mistake, and this wasn't the job I was originally assigned to."

"But it wasn't a mistake," he rummages for the paperwork. "You specifically said you would like to be an architect."

"No. I specifically said I liked to draw. I thought it would be more like art, more creative, like cartoons, not drawing a bunch of lines with a ruler."

"Do you like flowers?"

"Flowers? Who doesn't?"

"People with allergies. I pray you don't have any." He hands me a slip. "It's for tomorrow, but go now, before they hire someone else."

The next morning, I'm sitting in front of an old wrinkled man, that has three chins. His pasty skin looks like toothpaste and his belly looks like it's about to give birth to a large creature. He asks me if I can do books and tries to talk me into working in the office with him. I'm already in this office longer than I can stand, so I tell him I'm dyslexic, and because my creep alarm, is blaring inside my head, I add, "Unemployment is willing to pay half of the wages for the job listed on this card." I pass it to him. He speaks into an intercom and calls a man named Tony into the office.

"Teach her to stuff wreaths."

We enter a shed like room, at the end of the shop. It's filled with bins of wet soggy moss that smell like someone barefoot, wore the same sneakers for a year. One bench is covered with wire circles and crosses. Rolls of what looks like 3 inch strips of garbage bags are stacked in the corner. He moves a huge box of wires, the size of large paper clips, shaped like the letter u to one side.

"What are these for?" I ask.

"That's the last thing you need to know. First things first."

He hands me a wire wreath and grabs a handful of moss. Stuff it like this then wrap it like so. His hands fly as he tips the wreath up and down, and pins the plastic ends together.

"Oh. That's what they're for."

"Not just that. Your turn."

The roll of green plastic is half the size of a roll of toilet paper, cut in half. "Stretch and pull it simultaneously and wrap it under and over the wreath."

I try it.

"Are you double jointed?" Tony's hand halts my wrist.

"See that? You can see the top of the wire frame pushing against the plastic? It's flat. It needs to be round—curved. Think of the wire as a skeleton—maybe a rib cage, the moss as muscle and the plastic as skin. This thing is skinnier than a beanpole. The top of this wreath isn't supposed to be flat like that. You shouldn't be able to tell there is wire skeleton underneath. It needs more muscle. Put some meat on it." He orders me to make another one.

This time I stuff it with double the amount of moss. Water squishes out as I press it into the frame. It reminds me of picking bakeapples as a kid. It's a stench you never forget.

Tony yanks the wreath from me and pulls it apart. "This is morbidly obese. That is way too much moss." He throws handfuls back into the bin. In twenty seconds flat he fills and wraps the wreath, rips away the roll of green plastic and secures it with a two-inch wire that is shaped like an upside down u.

"Holy crap. How did you do that so fast? How do I get that quick?"

"You don't. Being the head designer means I'm the best. I spent my first six months in this room. At this rate you'll take twelve."

I make another wreath. He shakes his head.

"Too fat is better than too thin, right?"

"Come with me." He wears the flat and fat wreaths I made, along with his piece of perfection on his arm. I follow him and his giant bracelets back to the design room. Three rows of tables that look like full sheets of plywood with legs are half-vacant. Each row has four tables.

"Wow twelve design tables?"

"Nine. The last one in each row is a wrap table."

271

The floor is white linoleum and the walls are beige. At the front of the room, the owner sits on a red velvet chair edged with gold wood. It's elevated on a large platform covered with red carpet.

Tony works at a double table that is at the edge of the room, facing the sides of the other tables, and the throne is at the front, facing everyone.

I watch as Tony ties wired toothpicks to the stem of leaves and sticks them at a downward angle along the outside of the wreath. He repeats the process for the inside portion. The wreath reminds me of the owner's head—nothing on top, just on the sides.

Tony's fingers fly like lightning as he randomly snaps the heads of some white flowers from several stems. All the broken heads seem to be exactly half inch long. I watch the flower spin as he twists wires around the stem. One by one, he sticks the peg leg flowers in a double row around the top of the wreath.

"Now watch this," he tries to stick a flower into my skinny flat wreath. The plastic bends until the stick breaks. "Not wrapped tight enough. You have to stretch it until it almost breaks. Now look at this one. Not only is it enough moss to make two wreaths I'd have to use three or four rows of flowers to cover it. Three rows on this size wreath we make no money and four rows means we're losing money."

The owner claps. The chair looks undersized with him stuffed in it. He watches every move I make. I try to pretend I don't notice his prying eyes. I try not to squirm under his stare.

By the end of the day, my clothes are soaked and I smell like a marsh.

I leave the car windows open and drive home.

Sidney meets me at the door and grabs the keys from my hands. "I need you to start recording me on TV okay, so I can watch it at home."

"I need to get a bath. Can't you replay it at work?"

"No, that's what amateur's do." A quick peck and he's gone.

While I feed Sid, he points to his diaper and says, "Boo-boo."

I check his diaper. It's clean. It takes me a full ten minutes to realize I'm the boo-boo. I shudder to think I'm actually adapting to the stench of marsh moss. By the time I pour a bath, it's time to record Sidney.

By now, the bath water is on the cooler side of lukewarm. I pull the plug until it's half-empty and turn the faucet to hot. While it's filling, I jump in and lather. I rinse and lather again but the water is so soapy I have to rinse in the shower. I just want to soak in a hot clean tub of water. I drain the tub, rinse it and refill it. I have one foot under the tap, when I hear the timer ring. I turn the faucet to a dribble and rush back to the room and hit record.

I tap my foot on the floor waiting for him to sign off.

"Mommy. Mommy."

"Ssshhh." I whisper. "Mommy's recording Daddy and we're not allowed to talk when this red light is on. Go in my room and watch TV."

Part of me wants to trust the recorder but the tape looks like it might run out. Luckily it doesn't. I switch off the TV and check on the tub.

The floor is wet, and the bath is filled to the brim, yet the faucet is turned off. I gather up towels and spread them over the floor. The muscles in my chin tremble. I press my forehead against the tub.

"What's the matter?"

I wrap my arms around my son and hold him close. He pushes me away, points his stubbly little finger to his chest and brags, "Mommy me did it. Me turn-ded it off wif bof my bare hands." Water drips from the edge of his pajama sleeves. The cuffs of his bottoms are underneath his wet feet. I tug at them. "Lift your foot. No—leave your underwear on."

"Mommy are you mad?"

"No, I'm frustrated. Actually I'm not frustrated. I'm so glad this happened because Mommy needed to wash the floor anyway." I soak up the water, hold the towel over the tub and wring it out. "Go to your room and wait for me. I'll be there in a second."

Two minutes later, he returns stark naked, holding a boat.

"No the water is dirt—"

Water splatters everywhere as he lands in the tub. Bubbles roll from his lips. "Brrrrr-brrrrr." He swerves the boat in erratic circles.

"Fine I guess it's no worse than the lake."

Within five minutes he's yawning. I dry him off and he's asleep before I reach his bed. I tip toe out of the room, record Sidney's final broadcast, and lie back on the couch.

I slip into a pair of Sidney's pajamas and drift in and out of sleep for a few minutes. My head bobs forward waking me up. According to the clock it's been two hours since I recorded Sidney's last newscast. Where is he? Maybe he's been in an accident. Maybe he had an event to cover. Maybe he's at one of those late night parties or premier events. If that's the case, he'll be home in half an hour.

I curl up on the couch and drift off. I wake up and glance at the clock. Three am? I spring to my feet. A bolt of panic hits my chest. He must be in an accident. I pick up the phone and dial 91—what if he's working overtime. I hang up and call the newsroom three times but get a recording. I call the emergency news line and get another recording.

I turn on the TV and bite my nails until the news comes on. Nothing. There are no big headlines. The news is the same as it was at ten o'clock. I pace the floor, sit, pace again and flop onto the couch. This reminds me of the night back in Harbour Breton. I must have walked a hundred miles circling the kitchen table that night and for what—for nothing. Once again I don't know if I should be furious or scared. Right now I'm both. If he's with another woman, I'll kill him.

What if he's half dead somewhere? I pick up the phone and put it back down. Who can I call? If I call the police and he's okay, will they fax a police report to his newsroom? If so he'll go berserk. Where would I even start to look for him? He never tells me where he goes after work.

I hear the car in the driveway. I stand at the door ready to wring his neck. Now I wish he was half dead somewhere. The door slowly opens. I pull at the knob and fling it open wide. He jumps back a foot.

"Where the hell were you? I was worried sick. I thought you were dead. It's four in the morning WHERE WERE YOU!"

His eyes are glassy yet he isn't drunk. He looks tired. Maybe he was working after all. "God I was worried to death about you, are you okay?"

"Yes," he chuckles.

"You scared the living hell out of me. I thought you were dead. Now I want to KILL YOU myself. You have your NERVE!"

"I'm a big boy. You don't need to worry about me."

"Where the hell were you until three-thirty in the morning?"

"Working. I had to attend the after party for the awards show. Get some sleep. You have a job to go to in the morning, or did you lose this one too?"

I grit my teeth.

I follow him into the bedroom. "FUCK YOU!" I grab my pillow and a change of clothes, rip off his pajamas and throw them at him.

"I'm sleeping on the couch." I twist around and pull the blanket off the bed and tuck it under my arm, "And I hope you freeze to death."

I glance sat the clock every five minutes. It's three-forty-five am and I'm scared to death I'll mess up and sleep in. I get dressed and lie back down. All night I toss, turn, and plan the best way to cancel this Saturday's party. Now I wish I had not baked all those desserts and bought all that food. I throw the pillow over my head. Who needs a party when you go to one every night of the week anyway?

The next morning, only five minutes late, I cover my wrinkled clothes with my apron and rush to my bench.

I pound out wreath after wreath until I have the shelves of the room lined with them. I have run out of moss by the time Tony comes.

"I need more moss."

Tony eyes dart around the room. He tries to hide his surprise. "I'll notify inventory. Let's go. Mr. Floors wants you out on a station pronto."

"Why? I . . . I . . . uh . . . I'm not ready."

"He wants me to teach you design."

"But I don't know how to prep vases or baby boots yet. You said—"

"You should be flattered. You're advancing quicker than I—most."

"I'm not flattered. I think I'd rather stay here."

"Does he make you that uncomfortable?" Tony smirks.

I nod.

"He's harmless. He's just a looker." His voice lowers, "But be careful what you say. Don't even mutter under your breath. He has microphones and cameras hidden everywhere."

"Good thing I wore slacks."

Tony tosses me a brief nod.

I follow his wide hips to his work area. Tony is wearing the same blue shirt he wore all week but it's freshly laundered. He slides his thumb inside his brown belt and juts out his right hip. "You'll be working beside me. I'll be training you until you get assigned a permanent station."

By Friday, I still don't have my own station and I'm too exhausted to care. I have worked until ten for the past two nights, just to get Saturday off. Sidney's been cleaning the house and sucking up big time. All I have to do is cook. But when Saturday arrives I cook all day and don't get time to take a decent breath. I work nonstop preparing for the party.

I cut the rest of the vegetables for the veggie trays while Chile simmers in the slow cooker. I fill an empty ice cream container with sauce and toss in the wings, and shake them. Sidney should be back from dropping off Sid but there's no sign of him. The more I shake the tub the less frustrated I feel. I put down the tub and check to see if any of the skin separated from the wings. I'm rolling Swedish Meatballs, between my palms, when Sidney walks in with bags of ice and bottles of liquor.

According to the clock. I'm out of time. I shove all the dirty dishes in the oven, make myself a rum and seven and dash to the bedroom. I'm barely dressed when guests arrive. I doubt anyone notices my absence. I'm on my second coat of mascara, when the door bursts open.

"Jim Swirling is here. Hurry up."

I groan, examine my reflection in the mirror and remind myself to be a good wife. I smile at me, until I find a warm smile suitable for company. Jim Swirling stands when I enter the living room. "There you are. Undoubtedly worth the wait. Tell me, does beauty run in the family? Is your mother a beautiful woman too?"

I blush.

"Hmmm. And bashful."

"She—unlike me—didn't need makeup."

He raises his eyebrows. "I doubt a little lipstick constitutes makeup."

We spend the night discussing Patty Hearst and the SLA movement. By eleven, I feel my eyes drooping.

"Well, it's past my bedtime. As always, it has been an absolute pleasure."

When he leaves, so do the majority of the others and by midnight things come close to dying down.

Everybody, but a few single newscasters, have left. The men are huddled in the kitchen and surprisingly they are clearing the kitchen table. Sidney's mentor, the number one newscaster in ratings, climbs up on the table, lies on his back, raises his legs in the air and spreads his butt cheeks wide apart. The threads in the seam of his pants stretch to the breaking point. He flicks a lighter a few inches from his butt. I hear a grunt, followed by a long loud fart and see a two-foot blowtorch type of flame, burst out into the air. Everyone laughs. He rolls off the table, hands Sidney a cigarette lighter and my husband does the same thing.

After several nudges fail, I grip Sidney by the elbow and squeeze tight. "Can you help me unzip my dress?"

"Whoo-hoo." Cat whistles resonate behind us. I drag him into the bedroom. "Get rid of them. Get rid of them now. You promised no drugs. You promised you wouldn't allow anyone to do any drugs."

"Juanita it's nothing. Hashish is just a form of weed."

"I don't want it in my house or my life."

"Don't be such a party pooper, grow up."

I puke three times before I go to bed.

From my room I can smell the pungent smell of weed. Anger seeps up my spine. I rush down the hall into Sid's room. He's fast asleep in the top bunk. I pull the blanket off the lower bunk bed, jam it under the door and tape up the vent.

I wake up to Sid flicking my nose. I look around and groan.

"Wake up, silly. You slept in the wro-ooong room."

"I'm awake," I grumble. I shiver and shut the window. "Hey Sid. I have a great idea. How would you like to spend the day with Grandpa?"

277

He nods eagerly. "Grandma gives me ice cream and cake!"

I nod back. "And cookies. If you ask nice, she'll bake you some cookies." I force a smile as we play a shush game and sneak past Sidney, spread eagle, face down, across the hall floor.

I resist the urge to stomp on his outstretched hand.

I knock on Mrs. Simon's door three times before she answers it. She scoops up Sid and says, "You are such a beautiful boy, Sid, Grandpa is waiting for you in the living room."

Sid slides out of her arms and says, "Daddy's sleeping on the floor. Mommy said he drank too much." He giggles and runs down the hall.

"I didn't know Sidney drank."

"Neither did I," I say. She looks shocked enough so I don't mention his drug use. I suspected Sidney was smoking up months ago. When he started using eye drops. How many recurring eye infections can a person get?

I head back to the apartment and find Sidney still passed out. By late afternoon he walks into the kitchen and does a double take.

"Where's the table."

"It's garbage day tomorrow. Check the roadside trash."

"Are you crazy? You threw out the table?"

"No. I put it in the bedroom."

He walks down the hall and opens the door, slams it and gives me a dirty look. I shrug. He swings the front door open. It crashes against the wall leaving a round dent in the wood. Within minutes, he's back panting. "Where's the rest of it?"

I stop humming but continue to sanitize the counter top. "Rest of what?"

"You know bloody well what. The table?"

"Oh your fart platform? It was by the trash. If it's not there, you'll have to hunt it down, house by house."

I slam the crock-pot into the sink. Chile splatters across the counter and drips to the floor. "The next time you do hashish I hope you swallow the roll and choke."

"For your information you don't roll it you hot knife it." He slams the door so hard the house shakes.

Stalked

For several months, we are strangers passing keys back and forth. After he finds me circling, rooms for rent and has a giant panic attack, I agree to stay on the condition he never does drugs in the house ever again.

It takes him exactly one year to break his promise.

"Get the hell out of my house," I yell. "Everyone get the FUCK OUT." I glare at Sidney, "ESPECIALLY YOU!"

"But it's my birthday."

I pick up the phone. "I'm calling the cops, if you, aren't out of here in two minutes."

Bodies fly.

"I'm not leaving, my house. If you don't like it, you can leave."

"I am not leaving my son with you, not while you're high."

"It's freezing out what am I supposed to do sleep in the car?"

I nod and point to the door.

Legs Eleven

Sidney lowers the volume and says, "Remember this song. This is the first song we danced to . . . Brown Eyed Girl. I love your eyes, even when you're angry—and the doe eyed look you have now."

"When I was a kid, I counted footstep and icicle drops and almost froze in the back yard. I survived by convincing myself that one day I would grow up—be somewhere warm, with someone to love—who loved me back. What the heck happened to us?"

"We grew up."

I walk into the bedroom and start packing. I stay up all night and by dawn I'm taping the last box shut

At the last minute, Sidney protests, and asks for a second chance. He promises to stop drugs, to quit his job and to go back to teaching.

"Please don't leave me. I can't live without you. I'll do anything you ask—anything you want—"

"I want a divorce."

Sid looks up from playing and asks, "Can I have a divorce too?"

Sidney scoops him up, bends over the couch and drops him onto the cushions. He bounces and yells, "Do it again, Daddy."

"Later. Mommy and Daddy need to have a talk." He switches the TV to a cartoon station and pulls me down the hall towards the bedroom.

"No. Whatever you have to say you can say it here."

With one eye on the couch, he whispers to me. "Just give me until Christmas. Stay for Christmas, for Sid's sake. If you still want to leave after Christmas, I promise I will not try to stop you. Please. I will never ask you to do anything else again. Just this one thing. Come on . . . if you can't do this for me, do it for Sid. Please don't ruin his Christmas."

"Have it your way but I'm doing this for Sid—not you. And don't expect me to change my mind. It's made up. After Christmas is over, I'm done. I'm moving out in January."

––––––––

At work, I finally have my own station, but it's directly in front of my boss. Christmas wreaths and swags are flying out the door. The delivery drivers are stocking up the vans but it's too late to deliver them. It's almost midnight. Lately I've been here until two or three in the morning. But today is Christmas Eve and we should be home at a decent hour.

My thumbs are raw from wiring party corsages. Every now and then, I peel red spray paint from my fingertips. I glance up and catch my boss's eyes riveted to my station. His eyes bulge out at my every move. The only time he takes them off me is when he points at a designer and motions her over to his throne. She looks scared, cautiously approaches him, turns back, rolls her eyes, digs a broken stemmed rose out of the trash and floats it in a bowl of water. She ties a burgundy ribbon around the neck of the bowl, stores it in the cooler and rolls her eyes for a second time.

Despite the fact he manages to catch every minuscule bit of wastage and misses nothing, I feel his eyes pierce me the majority of the time. Finally, he calls it a night and leaves.

For the next hour, we joke and laugh but manage to push out twenty more orders before Tony dims the lights.

I'm still wearing my apron when I get in the car. For a moment, I think about returning it, but I'm too tired to race back before they lock the door.

"You must be exhausted."

"I am." I lean over the back seat and stroke Sid's cheek. "The hardest part was only seeing Sid when he was asleep."

"At least you get to spend breakfast with him. He seems to have adapted much better this past week."

Sidney managed to change his shift to days, which meant no more prime news for him. For the past week he's been the one picking up Sid, putting him to bed, cooking and cleaning. I've been living on four hours of sleep but last night I skipped sleeping and put the house back in order. Right now, I can barely stay awake.

I lean my head against the window and watch my breath steam up the glass.

"Sorry you've been carrying more than your share of the load lately. I can't believe how this industry relies on holidays to thrive. You must be more exhausted than I am."

"Actually we went to bed, most nights at eight, sometimes nine, so I got plenty of sleep. It's you I'm worried about."

"I can't wait for next month. I'm actually getting an entire week off."

"When?"

"At the end of January."

"Why the end of January?"

"Seniority gets to choose first and they all picked as close to New Years as they could get."

"Is your boss still being a jerk?"

"It's like every time I turn around his beady eyes are drooling at me. It's not just me it's all the girls. It feels like he's stripping us naked."

"Why don't you quit?"

"I don't want to quit. I finally have a career. I love doing this. It won't always be this hard. After Christmas things will be more normal."

"Mother wants us over for Christmas dinner, or did you want to cook and stay home?"

"No I'm good with going to your mother's house. Have you told her anything yet?"

Sidney shuts off the engine, grips the steering wheel and pushes his body backwards in the seat. "You're still going to leave me, aren't you?" His eyes are closed. "Can't you see I've changed?"

"Yes I can. But you changed too late . . . Sidney I . . . uh . . . too much has happened. I still love you but it's not the same. I know it's not the same for you either. Admit it—"

"I will quit my job—whatever it takes."

"It isn't your job. It's the trust. It's gone. For me trust is everything. Yeah, I hated that your image was more important than me. I hated that I was less important than peer pressure from work friends. But the main thing is I don't trust you anymore. You lied to me too many times—too much disrespect. I'm sorry but this can't be fixed."

He grips the wheel tighter. "But I've changed. You know I have." His glasses bounce around while he wipes his eyes.

I catch a runaway tear. "You took too long, Sidney. You changed too late. The damage was already done."

<hr/>

The light flickers above my bed. For some reason leaving it on makes me feel safer and less alone. I live in the eighth apartment on the fourth floor of a house. It was advertised as a loft apartment which sounded really romantic but the reality is it's actually half of an attic. A midget couldn't stand under the ceiling unless they stood two feet out from the far wall. The opposite wall runs along the peak of the roof and is ten feet high. The thing I dislike the most about this place is the bathroom. It's at the end of the outside hall, and I have to walk past the other loft apartment to reach it. Maybe why this place gives me the creeps is because it's one street away from Barters Hill. Every time I see a flight of stairs I think about that Clara and her drunk ex-boyfriend.

Despite Sidney's arguments I insisted on moving in here right after Christmas. It seemed like an ideal time. With all the overtime, Sid had adapted to me not being home much. He had grown comfortable with not seeing me at night and liked having his Daddy tuck him in for a change.

Sidney and I initially argued hot and heavy over who got Sid. I had an answer for almost every objection but lost the fight when it came down to being selfless and doing what was best for Sid. I couldn't argue the fact that Sidney was better equipped with a set of grandparents and doting Uncles and Aunts while I came from a broken dysfunctional environment with loose family ties. It was no secret that I wasn't a favorite choice as a daughter-in-law and had to agree when Sidney suggested he would be the better one to nurture those family relationships.

He made it clear that his goal was for us to get back together. My goals are different. My goal is to get a car and move to a safer place for Sid to live in and get joint custody. For now, on my salary, the best I can do is wait.

There are no steadfast rules. Whenever we want to do things together, we can. The first thing we do is enroll Sid into daycare. He spends weekends with his grandparents because Sidney and I usually work every Saturday and Sunday. Luckily my boss likes that I take my lunch at three, because that's when Sidney picks me up, and drives to his work, so I can have the car to pick up Sid after I get off. Sid and I hang out at Sidney's place until I pick him up, after the eleven o'clock news. Tucking Sid in the car seat, without waking him up is the hardest part. Every night Sidney tells me he'll see me tomorrow, and waits until I get inside my apartment building. But tonight he reaches for my arm. And says, "I won't be seeing you for a few days."

"Why not."

"I'm taking Sid on a camping trip. Not far. Just a local park but it should be fun."

"For how long?"

"One week."

"Swear on Sid's life you're not running away with him."

"Geez, give me more credit than that."

"Swear on his life."

"Angel, give me a break. I would never ever do something like that to you."

"Good. I want it in writing."

"I promise. I swear on Sid's life I am only taking him camping and we will see you in a week."

"You'd better or I'll hunt you down and murder you." Despite my comment he waits, then honks once I get inside.

The hallway to my apartment is quiet and it seems like I have the entire floor to myself but I know I don't. Some weird girl named Deidre rents the other half. I met her when the landlord showed me the place. Her eyes avoided mine when we were introduced. She appeared guarded, almost embarrassed. She had no makeup on and her hair was a mess. I was relieved she was a neighbor and not a roommate.

My room reminds me a little of the small place that Sidney and I had off Barters Hill, except for the one side where the roof peek meets the wall. That end wall is so short, you couldn't put a dresser there and stand at it. The other odd thing about the units is unlike other apartments these have no numbers on the doors.

Having my evenings back enables me to unpack and for the next two days I make some progress, but tonight I've had my fill. I'm bored with unpacking the boxes. I pick up the phone to call Sid, but halfway through dialing, I remember Sidney took him camping for the week.

I spend the evening drawing eyeballs on the unpacked boxes and have a stare down contest with them. The boxes win.

I grab a small box of toiletries and head outside to the bathroom. I open the medicine cabinet door. It's filthy but the top shelf is free except for three medication bottles. Two are empty. I read the label. Phenothiazine. Never heard of it. I carry my toiletries back to my room, lock the door and draw too closed eyes on the spare pillow.

I toss and turn between brief moments of sleep. Twice I get up to make sure I locked the door. The third time, I jam a chair against the knob. I spend the majority of my waking moments regretting my decision but at the first sign of light I feel relief and the regret slowly ebbs away. I grab a towel and head for the bathroom.

"Nice pajamas," a seductive voice says. Mr. Fabio wannabe is leaning in the other loft doorway. I hastily close the bathroom door and get a shower. As soon as I open the door Deidre confronts me hissing, "Stay away from my boyfriend."

"That won't be a problem. I just got out of a marriage and the last thing I want is a boyfriend."

She glares at me. "You're just a fucking whore aren't you?"

The blood rushes to my head. Her boyfriend pulls her inside and slams the door. While they scream and argue, I run back to my loft, wedge the chair back against the door and wait for it to jolt loose. When I don't hear footsteps, I slump over the counter and cry into the sink.

An eerie sensation creeps over me. It's a feeling I left behind when I was fourteen. Stop it! You're not nine. You're going on nineteen. Stop waiting for holy terror to break loose. This isn't the past. Get dressed and go for a walk. You have choices now. I'm a nervous wreck and my first instinct is to run back to Sidney. He was right. There is no way I am ever, ever, ever bringing Sid here.

I force myself to get dressed and creep downstairs by pressing my weight against the railing, an old habit I practiced for seven years of my life. I chant to myself, F.E.A.R. is False Evidence Appearing Real. This isn't real. There is no threat.

I aimlessly wander around town for two hours, thinking and rethinking until my mind is exhausted. I sit on a bench and try to imagine how I would be feeling, this very moment, if Sidney lived at the loft and I had stayed in the apartment near his mother. Would I still be thinking about reconciliation? The answer is a blatant no. I just need to move. I need to find a place suitable to raise Sid. I need a better job or an extra job. Maybe if I have two jobs I won't spend any evenings at the loft.

Back on the main drag of downtown, the windows are all the same. Everybody is selling something and my reflection hovers in front of every window display until I reach a flower shop window. A poster covers a third of the window. Hiring Please Apply Within. A mild curiosity entices me to saunter inside.

Stalked

It's a small quaint shop one-eighth the size of the Floors of Flowers. Inside two men are embracing. Should I wait until they finish hugging or interrupt them? Maybe a cough would work.

The one with the pencil like physique, adjusts his glasses, pats the man on the back and gives me a somber look. The other thick haired man has a warm stocky face and looks like he indulges in the odd dessert—or beer. He says, "I'll see you tonight. Bring a bottle of wine. A Pinot Noir."

"Excuse me . . . is the owner in?"

The slimmer gentleman points to the man leaving and says, "If it's bad news it's him, otherwise it's me."

"The sign . . . I was thinking . . . I have a job but I was thinking—"

"I'm hiring a doer not a thinker."

"May I ask how much the job pays?"

"That's all you want to know? You don't care about the hours or what the job is for?"

"I'm assuming it's for something to do with this shop."

"It could be for cleaning the bathroom," he grins, "or organizing our collection of pornography. How about we do this. How about you tell me what you can do that someone with a flower shop might benefit from."

"I work at Floors of Flowers and—"

"He sent you here to spy on me didn't he? That lowlife prick will resort to anything."

"He didn't honest. I have this week off and I saw your sign—"

"Why would you want to work here?"

"Because Mr. Floors is a big pervert that likes to stare at women all day and I'm sick of it."

The owner laughs, "He looks at everyone that way. Me, my wife—"

"You and your wife?"

"Ha!" He points at me grinning. "You pegged me as gay."

I look at him shocked. "No, no, I didn't mean it that—"

"I tried it once but I didn't like it," he glances at me sideways and smirks.

I am at a loss for words.

"Kidding! Jesus, you're going to be loads of fun," he chuckles. "Well don't just stand there, do some work. Show me some magic."

He has orders pinned to a line. He removes a clothes pin and slaps an invoice on the counter. "Wow me."

"I don't know your prices. What do you charge for a stem of chrysanthemums?"

"Ha-ha! I called it! You are a spy!"

"Tim, knock it off. How's she supposed to make a wreath if she doesn't know prices." The heavyset man reaches under the counter and dangles his keys. "Won't get far without these." He flashes a quick smile and pats my shoulder. "I'm the normal brother—John Walters. Forgive Tim. He doesn't get out much." He winks and leaves.

"Are you Tim Walters? The Tim Walters?"

"That's me. The one and only infamous former head designer of Floors of Flowers. Is he still bitching about me?"

I laugh, "Everyday. He calls you Traitor Tim."

"I like you." He points to the cooler. "Mums, $1.75 a stem, the flower filler of funeral work. Let's get you started." He opens the sliding glass door and pulls out stems of salal, mums, baby's breath, leatherleaf, plumosa and three carnations. He tosses them on the desk, folds his arms and nods at the stool. Then he tilts his head towards the far back corner. "The frames and moss are over there to your right. Make the order."

After fifteen minutes I look up and say, "Done."

"What about the card?"

"Designers don't write cards."

"Here we do. We order stock, unpack shipments, wash buckets, clean coolers, stock shelves, wash windows, you name it, we do it, even the books."

The books? Now I want this job no matter what he pays. I need this job. I'll get to learn everything I need to know about the business. Then, I can quit working for other people, who can fire me.

"Tell you what," he points to a clothesline of invoices. "You work on those orders for the next two hours and I'll consider it an interview, and tomorrow I'll decide if you're worth hiring or not."

"Which bench?"

"This isn't Floors of Flowers. Until I unpack the shipments, sitting on top of that one. You'll have to share mine."

"Can I help?"

"I take it you've never touched dry packs before?"

"No."

"There's a secret to flowers that look fresh for a week, so keep your hands off mine."

After two hours I'm five minutes away from finishing the last order. I select the card, write the greeting, sign it, and pin it to the bow. At Floors of Flowers, we used eight-inch plastic prongs to hold a card, but these people use straight pins or staples stuck to the bows.

I leave the wreath on the table, grab my brown ankle-length leather coat, and stand by the door, waiting for Tim to finish his phone call.

"Where do you think you're going?"

"The two hours are up."

"Sit back on that stool. You don't get off work until five pm."

"Does that mean I got the job? I get paid?"

"Can you work for free?"

"No."

"Then yes, I guess I'll have to pay you."

He tosses me a form. "Just fill in your contact information, driver license and social number. Skip the work history and reference parts."

He picks up the phone. "Mr. Floors please." I twist around on the stool. My jaw is tight and my eyes are bigger than basketballs. A strange whimper escapes from my throat.

He smirks at me. "Hey Wally, it's me Tim Walters. I just stole one of your better designers. Her name is Juanita Simon. You can send her final check here." He hangs up, slaps his knees and howls. "Bet that makes the old bastard croak.". I twist back in my stool facing the application.

His laughter becomes louder. "Legs Eleven. I'm going to name you, Legs Eleven." A flash reflects off the wall. He is busting up as he shows me the photo. All you can see below the hem of my coat is the bottom of the stool. I look like I have two wooden peg legs. "Legs Eleven it is," he grins.

He slides his glasses to the top of his head and rubs his eyes and lifts some boxes onto the bench. "These are containers and floral picks for Valentine's. I don't have anywhere to put them right now." He scratches his head, "What I can do is move that book shelf upstairs to the bathroom and build you a work bench. It'll probably take me into Tuesday, so how about you start Wednesday and work through to Sunday."

At five o'clock, I head home, crash on top of my bed and daydream about opening my own shop one day. At Floors of Flowers, all I did was design but now I get to do the books, see where the stock comes from and learn how a small, one-man operation is run.

I roll off the bed and look for something to eat. I open a can of beans and pour them into the frying pan. I turn them on low and sink into the recliner. I close my eyes, take a deep breath and for the first time ever I'm glad I left Sidney. Sidney would never want me working downtown but now it's none of his business. He has no—Thud! I'm face down on the floor, frantically try to pry two hands from my hair. Someone is ripping my hair out of my head dragging me across the floor. I bend fingers backwards until the grip loosens. I lift my head. Fingernails dig into my skull. I scream at the top of my lungs. "Help! Help me."

"You fucking whore trying to steal my boyfriend." She drags me out into the hall towards the bathroom. "He left me for you! How long have you been fucking him?"

She's backing into the bathroom doorway. Her wild eyes hung above mine. I can't let her get me into the bathroom. I jam my hands against the door frame. She kicks me in the knuckles.

"He's standing by the sink," I yell. She releases me and turns. I desperately yank her feet from underneath her. She topples and screams. I bolt for my room and lock the door. I try to move the dresser against it. It's too heavy. She rattles the knob and kicks at it. I grab the chair and wedge it like I did earlier today. Everything goes quiet. I huddle in a corner, shaking.

It's too quiet. I desperately look around. How the hell do I get out of here? There's no window! I try to get the vent off the wall with my nails. Suddenly a splintering sound breaks the silence. I see a knife blade slashing through the wooden door. I freeze. I see the tip wiggle. She's cursing and yelling. I open a drawer and throw the contents on the floor. Why didn't I take some pliers or tools with me? I panic as the knife wiggles more and retracts. Slash. Slash. Slash. I see her hand coming through the hole reaching for the lock. The smell of burning beans and fear permeates my nostrils.

I grab the red hot frying pan, slam it against her hand and smell searing flesh. Her hideous screams accompany mine. I back away. From the other side of the room I watch beans drip down the door to the floor. How did I find the strength to do that? Her screams echo from down the hall and disappear. I'm too numb to move. My skull is sore and strands of my hair are twisted between my cramped fingers. I'm scared and angry at the same time. I'm glad I hit her back and I hope every bone in her hand is shattered.

First, I hear male voices approach my door. Then I hear a scuffle.

It takes an hour for Officer Dooley, to realize my black eyes are from mascara and not a head injury. I grab a paper towel and clean my face with cream

"I'm okay," I whisper.

He doesn't seem convinced and suggests I spend the night with family. I tell him I have no family.

"You can't stay here."

I protest as they remove the door from its hinges. "Your door is evidence. Maybe there's a friend you can call?"

I try calling Gillian. A nasally recording says, "The number you have dialed is no longer in service—" I hang up. I swallow hard, "I have no friends. There's nobody I can call."

His thick salt and pepper eyebrows rise. His knees crack when he stands up. He seems to be at a loss for words.

I close my eyes and imagine Sid's small trusting face but a thumping sound in the next loft, drives the image from my mind.

I tense up. It's Officer Dooley. He slides a door towards my loft. "She won't need this anymore." He screws the hinges to the framework and tests it. "Fits like a glove."

Over the course of an hour, I learn she is a known stalker formerly convicted of aggravated assault.

"So she violated her parole?"

Officer Dooley stands in the door with one eye on the hall.

"Not quite. She wasn't on parole. She was convicted to a mental institution two years ago but managed to walk out of it three months back. She's not the first and won't be the last." He glances around the loft. "Guess you've got no space for a roommate." His mouth pulls towards his left ear. He clicks his teeth rapidly, studies my face and rapidly asks, "Are you sure you have no friends to call? Not one? How about coworkers? There must be someone you can call."

"No. There isn't."

Dooley's broad shoulders lift and fall. "We'll be patrolling this area all night. We'll make sure you stay safe." He tips his hat and turns away.

"Patrolling for what? I thought you had her—are there more crazy people like her, on the loose?"

He halts and taps the open door. "Keep this locked. We don't think he has a key."

"Who?"

"The boyfriend is still on the loose—" His blue uniform fills the entire doorframe. His sharp hazel eyes take in every inch of my room. "—also a patient."

"How can people just walk out of a mental institution in broad daylight? How can they rent an apartment?"

"Welfare."

"But it doesn't make sense," I say.

"Tell me something that does."

Sidney makes sense. Right now going back makes a ton of sense.

"Is there going to be a police report? Will people—will the news know what happened?" I ask.

"It's already all over the news. They're swarming the institution like rats to cheese."

"Oh. I see . . . well, what are the chances of her coming back here?"

"I wouldn't count on it." He glances at his watch. "By now she should be in a straitjacket, watching bubbles float in the air but you never know. Play it safe and don't forget, this door has her lock on it."

I take a sharp breath.

"At this point it's him—not her—you need to be more worried about."

I feel dazed. As if someone hauled off and hit me in the head with a baseball bat. "But—but he seemed normal."

"Most of them do," He mutters as he walks away.

For several days, my world is a haze of fear. I thought I would sleep better once they changed the locks. I was wrong. The night of day two, they apprehended him coming back for his things but I still spend my nights staring at the door waiting for footsteps or for something to rattle. It never does. My only reprieve from fear is work and for once in my life, I dread going home. I dread the hall.

I fumble with the key to the door. Inside I jump out of my skin when the phone rings.

I hover my hand over it. It can only be one of two people. My boss or Officer Dooley.

"I thought you went camping for the week."

"I did but a big news story broke. Some mental institution is losing track of its patients. I'm a block from you, at a payphone. Can you take the car, get Sid and pick me up after work?"

After a minute I realize I'm listening to a dial tone. I get outside just as the Javelin pulls up.

"I wish all women could get ready as fast as you. I'm cutting it close. I have five minutes to get to work."

"All women? What's that supposed to mean?"

"I just meant—er—like Mother and Deborah—they take forever."

I can tell by his tone, he's hiding something. It's a short awkward drive. I wait until he hands me the keys, then I say, "I'm not off for the week. I got a new job downtown and I work Wednesday to Sunday."

"Gotta go. I've got to spin a new angle before the story gets stale."

I suppress a scoff and say, "Some things never change."

"That's a perfect angle. Everyone is focused on the institution but not the patients. Where do you suppose they change, eat or sleep?"

My voice cracks. "Probably at shelters or chur—"

"I've got to go. That's the crew, loading the van."

It takes twenty minutes to reach daycare and twenty more to get Sid home. All Sid wants to talk about is his camping trip. I sit a glass of juice and a hotdog in front of him. Ketchup squirts out of the bottom of the bun and smears between his fingers. The wiener plops onto the table. He picks it up and chomps on it. "Daddy doesn't make me eat the bread part." His eyes light up. "And I saw a bear. It was this big." His outstretched arm smashes into the juice glass.

His shirt is dripping wet. His chin quivers. "Am I in trouble?"

"Only if that glass say sorry."

We both burst out laughing. His laughing abruptly stops. "Mommy I'm tired. I want to go to bed."

"After we get a bath."

"I don't get baths anymore."

"Why not?"

"Because big boys get showers."

By the time I turn off the shower, the floor is soaked. "Daddy doesn't make the floor wet. He dries me off, in the shower."

"Yes but I bet Daddy doesn't have water fights like we do, and I bet I'm a better tickler."

I sling him over my shoulder and toss him on the bed.

"Where's Mommy's good night kiss?"

His lips pucker up. But instead of kissing me he tosses several over each of my shoulders and says, "Nite Mommy, and Mommy and you too

Mommy." I twist around. A bunch of pictures of me are taped onto Sid's walls.

"Sid when did Daddy—" He murmurs something inaudible and rolls on his side. I tuck him in bed and tiptoe out of the room.

I gather up Sid's clothes, and gather several towels from the corner pile. A red bra drops to the floor. I gasp out loud.

I drop the load of clothes on top of it and pace up and down the hall. "He can walk home. I'm not going to go get him. I know what—I'll move back in just for the spite of it." My mind is seething. I turn and stare at the bedroom door. "I wonder what I'll find in there?"

"Mommy who are you yelling at?" Sid is staggering in the doorway rubbing his eyes.

"Nobody. Go back to sleep." I tuck him back in bed and head for the master bedroom. My hand trembles on the door knob. My mind replays every time I slammed this door and every argument we ever had.

Let it go. You did the right thing. I pick up everything, including the red bra, and toss it in the washer. For a moment I watch the towels twirl and tangle. I slam on the stop button. I pull out the bra. I hit the start button and walk towards the bathroom dangling the dripping bra on my middle finger. I hang it over his toothbrush and reach into my pocket for my lipstick. I choose a spot on the mirror that would be Sidney's eye level and write in big capital letters, SHE HAS TINY TITS.

I walk into Sid's room and wrap him in a blanket and carry him outside into the back seat of the car. For the entire drive I think about the most painful way to rip Sidney a new asshole. I'm still mulling over what I plan to say to him, when he sprints from the building.

"My place or yours," he grins.

"Mine."

He smirks. "Do I get an invite up to check out what you've done with your new place?"

"No . . . sorry . . . I can't. I have a hot date waiting inside."

His smirk disappears.

At Nineteen an Entrepreneur

I love my new job and my new boss. He doesn't micromanage and he's not one bit creepy. Tim is the funniest person on earth. He missed his calling. He should have been a comedian. The hardest thing about working here is keeping a straight face when customers walk in. For some reason Tim's shop doesn't do that many hospital arrangements. Most of the time customers are ordering flowers for someone dead.

Tim pulls out a long order and rubs his hands together. "It's been six months, Legs Eleven. Ready to do a complete wedding on your own?" He slaps a long order on my bench, sits back on a stool and smiles.

"You're joking right?"

He tilts his head backwards, folds his hands behind his neck and yawns. "Wake me up when you get done."

"Has anyone ever told you a bald head is the first sign of a pervert?"

"Shut up Legs Eleven or I'll fire you." He reaches into his pocket and tosses me a quarter. "Tell you what. I'll pay you to shine it and let you keep the change." He sits back and yawns again.

I pick up the order and read it. "Are you serious? You actually expect me to do this, all by myself? How come you're not doing it?"

"Because I would rather watch you earn your paycheck."

For the next two hours he scrutinizes my work. I glance around for a box to put the bouquets in. I mutter, "You need a bigger shop."

"The funny thing is, I was thinking about that just last month."

"Make sure the design room is big enough to build a platform so you can sit—" He tosses a bunch of leatherleaf at me. Several leaves of the sculpted fern crack and bend as they hit my arm.

"Maybe you could put a bed in there. Watching me work seems to be wearing you out." I fire the leather leaf back at him. It breaks apart.

"That's coming out of your check."

"No fair you fired it first."

"So you noticed I've been slacking huh?"

"I'd say. I'm soon going to start calling you Mr. Floors."

"If you're bothered by me watching you work I could always head up to the bathroom and jerk off to porn magazines."

"Ewwww. Gross. I'm quitting."

"Can't take it huh? Bet that's the last time you compare me to the old pervert," he smirks. "I'm thinking about taking my beautiful wife on a well-deserved vacation. Think you could handle things for seven days?"

"Yes. Do you?"

"Yes! Looks like I'm going on vacation!" He lifts me from the stool and swirls me around the room. A woman coughs! Tim stops and bows to her. Her long legs are crossed. Her dark arms fly up in the air, as a look of amusement crosses her face. "Can't trust you as far as I can throw you, can I Mr. Walters?"

"You are absolutely right Mrs. Walters. Legs Eleven this is my better half, June." He rubs his hands together and tosses her a boyish grin. "I know what this looks like, but rest assured, training her on how to waltz with old Mrs. Gleason, is crucial training, especially if she's going to run the shop while we're in Vegas."

"Vegas? When? Us? When did you decide that?"

"When I hired Legs Eleven."

June squeezes my cheeks and kisses me square on the lips. "Thank you dear! You are the answer to my prayers."

Tim flings his hands up in the air. "What am I chopped liver? If Legs Eleven charges you with sexual harassment, I—"

"Tim we have to leave tonight, before you change your mind!"

"You will have to excuse my overzealous wife, but we haven't been on a vacation since I opened this place six years ago." He looks at his wife and laughs, "If you liked it, and Legs Eleven doesn't mind I give you permission to kiss her again providing I get to photograph it."

June blushes but her voice is curt. "Settle down Tim."

His face turns serious. "Snap. Snap. Let's get this wedding boxed and on the road." He kisses his wife. "I'll be an hour late. I have a shipment coming in and I have to place an advanced order for Easter before suppliers sell out. Legs Eleven, go clean the cooler."

June folds her arms. "I don't trust you. I am not leaving here until you leave with me."

"What? You don't trust me? Allow me to refresh your memory. I'm not the one who kissed Legs Eleven."

"Tim Walters I don't trust you to keep your word." She turns to me "This isn't the first vacation he promised." She removes her coat and shakes her finger at him. "We are leaving this shop together, tonight, even if that means dragging you out of here by the ear. Anything she doesn't know, I suggest you teach her in the next five minutes."

She takes a long deep breath. Her wide green eyes glitter. "It's been sooooo long."

"Wait—" he flicks at the calendar with his fingers. "Don has a convention this week. I can't leave her here alone. We'll have to wait one week, until Don is available to watch over her."

Her wide green eyes pierce mine. "Do you know how to take, make, and place orders as well as how to handle shipments and unpack them?"

"I do."

She puts her hands on her hips and faces her husband, "She knows how to lock a door at five and unlock it the next morning at nine, so I don't see any problem whatsoever with leaving tonight, Tim."

"She has never done an order."

Her eyes open wider, "Customer orders?"

"No orders for shipments."

"Oh that's nothing." She looks at me, winks, and says, "It's the easiest part of this job. That's why he always handles it himself." She throws on an apron. "I'll handle the customers and make sure the delivery is boxed for the driver while you teach her how to place a supply order."

After a few minutes of training, I excuse myself, grab a note book from my purse and run back to the tiny office.

"What are you doing? Writing a letter?"

"Writing down the supplier's names and numbers."

"What for? They are listed right here." He pulls a binder from a stack. The first page has the contact info and a business card clipped to it. The next pages look like a catalog. Some are black and white. A few are in color.

"Where are the prices? If something goes up, what do I do?"

"See this number here. It's the item number. The reason some of these have more than one item number is because they come in different sizes or different colors. The sizing for wire wreath frames ranges from 8-inch to 36-inch." He grabs another binder and flips past a few dozen pages. "Never mind this section it's for silk flowers." He flips to the next tab. "Here we go. If we ran out of baby booties, which we won't, then you would have to pick sizes and col–" he throws the book back. "Forget everything I just told you. The only thing you should need is fresh stock. Other than booking the odd wedding, this is our dead season." He rushes out to the counter and flips through a book. I wait behind him, "Whew," he wipes his brow. "For a minute I thought I had booked another wedding but it's not until the weekend after next."

"What about the fresh flowers?"

He points to the fax.

"I've only seen the FTD orders coming by fax," I say.

"Have you never sent a fax?"

"No."

"The fresh flower price list comes by fax, because prices fluctuate depending on the market. Here's where we keep those lists."

Below the counter he pulls out a cardboard box. "When the faxes come in throw them in here. Now follow me." He feeds a piece of paper through a calculator and tears it away from the roll. He stands in front of the cooler. "We'll need roses. These will be sold or dead in three days. Those mums are starting to droop so unless someone orders a wreath, we know where those will end up in two days. You get it. Right?"

I nod.

He tears up the paper, "The trick is to order what you anticipate will cover an average weeks' sales."

"Do I pay the driver and how long does a delivery take?"

"No and delivery is always next day. Speaking of the devil, the truck is here. We need to clean the cooler."

June turns up her lip and says "I hate doing this especially after Valentine's Day."

"You worked here on Valentine's?"

"And every other major holiday. But thanks to you that might change. If we don't do this now, it will be too close to Valentine's, too close to Easter or too close to Mother's Day . . . this vacation is really now or never."

After we unpack the shipment and restock the cooler Tim pulls another box from under the counter. "This is where I put the Order Receipts after you fill them. They are in numerical order. The customer keeps the yellow copy so just match the white with the pink."

I grin at June. "It's official. I'm trained. You get to go."

Tim dangles a key at me. "Don't lose this Legs Eleven."

"What if there is a funeral and I can't handle all the work?"

"Only take orders for what you can handle."

"No I meant remember three weekends ago when you worked through the night because you had four weddings booked, the morning you slept on that cot in the closet? If I get really busy and have to work until really late, like too late to walk home, can I sleep on it?"

"I don't expect you to do that."

"But if I wanted to. Like if there was a big funeral or something."

"She has a point Tim, especially if it's a regular customer."

"If you do, I'll pay you time and a half."

"What if the weather is too bad to walk home?"

"Then I pay you nothing and charge you rent," he laughs. "Do you need a drive home?" He hands me the key.

"No I live real close," I say. "Want me to lock the door?"

"No let's keep it open in case the homeless get cold. Of course I want you to lock the door."

I lock it, hand him back the key, and walk away.

"Hey Legs Eleven."

I try to contain my excitement, "Yes?" I look back and see he's dangling the key.

"You planning to break in here tomorrow morning?"

I walk home with one eye peeled over my shoulder. I tiptoe upstairs and silently unlock the door. Then I slam it shut.

I feel strange being so alone. No TV. Not much furniture. I drop to my knees, remove the drawers from the dresser, and push it beside the door. Twenty minutes later, I'm moving it away and rushing to the bathroom, peeing as fast as I can and running back to my room. Stop being paranoid. It's safe here now. Smarten up.

I sit on the floor and try to figure out what to do on the far wall. If I bought some kids furniture, this wall could be a perfect play area for Sid! If I work enough overtime, I can buy a little table and chair set, a chalkboard, and maybe a bike! Sid could easily ride a bike in here.

That idea is crushed the minute I phone and suggest it to Sidney.

"Because it's not a good idea. Hang out with him here, it's safer and what he's accustomed to. Don't forget we agreed to no drastic changes."

"Oh, but red bras are not a drastic change?"

301

"It's not what you think. Deborah was babysitting him. The bra belongs to her."

"Sure it does. And exactly when did she get her breast reduction? How about this drastic change? How about you shut up lying?" I hang up, pull the blanket over my face and sleep until dawn.

I spend any spare work time I get during the week, browsing through supply catalogs and visualizing how I would change this place if it were mine. On Wednesday, the supply person brings in some boxes along with a paper cutter.

"I didn't order that."

"Yes you did."

"No I didn't."

"I'm going to have to call the boss."

I hesitate.

"Tim calls us all the time. It's toll free I don't see the problem."

I stare at the skinny kid in the oversized hoodie and nod.

He exchanges a few words with his boss and says, "He says you ordered it."

"I must have made a mistake. Can't you just credit it off and take it back."

"Nope."

"Please. I don't want to get in trouble—I'll buy it. But can't you fax me two invoices? One without this cutter and one for just the cutter?"

"Boss, the lady wants to know if you can fax two invoices one for the cutter and the other one with everything else. She's going to take the cutter for her shop . . . Nope, Tim's not here. He's on vacation. It's for her, not him. She's here helping until he gets back." He looks at me and pauses a moment. "She said that was okay. She knows it's C.O.D. for her." He covers the phone and whispers, "He wants cash for the cutter."

I nod.

"He wants to know what name to put on the invoice."

I tell him my name.

He whispers, "It's got to be a business name."

I shrug and mouth the words, "I don't have one."

He winks at me, "She said it's called The Flowershop."

I grin.

"Yep that's it, F-L-O-W-E-R-S-H-O-P . . . Yep . . . Nope, just one word. No space."

He hangs up. "Congratulations you own a paper cutter. I'm back in town in two days. Do you want to order a roll of paper for the cutter?"

"What kinds are there?"

"Tons. Plain, patterned, seasonal, you name it we got it."

"Something suitable for all seasons, but nothing pink or blue. White with green vines or leaves would be good."

"It has to be C.O.D."

"Can I order a few other things?"

"Sure. The more you order the better I get paid. Plus, I get a bonus for new accounts."

"You can't ever mention this to my boss."

"It's not his business. I deliver to his competitors all the time."

"Oh I'm not a competitor."

"Not yet. Tell you what. I have a delivery eight blocks away. Got to pass by here on the way back. If you're still open, I'll pop in and grab the order. Whenever you want anything, all you have to do is call me. If you fax the office, I don't get commission. Deal?"

"You bet!"

This is really happening! I am going to open my own flower shop. I don't know where, when or how but I am going to do it!

Several days later, I'm ecstatic that Sidney said no to Sid coming to my place, because the space I was going to designate as Sid's play area is now being used to store floral supplies. But by the day Tim is due back I'm almost broke, and having second thoughts, about how I'm going to pull this off.

"There is still so much more I need to buy . . . but Tim is due back today. Promise me you won't say anything to him."

"What are your days off?"

Oh God no, please tell me he is not going to blackmail me for a date.

"My wife and I just had a baby. I need any extra cash I can get. Maybe we can do business on your days off?"

"Really?"

"Yeah. That's how Tim opened this shop."

"Ordering products on the side?"

"Yeah. On his days off. Back when he worked for Mr. Floors."

"I used to work for Mr. Floors before I worked here. He doesn't let people near the office. He keeps designers restricted to the design room."

"It's called good business practice. Every flower shop owner I deliver to worked as a designer for Floors at one time or another."

"Now I get why the man was so paranoid and spent days upon days watching my every move."

"What days?"

"Every single day. That's all he ever did."

"Not him—you. What days are you off?"

"Oh. Monday and Wednesdays. But after Tim gets caught up, I'll get four days off next week because I've worked straight through."

"Call me the morning before your day off. Before you go to work. I'm up at six."

The day Tim appears to be caught up is the day funeral orders pour in for some poor soul who is still at the hospital morgue. When I do get time off, it's a week later and I am owed six days with full pay.

The first thing I do is borrow the Javelin to pick up groceries. I tap on the wheel and plead the red light to turn green.

I pull into the parking lot. I expect Sidney to be waiting in the parking lot, considering I'm twenty minutes late, but he's nowhere in sight. After ten minutes, with Sid in tow, I head into the station.

A suit directs me down the hall to the studio.

"Juanita!"

"Sorry I am so late."

"No it's fine. I thought you were outside waiting all this time. There's a news story breaking. Can you bring Sid home and wait until I get there? I'll get a run from someone here."

"Sure." A cute blonde with deep dimples holds out his right hand. He tosses Sidney a sarcastic grin "Thanks for introducing us. Hi, I'm Bob. And you are stunning."

"Thank you."

Sidney scoops Sid up and sits him on his shoulders. Holding both of Sid's feet in one hand, he motions towards me. "Bob this is my wife Juanita—and don't forget the spare microphone."

"Your wife? I thought . . . What about Pa—" his eyes open wide. He covers his mouth with his hand.

I take a deep breath, "Let me guess Bob, she wears red bras? Right? Don't worry we're separated and lucky for you I have a fetish for younger men."

"Wow. Are you serious? How about a date?"

Sidney points down the hall and says "Maybe in two years. She's joking. Go get the spare."

"If you're around in two years I'm marrying you." He shakes his head at Sidney, "Man you're stupid."

Sidney points to a door down the hall. "And change your diaper while you're there." He waits until Bob disappears and says, "Don't lead him on. He's a little pervert." He glances at his watch and frowns. "I have to go but you won't need to pick me up. If you have plans for tonight, Mother said she can babysit after five. Her shift ends at four."

"How will you get home?"

"Like I said, I'll get a run." His eyes cast downward.

"Say her name."

"No."

"I'm not leaving until you say her name."

"Paula."

"Tell me one thing. Were you seeing her when you lived with me?"

He looks me in the eyes, "No. Believe me. I stopped lying to you a long time ago." His eyes open wider. "Are you doing okay? You look too skinny and your eyes look tired."

"Actually I'm the same weight I've always been."

He looks at me confused.

"I'd better let you get back to work."

"I'll walk you out."

As I drive towards the Gould's I see a plumbing shop with a huge parking lot. One large window on the left seems to have cardboard inside it. I stop and look. On the right hand side, they have signage and I can see a dark haired skinny girl inside.

Gravel crunches as I pull in front of the window. The girl smiles at me through the glass. I turn off the car and whisper, "Sid, Sid, wake up sweetie."

He's solid as a rock. The cold wind hits me as soon as I open the door. I lock the car and hurry inside. A paper-thin girl with long jet-black hair stands nervously at the counter. She's wearing a white angora sweater and skintight blue jeans that make her look like a walking skeleton. But she has the most beautiful haunting eyes I've ever seen. Something about her reminds me of Gordon. She looks the age he would been by now.

"I hope you don't think I'm weird but you have the most beautiful eyes."

She smiles bashfully. "I love your hair. How long did it take to get to your waist?"

"Too many years," I laugh. "And I never cut it. Is the owner in?"

She calls out, "Dad. It's for you."

"I'll be right back. I have to check on my son." I run outside, breathe a sigh of relief and rush back in.

Two worn hands with greasy fingernails are leaning on the counter.

"I'm not here to buy or sell anything, I was wondering if that room might be for rent. The one with the cardboard stacked against the window?"

He scratches at his three days of beard growth and asks, "You want to rent the storage room?"

I take a deep breath. "Sir I was wondering if I could rent that space The one with the cardboard window."

"To live in?"

"No. I want to open a flower shop and it seemed empty and I thought maybe it was for rent, and I'd like to rent it from you . . . if I can afford it."

"Hmmm. Well right now I'm using it for storage."

"Is there any way you could move the storage to another spot? Please? The window is perfect for a flower shop."

"What if I expand and need it one day?"

"You can kick me out."

"Dad, please, I like her. Say yes."

He looks at his daughter with the warmest eyes I have ever seen.

"How do you know it's perfect if you haven't seen it yet? Maybe after you see it you won't want it. How about I show you it first."

"Does that mean you'll rent it to me?"

"It's possible but not unless you see the space."

I keep looking out the window at the car. Sid is still sleeping.

"You didn't steal the car did you?"

"No. It's my husbands—well we're separated and our son is sleeping and I'm afraid he'll wake up."

"I can watch him from here. If he stirs at all I'll call out," she smiles.

"Thank you. I'll be quick. I promise."

The space is perfect. It already has a counter and unlike my loft, it has a private bathroom. I point to a door at the far wall. "What's in there? A closet?"

"No that's another room half the size of this." He shows me it. Down the hall is a huge space. It looks like a warehouse. "It's pretty deep. But we don't need all the space any more. We used to do plumbing and automotive but we're giving up the plumbing side."

He points to a sign on the floor. "Just Riff Automotive now." He pulls at his ear and shrugs. "I s'pose we could use a flower shop around here. There's none for miles. You want two rooms or one? I can give you both for three hundred a month and I'll even install a laundry tub for filling up flower buckets."

"I only have three hundred dollars to my name. Can't I just rent the first one and opt to add the second room later?"

"You know my daughter doesn't like many people but she seems to have taken a liking to you." He takes a step closer and whispers, "She used to weigh two hundred and thirty pounds when she was eleven. All the kids made fun of her called her Tubs. Then one day the weight started peeling off her. Almost killed her."

His story is making him cry and his eyes are making mine water. "That must have been harsh on her . . . She's so thin. It's hard to imagine her having a weight problem."

"One day, last fall, I found her rocking back and forth delirious in the bedroom. She'd been eating nothing but one apple a day. I almost lost her. Didn't pay as much attention to her as I should have with her mother just passing the year before . . ." His eyes lower to the floor.

"She's a beautiful girl. You must be incredibly proud of her."

"I am." He kicks at a pile of tires. "Here's what I can do. I'm going to clear out the front room and repaint it any color you like. I get paint wholesale anyway. I'll connect a laundry tub and I'll charge you one fifty for the first month starting at the beginning of next month. By the time I get around to cleaning out the back you'll need the space and be able to afford the three hundred a month. How's that sound?"

"Oh thank you so, so, much . . . but there's just one problem. I need the laundry tub to be in the back space. Away from the customers."

He kicks at the tires again.

"Tell you what. I'll clear a corner of the back room near the bathroom wall and set you up. Today is Monday June 2nd, so you can move in this weekend and you get three weeks free rent to get organized. No need to pay me yet." He waves me off.

"Please . . . I insist. I need you to take it now before you change your mind."

My Long Lost Brother

From the flower shop counter all I see is an empty parking lot. It's been two months since I quit Tim's shop. Quitting that job was a lot harder than I thought. He begged me to stay, offered me a raise and even offered me a small percent of his business. He was convinced I was going with his competitor eight blocks away. I told him it wasn't a competitor it was a small shop in another town, too far away to be any kind of competition. He said he felt better about that but once he realized he couldn't change my mind, he let me go immediately.

I managed to pick up a used soda cooler with sliding glass doors. It can only hold eight buckets of flowers and the odd arrangement, which isn't much, but I'm having a hard time filling it. In order to buy fresh flowers for a decent wholesale price, I have to buy them by the carton. That's tough to do with a small cooler and a tight budget.

Lucky for me every week some supermarket or other chain store carries plants or flowers as a lost leader. They sell them at prices lower than the

Juanita Ray

those offered by my wholesaler. So far, most of my fresh stock, including plants, are from those sources.

A few of the plants are four feet tall but the majority are eight inches high. Two months ago, I bought a dozen, at half price, for two dollars each. They were only three inches tall. I treated them with insecticide, fertilized them and priced them at $4.99 each. Now they need to be transplanted again. This means higher priced sales, but the bigger pots and extra soil steals from the profits.

In the back room, I focus on making some more silk arrangements. They sell really well. So far my best sellers are wreaths. Customers who buy flowers for funerals seem to like the idea of buying something that doesn't die. The reason I like wreaths is because I don't need shelves. All I need is a nail to hang them on.

I lean against the counter and watch the odd car drive by. Come on! One of you must need flowers. Before I opened the store my biggest worry was how I could manage deliveries and be here at the same time. Now my biggest concern is how I'm going to pay the rent. How foolish of me to think that people would swarm in once I opened.

I retreat to the back room and shake my head at the mess I've made. Should I clean it or make some more stuff to sell to nobody?

The bell rings, and a muscular looking guy walks in with his head hung down. His eyes are peeled to the floor.

When a guy hangs his head like that, and avoids eye contact, it usually means he's desperate to buy flowers. If he's not in the doghouse and looking to get out with flowers, he's cheating and trying to suck up with roses.

I notice he appears to be avoiding the counter area. Guys who celebrate births, anniversaries, birthdays or even mourn deaths never beat around the bush. They head straight for the counter.

I watch him shuffle plants back and forth. No doubt this one has OCD.

After ten minutes I break the silence, "Can I help you?"

He turns his back to me and looks towards the window. "No thanks."

I purse my lips together. I've already sorted the books on the counter three times since he's been here. I grab one and flip through it.

Five minutes later, I'm burning a hole in the back of his head, thinking, buy something or leave. I say, "Is it a special occasion?" and wait while he thinks about it.

"I guess you could say that." His voice is slow and deliberate.

"What kind of special occasion?"

It takes him two full minutes to answer. "I dunno." He starts messing with the plants again.

"How much?"

For him I raise the price a buck. "$5.99."

Thirty seconds later, "Humph."

He reminds me of an Indian. The fictitious kind. The Tonto kind that grunts a lot.

Finally, he walks out the door. He pauses outside of my window, shields his eyes from the sun and looks up at the roof.

Is he chuckling? I glance around the back room. What was I doing before he came in and wasted my time? I can't remember. I notice a silk wreath and a nail sitting on the counter. That's it! I climb onto the counter and take off one boot. I lean over the edge and use my heel to nail the wreath onto the wall above me. The bell rings. I slide off the counter, sit down on the floor and struggle to put my boot back on. I can hear him grunting. Maybe if I hide here, he'll go away.

I lean on the shelf to get comfortable. A stapler falls off.

"You okay back there?"

I peek above the counter, "Yes. I'm fine, thank you." I brush off my jeans.

He slides his finger along a larger plant leaf, "Pretty dusty."

I say nothing hoping he'll go over to cacti and do that. He lifts up a plant. "There's little bunches of soil on the shelf around the plants. It reminds me of ants building hills. You should clean it up."

"That's what happens when you water real plants. Soil tends to come out of the bottom."

"Really? Huh." He rubs a leaf between his fingers.

He goes over near the cacti. Yes, yes, yes! Feel those leaves you big jerk. He doesn't.

"I'd appreciate it if you don't rub the leaves of the plants."

"Why?"

"It kills them."

"Really?" he seems genuinely surprised. He doesn't lift his head. It's as though his neck is glued to his chest.

"Really," my voice sounds irritated. "They have fine, spider web type veins that they use for photosynthesis. They're easy to crack."

"Humph. Spider webs are usually strong." He actually looks at me from the corner of his eye and asks, "So what is photosynthesis?"

I point to a rack of plant books. "Prices are on the back cover."

He takes a deep breath and chuckles. "Where's your sign?"

"What, price signs? I told you that the prices are on the back cover of the books."

He lifts his chin a few inches. "No, the sign for your shop."

"I'm working on that."

"Oh." He glances back up at me. "So what's the name of the shop?"

I purse my lips together and give him a sideways look.

He lifts his chin further and actually looks straight at me. "I get it. You're working on that too."

I glare at him.

He lifts an eyebrow. "Don't you think your prices are a bit high for such little plants?" His voice sounds cheeky.

Who the heck does this guy think he is? My eyes are hurling fireballs at him. I try to control my tongue but I can't. I'm a melting pot of hostility. "That way. Half a mile. They sell bug infested ones for half the price. I suggest you go there."

He chuckles, "You don't even know me do you? It's pretty bad when you don't know your own brother."

My eyes bulge out of my head.

"It's me, Drake. Your brother . . . Drake."

"Drake?" I run from behind the counter and hurtle myself into his arms. "How did you find me?"

"Adam." His mischievous lopsided grin flashes in my face.

"I can't believe I didn't recognize you. How long are you in town for?"

"Oh a few days. I think I still look the same."

"You certainly don't sound the same."

"That's because I've been living in Alberta." He doesn't say all that much, he mostly listens but I learn he's married and has children. Then comes that dreadful hug. The goodbye hug. It leaves me empty and lonely, but I don't show it. It reminds me of my childhood. Each sibling forced apart, fighting for survival, going their different ways. I wonder what would have happened if we had banded together to fight Irma. Probably nothing good. We'd undoubtedly be in jail for murder.

I turn and trip over the broom. Maybe it's a sign I should sweep the floor and toss out the trash. Instead I evaluate the silk inventory left in boxes and sort it by color. Two minutes later I hear the door jingle. Drake's back! I rush out with a huge smile on my face.

"Drake!"

My smile disappears. It's Sidney. He has flowers in his hands but he looks like someone just died.

"I waited for the guy to leave but I sort of figured it wasn't a customer when you flew into his arms." He tosses the flowers on the counter. "I came in anyway thinking there was still a chance for us but I'm not blind. I saw that smile vanish from your face."

I'm speechless. I open my mouth. What does he expect me to say to that? Nothing comes out. He jerks his head towards the flowers on the counter. "Maybe you can sell them to someone," he says and walks out.

A Shop with No Name

Finding a van wasn't easy. Keeping it in good shape was harder. The slow crunch of scraping metal, makes me cringe. My foot slams against the brake pedal. Why didn't I get a van with side windows? This is the third time, and it's always in the same spot. I pull out my purse and rummage around for my checkbook. I circle the van to the passenger side.

"You parked there on purpose!"

"Juanita I'm three feet away!" Sidney shakes his head and laughs. His bumper is barely scraped. "Maybe you should hire a delivery driver before you lose your license."

"I did. He's up at my other shop."

"You opened a second shop? Why?"

"The funeral home is fifty miles away and I got their account but the gas prices are killing me between the funerals and the weddings."

"You opened a second location?"

"A small place, rented. It's cheaper than the gas I'm using."

"What did you call it?"

314

"Nothing."

"Nothing? What is with you and not naming shops? If you had a sign it would help with business."

"I can't handle any more business. But you're right I need a name but not just any name, something fitting."

"How about The House of Roses."

"I thought of that but people would think I just sold roses."

He examines my fender. "There's three different colors of paint on this thing."

"That's because people like you keep parking too close to me."

He walks into Riff Automotive, and comes out with a rag and bottle. He rubs the fender until the paint disappears. The fender takes on a glossy sheen.

"This reminds me of the time back in Harbour Breton when you went for your driving test and knocked down the stop sign. I'll never forget how fast the examiner ran from the car . . . you have this way about you—that's why he passed you. You draw people like a magnet but you never let them in. You're remind me of a cute scared doe."

"He didn't pass me because he was drawn to me, he was afraid I'd come back for another try. People drawn to you don't run away."

"I miss you Angel . . . so freaking much. I really do."

"I see you more now than I did when we were married. We do things together with Sid. It's better."

"Exactly, better. Look—I don't want to get divorced."

"We don't have to. Not unless you plan to marry what's-her-face."

"I want things back the way they were—before we went wrong. Do you ever think of us and miss the good times we had?"

I look at his purple Javelin. "You really should get that dent fixed."

Sidney rubs the bumper. "You didn't dent it."

"The dent from the stop sign. The one I ran over."

"I like it. It's a good conversational piece."

"Please don't tell me that's what you're using to pick up women."

"If you're asking me if I'm still dating, the answer is no."

"Are you stalking me or did you actually visit for a valid reason?"

"I'm here to offer you some help."

"You help me with flowers?"

"I could help you with deliveries. You should say yes before you completely obliterate this van." He waits for an answer. "I'm on vacation, and Sid's in daycare. My time, in exchange for a dinner date?"

"What about Paula?"

"Paula who?" he grins.

"If I agree, will you swear you won't try to get back with me?"

"That depends on your definition of get back."

I unlock the shop and bring him back the keys.

"Listen. Isn't that your phone ringing."

"It's probably the line for Riff Automotive." While I check the deliveries and make sure they have tags, Sidney dashes for the door. I chase after him. "Stop. Don't bother. Let the machine get it."

"Good morning. Thank you for calling—" he coughs. "Excuse me. I seem to have a frog caught in my throat." He presses the phone against his chest and whispers, "How do you answer the phone with no shop name?"

He winks. "May I ask who is calling?" He flips an order form over, draws a heart, and writes Sidney & Angel inside of it. He smiles and touches his heart and point at me. His smile, twists into a puzzled look. "One moment please." He covers the phone and whispers, "It's the Federal Business Development Bank about some loan."

"Hello, this is Juanita Simon, how may I help you?"

"This is the FBDB returning your call. Did we get you at a bad time?"

"Actually you did. My driver is trying to man the phones while I'm in the middle of a large wedding order. May I call you back?"

"Will it be today? If so, I will available up until two-thirty."

"Probably not. May I take your number and call you back on Monday? I assume you're not open tomorrow?"

"That is correct." The man proceeds to give me his number and extension.

"Thank you so much and have a good weekend."

Sidney shakes his index finger at me. "Naughty, naughty. What happened to the no lies rule?"

"I didn't lie. See this order on the counter? The one you drew on? See these color swatches? That's bridesmaids' colors for a silk wedding." I point towards the back room. "Behind you, somewhere in those boxes, are the silks for this order, so geographically speaking, I am in the middle of it. Technically, it's not a lie. Besides, the rule is for personal relationships, not business transactions."

"If I asked you to be more than a friend, would you think about it?"

"Maybe for a fleeting second—right before I said, tough luck."

His eyes glance up at the ceiling. Hope flitters across them. "What's that hanging upside down? Are those the roses I bought you? You dried them?" An astonished look sweeps across his face. "You're still in love with me aren't you?"

Half a laugh escapes from my lips. "Of course I'm not. You're the one who said to sell them. I'm saving them in case someone orders a dried bouquet."

He grabs me by the shoulders. "Swear on Sid's life you don't love me."

"Don't be childish. That's absurd and you leave Sid out of this."

He backs up and smiles. His eyes are dancing. "Deliveries for dinner?" He dangles the van keys, turns and leaves.

"Fine," I yell after him, "but you're paying for dinner and gas in the van."

Five hours later, I am on my third rum and seven and dinner hasn't arrived. By the time dessert arrives, I'm three sheets to the wind. The last thing I remember is the table spinning.

I wake up to the smell bacon and eggs. For a minute, I savor the smell. It reminds me of when Sidney and I were together. Every morning for the last month of our relationship, Sidney brought me breakfast in—I bolt upright. My head is pounding. Sidney appears at the door smiling with a tray. I look towards the wall hook for my clothes. I blink twice and look at the wall again. I love you and stay with me in black bold letters adorns the entire wall. I roll over on my back.

A shadow hovers above me. I groan. Sidney's hands are clasped around a breakfast tray. He's wearing his wedding band. There's a card leaning against the glass of orange juice.

"It's from Sid." The tray wobbles. He sits it on the bed and picks up a rose. It snaps. A bead of blood drops onto the envelope. He sucks his thumb and hands me the card. I read it aloud. "Daddy wants to be a full time husband and I want to be have a full time mommy. Love Sid xoxoxoxo."

I laugh, "The old Sidney would have said I want a full time wife."

"Is that a yes?" His eyebrows perform acrobatics on his forehead.

My eyes leave him and scan the room. "Where's Sid?" I ask.

"Angel, please don't avoid the subject. I swear I'm a different man. I've changed—but it seems you haven't at all, have you?"

"What's that supposed to mean?"

"When are you going to stop answering a question with a question?"

"Do I do that?"

He raises his eyebrows and half smirks.

I grin at him. "Old habits are hard to break. I trained hard to acquire that skill. Eight years of brain washing at the school of hard knocks."

"Angel, I'm not trying to change who you are. I hope you never change."

"Why did you come up with that nickname? Angel doesn't suit me."

"I think it does. Remember our wedding night?"

I laugh, "You're joking right?"

"I spent half the night watching you sleep. You looked so young and innocent. Your hair was hanging over the edge of the bed and you were wearing a white silk slip. You looked like an angel. That same morning, on my way to university, the first song that played on the radio was Angel of the Morning, and when that song ended they played Walk Like an Angel. And you are my angel. I'll never find another you . . . never. Half of the songs I heard—hear now, reminds me of you—of us."

"Exactly what happened last night?"

"You jumped my bones. Ha-ha-ha. I wish." He pauses, cocks his head and says, "It was a repeat of our wedding night—you got drunk and I spent the night admiring the most beautiful girl in the world drool. But before you passed out, you promised on Sid's life, to come back to us."

"I did? Me? On Sid's life?"

Sidney makes a cross on his heart. "Swear to God."

"How's your mother going to take this—if we get back together?"

"She's the one who told me to smarten up and get you back."

"Is she ill?"

"Believe it or not, she does respect you."

"You want me back because your mother finally approves of me? Why am I good enough all of a sudden? Is it because I own a shop?"

"No. She accepts how much I love you and she realizes now that you are the right person for me. That with you I'm a better me. When I told her you wouldn't have me back. She said any decent man wouldn't stop trying."

"Aaawwwwrrrrrgggg."

"I'm not asking you to take Mother back. I'm asking you to take me back. That day in the shop, I came to propose to you again. You should have told me it was your brother."

"How do you know that?"

"Adam told me."

"What else did he tell you?"

"Good luck figuring her out because I can't."

I laugh.

"Is that a yes?"

"I don't know. Maybe—" I glance around the room and nod. "But I'm not helping you repaint these walls."

"Maybe I'll leave them that way forever. Let's go somewhere. Somewhere special. Anywhere you want." He caresses my hand.

"Unfortunately, I don't have days off like you. I have to work."

"I'll come with you. I can answer phones. Whatever you need."

"Maybe you could hold a sign and wave people in, seeing you're such a celebrity," I laugh. "Seriously, what I really need is a sign for my shop. I need to come up with a name for it."

"How about the Rose Room?"

"I like it but, again, people would think I only sold roses. That call I got yesterday . . . was about me applying for a loan. There's this lot, up the road, that's for sale and I want to build a shop on it. That's why FBDB keeps calling me. They need the application sent back, but I can't finish filling it out because I don't have a business name. I need a catchy but professional sounding name, like Floors of Flow—"

"Whoa. Back up half a mile. Build a shop? On what lot?"

"There's a piece of land for sale, up across from the school. Next to that woman that cuts hair in her basement."

"I know the one. That's a nice spot, but it's residential. There's no way you'll get them to rezone that to commercial."

"Just like there was no way you would be a teacher again, or get the newscaster job. Look I'm doing this . . . you know, maybe getting back together isn't the right thing to do."

"Don't say that. You have a better chance of getting the loan with me. If we're together and add my paycheck as an income source, you won't need to show personal cost of living expenses which will make your business show more profit."

"They already preapproved me. I already qualify."

"Angel, I'm on your side, but are you sure you're ready for this?"

"Yes one hundred percent certain. Think about it for a minute. I'm virtually unemployable, I love what I do, and I get paid for doing it."

"But can't you do it without building a shop?"

"No I can't. I've outgrown my space in just seven months. Imagine how much room I'll need in a year or two. Customers walked away Mothers' Day because the store was packed solid with shoppers. I can't imagine what Christmas will be like."

"I'm not sure you're going to make this work. The zoning is the zoning and zoned residential means residential."

"I don't care about how it's zoned. If that woman up the road can have a hair salon, I can have a flower shop."

I turn the card over. "Pen?" Sidney passes me a pencil. I write Flowers & More. I scribble through it. I write down and scratch out several more names that we each come up with. None are good enough.

"Angel, I think we should finish this at the—"

"THAT'S IT! You're awesome."

"What did I do?"

"It's perfect. When people have a baby, they describe it as an angel, when they get married they want to look like an angel, when they die they want to be with angels. I'm naming the shop Angel Florists."

"Hmmm. Shouldn't that be florist not florists?"

"I have two locations, so it's going to be plural and it sounds more professional, like there's more than one florist working."

———————

I sit before the council meeting waiting for them to decide. "Mrs. Simon we accept your offer to live above the shop, know that the approval is conditional upon you residing there and keep the building foundation one hundred feet from the road. You must refrain from having neon signs or a paved parking lot. The building architecture must blend in and be similar to that typical of a house and not a business. This means it must not be concrete, brick or sheet metal. Do you mind telling us why you proceeded with excavating and constructions?"

"My understanding is that the lot is currently zoned residential and I can build a two-story house on it."

"According to this report the eight-foot foundation is large enough to erect a four-bedroom house on one level."

"I am planning to rent out the main floor, if I don't get commercial approval, and the eight-foot basement is for storage—my son has a bike and toys—and a tent, and likes camping."

I try to act calm and collected but my heart is twisted in a knot. For thirty minutes, I watch them huddle, ask questions and make notes.

"We assume you are building a wooden two-story structure."

"Yes I am."

"You understand upon change of ownership the property reverts back to residential?"

"Yes I do."

"You understand the property cannot be rented as a commercial location to any other party?"

"I do."

"I hereby motion that the approval of . . ."

I glance at Sidney and hold my breath. He nods my way, holds up two fingers and leaves. I start to panic. He returns and gives me a wink and a thumbs up. My mind screams, we did it, I can't believe we did it. I grit my teeth together but I can't stop the smile that is crossing my lips. I make steady slow steps out of the building. Once we reach the parking lot, Sidney swoops me into his arms and swings me in a circle.

"We did it! I was so nervous. Especially when you left. Where did you go? I was scared to death something was wrong with Sid."

"When I heard them stipulate the liability be increased, I called your insurance agent. He verified it was increased but he needs your signature. He's at the shop."

My agent is waiting inside Riff Automotive, talking to Lily. I catch her grateful smile as the agent walks towards me.

"So how can someone get hurt on an empty lot?"

"People fall in excavated holes and crack their skulls. It could rain, turn into a lake deep enough for someone to drown in. Initial here and sign here."

"I have another issue. FBDB wants the contents insured, not just the building."

He looks at me stunned. "How can you insure contents in a building that's doesn't exist?"

"I don't know. That's your job," I say and sign the papers.

"Listen I would love to sell you more insurance but I can't—unless you want contents coverage here at this location."

"My supplies don't last long enough."

"What about the cooler?"

"I could buy two more before I'd reach the deductible."

"How about medical coverage? What would happen if you had an accident? Who would take your place? How many people would it take to replace you? Who would pay your medical bills? What would it cost you in lost sales?"

Several minutes later, I'm signing another dotted line. I hear a car door slam. I glance up and see my father-in law.

"How about life insurance?"

"No thanks. It looks like I have a customer. Are we done?"

"Yes, but call me before you move in, so we can adjust the policy limits."

Mr. Simon waits quietly by the window until the insurance agent leaves. "There's something I want to discuss with you, at the job site."

"My full time employee is out on deliveries. Can we discuss it here?"

"Can you lock up? Take a lunch break?"

"I don't close for lunch. I only eat at night. Besides it's almost two."

"You look like you're wasting away."

"I'm the same weight I've always been."

"Maybe so."

"There's my driver pulling in now."

I walk outside before he can switch off the engine. Mr. Simon grunts and pushes the seat further back from the dash. We drive up around the bend to the site, wade through the mud and stop just short of the first mound of dirt. Mountains of soil surround a hole that looks deep enough to bury two houses. The footings are in place and the concrete walls are poured and dried.

"It's none of my business but you need to have your contractor dig out that soil and fill it with a dryer mix. The hole seems dry but I guarantee you it's damper than it looks. It rained last week and I am a little worried about them using the same soil. Who's your contractor?"

"What do you mean? Who's digging the foundation or who's doing the footings?"

"Who's in charge of the excavator? Who's ordering the materials?"

"Me. After they give me a list."

He pulls his collar closer to his throat. "Every job needs a contractor. He oversees the workers, makes a timeline." He coughs and makes me an offer I can't refuse. He offers to check on the site and manage inspections free of charge.

"No. Please."

He looks rejected. "I'm more than qualified. I've been a contractor all my life."

"I mean I am thrilled but I want to pay you something."

"No. Not one penny. I don't want the title. It'll be our little secret. I'll keep an eye on things, once or twice a day, and if something is awry I'll let you know."

"I trust you."

"Then if you trust me, replace that soil."

I cringe when I get the quote for soil. It puts me over budget. I grit my teeth and tell the drywaller, I have to cut out the texture on the ceilings. The ten percent saved will get me out of the red. He offers me a ten percent discount if I pay cash. I quickly realize I can stay back on budget if I get a break by paying as much as I can with cash.

The biggest break I get is from a man who drops by and offers me the lowest price in town to pave the lot.

"The zoning stipulates crushed stone or gravel but no concrete."

"I've been laying crush stone for two decades." He jingles some coins in his pocket. His demeanor is humble. He apologetically explains he needs the job bad enough to under bid any price I am given.

"What's a fair price?"

He hands me a piece of cardboard. "The number on the bottom. The one circled—but I can go lower."

"How much lower?"

"Twenty percent." He kicks at the floor. "I have five sons. I'm a widower—cancer. No insurance." His eyes mist over. His pants shake while he jingles more coins. A shiver runs up my spine. The morning my father introduced Irma, the coins in his pocket made that exact same sound.

His eyes focus on the floor, "I do good work but I can't take a check."

"You on unemployment?"

He shakes his head no.

"It's okay if you are, half of my crew were when I hired them."

"I don't qualify."

"Why not?"

"Always been self-employed. I need cash because the bill collectors attached my wages and froze my bank account. I got issues with medical bills. My kid has MS ..."

He presses his fingers into the corners of his eyes and clears his throat.

"What's the normal charge for that?"

"For the treatments? More than—"

"No, for leveling the lot."

He rubs his forearms back and forth and drops them to his side. Hope flickers in his eyes. "Five hundred above that." He points to the cardboard. "It's a good price and I can go down twenty—"

"You're hired. And you can keep your twenty percent off."

He shuffles his feet a little and says, "I'll need a little up front to fill the grader and then a few more dollars a week later to pay a helper."

"You look like a good guy. How about I give you half up front, but if you rip me off, that back hoe or whatever you call it, is mine."

He takes my hand and shakes it with both of his. His mouth twitches as if he doesn't know which sound to form.

"Sir, if you keep pumping my hand, you'll soon see water spurt from my mouth."

I reach under the counter and unzip the bank pouch. I count out half of the agreed price. He keeps one hundred and hands me back the rest.

"I'll be at the site come daylight."

I walk outside and shake his hand. Sidney pulls up and waits for the man to back out onto the street.

"What was that about?"

"I hired him to level the lot but I forgot to get his name."

"You didn't pay him anything up front did you?"

"Yeah, but I'm not worried. For some reason I trust him. The poor guy has had a truck load of bad luck. He's as broke as they come, trying to raise his kids. In some ways he reminds me of my father."

"Your father? The man with no soul?"

"I'm not sure that's entirely his fault. If Irma would have stayed with her husband or preyed on some other family, things would have been different. You don't know my brothers, but they call it like it is, and they swear up and down, that my father was a real nice person, once upon a time."

"Once upon a time doesn't cut it in the real world, and neither does hiring someone because you pity him, or, he reminds you of your father."

"He doesn't. This guy cares about his kids."

"Speaking of fathers, mine has good news for you. Father says the final inspection should be in four weeks and today they start the finishing details, so we need to focus on wall paint and carpet colors."

Each day seems to bring a new choice demanding another decision. Weeks fly by and turn into months and progress seems slower than anticipated. The delay in the finishing details is due in part to me. I seem to have a knack for choosing unusual colors and fixtures that are special order items.

Last week the workers tried to convince me to put more rooms downstairs. They think I'm making a big mistake by dividing the area into two large rooms. If it's not a structural necessity, building more walls on the shop level is inconceivable to me. Why would I pay more for walls that would serve no purpose? Especially when I'm building a huge center display are in the middle of the main room and need plenty of space for foot traffic? Even my own husband can't seem to get the concept that on the main floor all I want is one large showroom and one large design room. It's not rocket science. It's just a three-bedroom bungalow above a store.

The painter pries his screwdriver against the lid. "If I was you I wouldn't want to haul sacks of groceries up a flight of stairs."

"And if I was you I wouldn't be trying to sell me on yellow walls."

"This is a very nice yellow." He opens the can. "See?"

"I said I wanted lemon not the color of yellow rind."

I dump half the can into an empty bucket. "Fill the rest of this can with white."

The painter hesitates. "I have other color samples."

"It's my paint. Please do it. Actually I'll do it while you stir it." I pour half the white pail into the bucket and the other half into the yellow can. "There that's perfect. I want that color."

"Which one? This one seems a little brighter."

I pour the can into the bucket. "Once you stir this bucket, it should be the exact color I want."

"But it's not in the color samples."

"Just figure how much paint you need then buy half the cans in white and the other half in this yellow, mix them half and half and paint my walls. It'll go perfect with a silver gray."

"Silver gray? As in base boards?"

"The carpet is going to be a silver gray. It's the only color that seems to go with the burgundy top I'm wearing."

The drywaller leans against the wall and chuckles. He snorts twice and says, "The carpet has to match your top?"

"Don't you have something to mud?"

Bead sweats splatter as he shakes his head. He smells worse than a wet dog.

"For your information, the interior designer has ordered custom made burgundy drapes and matching sofas in exactly this shirt color. I'm using it as a reference."

"Are the kitchen appliances white or red color?" I can't tell if he's being serious or taunting me. "And those chocolate bathroom fixtures are going to be a bitch to clean." The man doesn't look like he knows what soap is. Why did I even hire him? His fat belly jiggles as he takes another sip of beer. A long loud burp escapes from between his lips.

"Aren't you supposed to be up stuccoing the ceiling?"

"Nope. I'm on break. Done for the day. But if I were you I would put flicks of red and diamond glitter in the stucco. Just a small touch. I'm dead serious. It would look sharp with those colors. Tomorrow I'll put some on a sample for you to take a gander at."

"Make it burgundy or nothing. Red is too Christmassy."

"Red's a fashion trend right now. But I can't say the same for this mural. It would be cheaper to put plants against the wall. You with a shop and all."

I wasn't sure if it was the bowl haircut, the bright green jeans, the purple tee-shirt or the fact that the cut of his clothes looked like something a decade back, but in my mind, this slob had no sense of fashion or trends.

"Can you please move away from the wall mural before you spill beer on it?" Sidney loves murals. It took me two weeks to find a mural guy and two more to compromise on a price for a mural that complimented the color choices yet met with Sidney's approval. It was a sunset shining through a grove of palm trees on a grayish colored beach.

The drywaller kicks the lid of his cooler with his foot, tosses in the empties, grunts, pulls out a beer and opens it with his teeth. Then he flashes me a twisted yellow smile before he steps away.

I walk down the stairs and face three doors. One leads straight out to the parking lot. The left is to the showroom and the right is to the design workroom. The design room is as big as the one at Floors of Flowers. I lean against the giant window and glance past the design benches. The back wall facing me has wall-to-wall shelving, and two laundry tubs, next to a bathroom. Next to that is a small corner office. The sidewall has a huge arched opening. I walk through it and lean against the counter. I sit on the wrap around counter and gaze at the show room.

The showroom is huge. It takes up exactly half of the main floor space. Everything looks great. Everything smells like new wood. I walk back into the workroom and walk down a flight of stairs that leads to the basement. I stop at the bottom step.

The finisher is kneeling on a floating plank, smoothing out the concrete. His dull rubber boots were covered with flat gray stains.

"So this is what you call feather edging?"

"Yes ma'am. Smooth as a baby's ass."

"Looks great. Thanks for doing such a good job."

"After I take a break, in half an hour, one more round of smoothing, and finito!" He kneels back on the board. "How much you renting this out for?"

"I'm not. I plan to use it for storage."

"Seems a waste of money to feather edge it. Why the nice set of stairs if it's just a basement for storage? Don't get me wrong. I'm not complaining. I need the work."

"In case I need to change usage. Down the road I might have to rent this out as an apartment. If business turned bad I could rent the top out and live down here. My commercial permit is conditional and you never know. I just want to cover all the bases. Sometimes things can go wrong."

"And if things go right, what goes down here? Boxes?"

"Moss. Big bins of stinky wet moss." I climb halfway up the steps and pause. "Can you tell the other workers to drop by the shop to get paid once they're done?"

"Yes ma'am. Can do."

Outside, Peter shuts off the backhoe loader, wipes the sweat from his brow, taps his heart and points towards me.

On the way to the gas station, I consider hiring him for delivers and wonder if he would appreciate the offer or be insulted by it. I pick up a paper, park in front of the tanks and flip through the pages. Perfect. I scrutinize the center spread announcing, Angel Florists grand opening and find no errors. It's hard to believe it's only a week away.

Tap. Tap-tap-tap-tap.

He steps two feet back from the window. The first thing I notice is his wide mischievous smile. His wind swept hair is sandy blond. He looks like he was born on a surfboard.

With a sheepish grin, he taps on my window again and points at the pumps. I shake my head no and put the van in drive. I look in my rear view mirror. He doesn't move. He's rooted to the spot looking in my direction. Something about him strikes me as familiar. Maybe it's the Rod Stewart haircut. He finally disappears from my mirror when I turn around the bend.

I pull into the shop and kiss Sidney on the cheek. It's an understatement to say it's hard to pack and still manage to maintain customer service. It's literally impossible. This week I have pissed off more people than I can shake a stick at. Between the workers who have a love hate relationship with one another, disgruntled clients who are upset because I've put a temporary hold on booking weddings. FBDB isn't happy either because I'm not psychic and can't predict the exact hour I plan to move in.

Fifteen minutes later, Sidney hands me a letter from the FBDB. I open it up expecting it to be another progress report request. It's not. I slam it down on the counter. "I'm not doing it."

"Doing what?"

"They want me to take a one year course in business management. Apparently, it's part of the loan agreement. I can't run a shop and go to school." I slump to the floor.

"Let me see that." He reads it and pats my head. "It says here it's night classes. It will be good for you and it's free. People typically pay for these courses."

"I probably have—hidden in the loan."

"Angel if things get that crazy, I can always quit my job and help you manage the shop, but until then I have a job to get to."

I lean against the cooler and draw in a long slow breath. The glass doors feel cool and refreshing. I catch a glimpse of a reflection my frazzled state. Keep it together. You're on the home stretch.

The cooler is empty except for a dozen white carnations and the bridal bouquets, I made late last night. I have one hour before deliveries have to leave. All I have left to make are a few boutonnieres. I'm on the second boutonniere when my sweaty drywaller appears and fills my door frame. He's shaking badly and stuttering.

"Are you here for your pay? How much do I owe you?"

He's out of breath. He wipes his dripping face with his tee-shirt.

"What did you do run here?"

He nods, choking. He coughs continuously and holds his throat.

I grab a bottle of water and hand it to him.

He waves it away. "Your building . . . it's gone."

"What do you mean it's gone?"

He hyperventilates some more.

"It's gone. Poof!"

My throat feels numb. Panic freezes my jaws.

"What do you mean gone?" My voice sounds slurred.

"Poof. Gone."

"What do you mean GONE? GONE WHERE?"

He slaps his hand against the top of my card rack and knocks it over. The cards scatter over the counter. "GONE POOF JUST LIKE THAT. DESTROYED."

My knees go weak. I can't breathe. "No. No. No. Tell me you're lying. This is a joke right?"

The stunned look on his ashen face tells me it isn't.

Destroyed and Stalked

I swerve out of the parking lot and say, "Anyone hurt?"

"No. That's the real miracle." He pants and wipes his sweaty brow with his trembling hand. "I ran all the way here as fast as I could."

I listen in horror as he describes the shaking, the noise, the bodies diving out the door—the mangled sparking wires.

"Is anything left standing? Anything?" I can barely talk. Every muscle in my face is twisting into spasms. Tremors penetrate my body—weaken every fiber. I grip the steering wheel for support.

"It's toppled forward. Bent like a branch in the wind. It's not going to stay up. The front foundation got sucked into a black hole. Destroyed."

"Is anyone left on site?"

"Some ran away yelling it was the end of the world, and some more are stunned, just sitting outside like swatted flies."

I pull into the lot and gaze at the falling building, as though my eyes were fisheye lens. A large gaping hole is where the front foundation used to be. It reminds me of the house we rented in Harbour Breton. The one on stilts. My eyes scan the site. The missing concrete—the drop-off—the ten-foot gap between me and where the front edge of the lot used to be.

Wires are sparking and dancing in pools of water. The plumbing lines and shut off valve obliterated into nothingness. "Use tree stalks! Get saws. Cut down the trees on the back of the property. Wedge them under the front like stilts. I'll pay people double the minimum wage and I'll pay you double your stucco rate if you stay all night and make them work. Just keep it standing!"

"Where do we get the trees?"

"The lot. The back of my lot is full of trees." My mind screams GO!

"There's no way you're saving that building." He shakes his head as though a bug is lodged inside his ear.

"No. Don't say that. And don't just stand there with your mouth hung open. Hurry for God's sake. GO!"

"I'll need more help than we have here." His voice is wavering worse than mine. "Double time, right?" he says as he closes the car door.

I nod and race back to the shop. I find my delivery driver inside talking to Lily. I open the deposit bag and remove the deposit slip. The Riff Automotive team piles into my shop.

"We heard the news. Anything we can do to help?"

"Yes. Rent saws, buys saws, whatever you have to do, just keep the receipts." I push the deposit bag into my driver's hand and say, "Take them with you. Hurry!"

"What about the wedding?"

"Never mind the wedding. GO! Bribe people. Give them twenty bucks. Tell them there's a hundred more where that came from."

I'm in too much shock to do much of anything. I pace back and forth like a lunatic. Somehow, I manage to make some phone calls. I call Sidney's father. I hang up the receiver wondering what I said. I stare at the phone wondering who else to call. Then it rings. I'm afraid to answer it. Afraid it's someone with worse news. I slowly pick it up and say, "Hello."

"Is this Angel Florists?"

"Yes."

"Are you open?"

"No."

I hang up.

In a trance, I break off several carnations. I spray blue paint onto a stem of baby's breath. The paint hits my shirt. I try again with the nozzle pointing in the right direction. I'm shaking so much I waste half of the can. I end up with blue wrists and hands. Even part of the cash register is blue. I wrap floral tape around the boutonnieres. I grab a box, kneel beside it, and line it with tissue paper. The tissue is splattered with tears—smudged with blue fingerprints. I'm about to open the cooler when I see my driver's reflection behind me. I slowly turn around. I read his face and cry harder.

"I'm not going to lie to you. It's bad. Real bad. It's bent over worse than when you saw it. There are live wires everywhere. The power company is at the site right now."

"Can't they just turn off the breakers?"

"No box anymore—got ripped out—buried under slabs of concrete. Wires are dangling and zapping."

"How can concrete walls just collapse? I'm bewildered out of my mind."

He shrugs and says, "Everyone is."

"What's everyone doing?"

"Watching."

"Not cutting down trees? Supporting the structure?"

"They did and—or were—but the power company made a perimeter. Everybody in town is gathered there. Whole families came. Most are volunteering for free. About a hundred or more. The police have the street blocked, and the electrical company is working up on the main pole. We can't do anything else to the building until they finish cutting the power. We kept cutting trees 'til they shut us down."

"Help me load this delivery into the van."

"I can't believe you're thinking about delivering the wedding with all of this going on."

"We have to. I have no other choice. But *I'm* not—you are. After you drop me off at the site."

I push my way past the crowd and stare at the yellow and black tape. I stare at the building. Then I stare at the ground. I duck underneath the tape and stare some more. Inch by inch my forced composure disappears into thin air.

An official sounding voice says, "Sorry kid, but the show is over." He points past the hazard tape and says, "Move along."

"But I'm the owner," I say in a weak voice. "This is my building."

He raises his eyebrows, then knits them together and says, "You mean was your building—and if that's the case, we have a few questions for you. Was this vacant, and if so what was the occupancy date?"

"Occupied with workers, doing finishing touches. I was moving in tomorrow. My grand opening was . . ."

"This is commercial, not residential?"

"It's both. The top floor was my house. The main floor was the shop." My voice breaks. I clear my throat and point my trembling finger toward the gaping eight foot opening and say, "and that area was the basement for storage."

"Are you aware the investigating engineer has deemed this a structural integrity failure? No longer under your authority? Now under our jurisdiction?"

My voice is barely a whisper. "And who are you? What agency are—"

A gentle tap on my shoulder startles the living crap out of me. It's a tree branch. Mr. Simon is holding the other end. I turn around, duck back under the hazard barrier and stand beside him.

"Did you call Sidney?" Mr. Simon says.

"I don't know who I did or didn't call," I say, and collapse into tears. He puts his arm around me. "We should go. There's nothing more to do."

"You're a contractor," I say. "What equipment holds buildings up? Keeps them from falling?"

"House jacks, but this building is a monster. You're going to need hydraulic jacks. The kind that look like cranes. And one jack won't do."

I don't remember much about the past few days. I don't know if my shop is open or closed. I don't even know if I locked it when I left. All I know is the insurance company said collapse is excluded in the fine print. They didn't even think about it. It's as if they expected my call and already had the answer made up.

The sun is bursting into the room. I have no idea who's opening the blinds, but it's not me. I get out of bed and jerk the blinds closed. They slam against the windowsill. I watch them jerk back and forth. That's what the insurance company is doing, jerking me around.

I hit the blinds and crawl back to bed.

A silhouette of a nurse hovers over me. She puts a pill in my mouth and urges me to drink water. I pretend to sip and hold the pill under my tongue. As soon as she leaves, I hide it under my pillow. Over the next few days, I have managed to collect twelve pills. I start feeling less black and more red as anger turns to rage.

How dare they deny my claim? I hate them. I hope every one of their homes burn to the ground. I bought an insurance policy fair and square and now they are ripping me off. I scream into my hands.

Sidney and his mother run into the room. But the door is on the left instead of the right. I look around. I bolt upright. Where the heck am I? This isn't even my room. I struggle to get out of bed.

"Lie back down," Sidney whispers.

My legs feel wobbly. "What's she doing here? Gloating?"

"Mother has been looking after you for three weeks."

I burst into uncontrollable tears. She hugs me and tells me how sorry she is that this happened to me. All I feel is dead. Her entire family forms a circle around the bed. Maybe I did die. Maybe I'm at my own wake. Their glum faces confirm my suspicions.

"It's okay Juanita it's going to be okay." Sidney's mother motions everyone out. Sidney hesitates.

"Especially you." She points to the door.

She sits on the bed and strokes my hair. "A long time ago, during the recession, when my hair was three feet long, like yours, I was three years older than you and married as long as you have been. Construction slowed down until it came to a grinding halt. The only people it did not affect were doctors and lawyers. But by the grace of God, somehow we survived. Those were the darkest years of my life. Two babies and no food to feed them. It may seem like the end of the world but I can assure you it is no such thing."

"Is that why you wanted your kids to be doctors or attorneys?"

"No. Not at all," she looks insulted. "My point was you can't quit and you don't need to be rich to make things work. I am sure you've been through worse. You were on welfare. Certainly you must have experienced times of hopelessness, yet you obviously surpassed them."

"Foster care wasn't by choice and it wasn't a bad memory. Some of the best moments of my life happened during foster care. And for the record, I wasn't in a foster home because my mother sucked."

"Do you mind if I ask what caused it?"

"Greed and jealousy. My stepmother was a retarded bitch from hell."

She shifts uncomfortably in her chair. "Couldn't you have moved in with your mother?"

"She's dead. She died of cancer when I was four. I tried hanging out in the graveyard when I was thirteen but that didn't work out so well."

"I'm glad you are getting your sense of humor back."

"I wasn't joking."

"I heard you have a rich father maybe he can help you."

"You heard wrong. I have no father. My father died when I was six."

"Oh," she looks confused, "I see. Well look at what you've made of yourself despite all of that."

I turn my head towards the wall.

"Sid wants to see you but I thought it better to say no."

"Not like this. I need to clean up. Where is he?"

"I usually bring him in for a visit while you sleep but lately you seem to be less calm."

"You mean less listless." I grab my pillow and shake it. Pills roll across the sheet.

"Oh dear."

"I'm done with those. If Sid's seen me like this already you may as well bring him to me."

"He's out with his grandfather at the site."

I look around the room. It looks familiar. The walls are lemon and the carpet is a silver gray. "Where am I?"

"My house. I saw your colors and loved them so much I redecorated. You were right about the stripes. If the shop doesn't work out, you might want to be a designer."

"I am a designer."

"I meant an interior designer."

"Can you ask Sidney to give me a ride to the shop before he goes to work?"

"Sidney hasn't been to work. He took off some family leave time, but as soon as he gets out of the shower, I'll tell him."

I watch the door close and see some of my outfits sway as they hang from the hook. I choose the one that sways the most and head down the hall for the shower. The shower is wet and the room smells like Old Spice.

When I come back to the room Sidney is sitting on the edge of the bed wringing his hands. I hold his head against my chest.

"I'm back. Everything is going to be just fine."

His breath catches in his throat. "Is this what I put you through back when I had a nervous breakdown?"

"No. You were worse but you can make it up to me by driving me to the job site."

I hold my breath and look to my right as we pull towards the left. It takes several minutes to get the courage to turn my head to the left.

The site is silent . . . abandoned. Yellow and black caution ribbons flap recklessly across the ground. Nobody is at the new shop. It looks like a haunted house. I tell Sidney I need to be alone. I have to tell him three times before he gets it and releases my hand. He turns back to the Javelin and leans against the bumper. "I'll be here waiting if you need me. If you need me, turn around and wave or yell. Just yell."

Yellow plastic ribbon snaps in the wind and lashes my face.

I yelp then yell, "I'm okay."

The front of the building looks like a tree house built on eight-foot stalks. Through the large gaps, I can see past the back windows, into the back lot. It resembles an abandoned underground garage. The eight-foot high concrete front foundation, the surrounding soil and crush rock is strewn randomly inside. It looks like a meteor hit my basement. The feathered floor is separated in parts, some jut up near the back wall. The front two-thirds of the floor, is embedded with chunks of debris and hunks of concrete. Large splinters of wood, and electrical wires are entombed in concrete, that hardened since the collapse.

The sides look like those ancient ruin rubbles where parts of the wall are missing. Two-thirds of the sidewalls are still intact and look normal.

I walk around the back. The emergency second floor exit is gone. Just a ladder nailed to the building leading to a door. No landing. Tree stumps, treetops and broken branches, litter the back lot.

The wind blows a gust of sawdust my way. I duck down, turn away and after the swirl subsides I walk toward the front. Sidney is still waiting in the parking lot.

"The entry's destroyed but we can still get inside."

I stare at the eight-foot ditch in front of the doors. One leads to the showroom, the other leads to the house stairs. "How?"

He pulls a long board from the basement hole. He props it against the shop door. "Wait here."

He disappears inside.

The right side of the basement is filled with water puddles and littered broken copper pipes. The water tank and furnace is on its side, poking out from a four by eight piece of concrete slab that once was part of a sidewall. I walk over to the left wall. Electrical conduit, once connected to a power box dangles from the basement ceiling. Now I understand why the power company came out.

"Stay back." Sidney pushes a ladder out and bridges the four-foot gap between my feet and the door. I panic.

"You can do this." His smile is too wide.

"I can't. I'm afraid of heights."

He walks out to help me but I freeze at the first rung.

He walks across it. A sheet of 4'x8' plywood slides my way.

I focus on Sidney's face. My arms waver up and down as I teeter towards him.

"Is the floor safe?"

"For our weight? Yes. They braced tree stalks to the sides of the bearing posts in the basement. Cabled one to each side. That was a good idea—tree trunks. What made you think of it?"

"I don't know—Harbour Breton."

A giant trash bin of glass is near the front boarded up window.

I walk into the back room. "How come this window didn't break?"

"Weird huh?" he says.

My grip tightens around the stair railing. The steps are slanting downwards. The walls have multiple cracks that fork out from the front corners. Up on the ceiling, some of the pinwheel swirls in the stucco look like fat spiders with skinny legs. Other than that, the upper floor looks perfect.

"I want to see the basement."

"There's nothing to see."

I ignore him and go downstairs. I walk past the office and head towards the basement entry.

"Don't go down the steps it's not safe, the bottom ones are missing."

I walk down one step and sit.

"This basement is the last thing I looked at, before this happened."

Sidney sits beside me. "What are we going to do? The bank wants their money. You realize we may have to go bankrupt."

"I need to reopen this shop."

"What for? Juanita it's finished. The National Building Code of Canada representatives practically condemned the place."

"I'm going to make it work. I'm going to the old shop and opening it back up."

"What for? It's the talk of the town. You'll have a shop full of nosy busybodies."

"Those busybodies are the reason this place is still standing. They're the ones who cut the trees and braced them between the openings."

He frowns at me and says, "I think you're wasting your time."

"I don't." I walk across the plank and look back at the building. It looks like the leaning tower of Pisa on stilts.

I yell at him from the parking lot, "You coming or not?"

At the old shop, I keep the lights off and the closed sign up. I call the wholesaler. The best thing he can do is give me roses for ten cents each. They are seconds with crooked stems. Roses are normally two dollars a stem. I call the newspaper and run an ad. I tell the representative that I want to design it and I want a prime half page spot.

I look at Sidney he looks like a lost puppy. "I want to help but I don't know how." His eyes remind me of Dork. My dead dog.

"You just did." My hand flies across the paper. I draw a person's head, with his tongue hanging out, looking out of a doghouse. In big caps I write the header.

Sidney laughs when he reads it, "ARE YOU IN THE DOGHOUSE LIKE ME?" I add a cartoon caption bubble and write, Buying Flowers Will Get Me Out! My finishing touch is a tree trunk stuck in the ground with a broken board nailed to it.

"What's that?" Sidney looks over my shoulder.

"It's a sign," I say and scribble, ROSES $3.99 PER DOZEN. "You don't get it, do you? Hopefully other people will."

"I get it, but how can you pay for the ad and the roses, while selling them for that?"

"Here's how."

I call the wholesaler back. I ask for a better additional deal. He tells me he got sent some crooked short stem carnations by mistake. He says they are a write off. By the time he returns them they'd be dead but if I wanted them I could get them for five cents each.

"How long are they."

"Twelve to thirteen inches. They come six hundred to a carton."

"How many do you have?"

"Six cartons."

"I'll take them all."

"When can you ship them?"

"When do you want them?"

"By yesterday."

I hang up and press my hands against my cheeks. I can feel my mouth scrunch up. "I've got three thousand, six hundred carns coming by air."

His mouth hangs open. He holds up six fingers and mouths the words six hundred.

I nod and grin. "Carns are normally a buck a piece. I'll sell them for two-ninety-nine a dozen. It's a markup of five hundred percent. The truth is I'll sell out before mid-afternoon."

"How can you be so sure of that?"

"Projections. Remember that six-month business course I had to take in order to get the FBDB building loan? Well, it wasn't such a waste of time after all. It taught me how to estimate instead of guesstimate. Based on the performance of previous seasons, and the ROI per season, I could sell eight hundred—but they only have six."

Sidney points to the cooler. "Holy shit. How are you going to fit them in there? And what are carns again?"

"Short for carnations. They come as dry packs. When carns come dry packed, they have to be put in hot water at room temp for a day but for roses it's crucial we get them in the cooler immediately—which means I have to clean it. Can you bring this ad to the newspa—why bother asking questions when you don't want an answer? You're not listening to one word and why are you rummaging through the cash register?"

"Do you know you have a bunch of checks here from a funeral home dated a month ago. And what are these?"

I shrug and say, "They're invoices I need to mail out."

"The police department? The hospital? Juanita you have some pretty decent accounts."

342

"I know," I say and wave the ad in his face. "There's a deadline for this."

His eyebrows arch. "This ad is no good. It's for roses, not carnations."

"I'm still getting the roses. The carns are for when the roses run out."

He takes the ad and says, "Shouldn't this ad mention both?"

"No. Are you going to help me make the deadline or not?"

"This invoice is for a different funeral home. It's for over a grand."

"I bill them every thirty days. People die daily."

"But you're not mailing them out. How are people supposed to pay you? How do you keep track of who owes what?"

"Here," I say as an exasperated sigh slips from my lips. I pull out a drawer and try to maintain a civil tone. "Look under B."

"B?"

"Blacks Funeral Home."

He waves the card, "What good is this?"

"Sidney," I say between grit teeth, "if you must know," I point near the top of the beige card, to the pale-brown highlighted line and add, "see the words typed on that line? Now see the columns below?"

"Mmm. Date, invoice number and description, charges, credit," he smiles and says, "and last but not least balance. I get that one. But you don't have any descriptions—only numbers listed in the second column."

"That's because those numbers are the invoice numbers. If you need details and descriptions, you look for the invoices—in here." I reach for a six-inch card board holder and slap it on the counter, barely missing his hand. "Fill your boots they're in numerical order."

"So you just have a thing about mailing out the original? They owe you over three thousand dollars, minus these checks I found. Oops never mind. The checks are from a different funeral home. They haven't paid anything for the past two months."

"I know. They always pay on time and when they don't it's because I've been too busy to send them a statement."

I grab the ad from him. "I guess I have to deliver this myself?"

"Are you sure you want to do this. Maybe you should focus on your receivables, not sales."

"Without sales there won't be any more receivables. If people are going to stand outside and spend half the day gawking at the shop they may as well come inside and buy something. Maybe you could come and sign autographs. I'm serious. Why not?" I tilt my chin up and toss my hair towards his face.

"Why?"

"I need people to see I'm still in business and I need to prove to FBDB that I deserve a second mortgage."

"I think you're wasting your time." He snatches the ad and leaves.

———————

In one week, I have my second mortgage and hydraulic jacks are shifting the house back. Each day it gets one-eighth of an inch straighter but I'm almost out of money. Desperate and scared I visit my attorney.

"My only chance of surviving this is if you to go after the insurance company."

"Juanita I don't know what you expect me to do."

"Can't we sue them? Can't we make them pay the claim?"

"I talked to the adjuster. Their defense is that they would if they could litigate a third party such as the general contractor but you can't sue yourself."

"Say what?"

"They deem the general contractor was you."

"That's ridiculous. Then I deem them to be a bunch of crooks. A contractor—that's the stupidest thing I've ever heard."

"No it's not. You did act in the capacity of a general contractor by hiring and overseeing the job, and apparently a concrete test was never performed on site."

"Then tell them to litigate against them."

"Who?"

"The concrete company."

"Juanita the odds are not in our favor. It's a waste of money and you will not win."

"So you're quitting?"

"Nobody will take this case on. What's happening is wrong but you don't have endless pockets to fund a losing battle."

"How do they know something like the furnace or boiler didn't explode? Explosion is covered right? The guy, working with the grader, thought he heard an explosion."

"Are we talking about the same guy? The guy who ran down the middle of the road, waving a rake, screaming at the top of his lungs, it's the end of the world?"

I nod.

"Juanita, it doesn't look good. Someone who acts like a lunatic is not a credible witness." He leans back in his chair and adds, "They are taking the defense that it was an act of God. Acts of Gods are excluded from your insurance policy."

"Tell them I said I hope they burn in hell."

Sidney looks at me and apologizes on my half as I drag him out the door.

In the elevator, I glare at the flashing numbers.

"You're not mad at me are you?"

"I'm mad at the world because the Engineering and Inspection Services Division is insisting on a new twelve-inch concrete wall with caging and rebar. They also want the existing sidewalls reinforced. By the time I do that, I'm out of money and I don't have enough to resurface the concrete floor. So right now I'm mad at everybody, including me."

The bottom half of the basement stairs are jimmy rigged with cheap planks. The top half is the original oak. I stare at the new electrical power box. The old concrete foundation, on the back wall, and the parts of the basement floor that are still intact are riddled with white swirls from the calcium. Nausea sweeps over me.

I head upstairs past the shop and climb another flight to the house. I'm sick of looking at the cracks in the drywall. I get some toothpaste and climb the ladder.

"What are you doing? Is that toothpaste?"

"Yes. You'd think after six months this building would stop settling . . . Aren't you supposed to be at work?"

He takes a deep breath, "I quit my job."

"Say what?"

"I'm coming to work for you."

"I don't know if I can pay you. What if we can't stand each other?"

"Us, get sick of each other, never."

"Besides you're never home. If I work here maybe I'll see you more," he grins.

"That's not fair. That's just the way it is during Christmas and Easter."

"Are you forgetting that on Mother's Day you're here making other mothers happy?" he asks.

It doesn't take long for Sidney to fill the manager role. He insists we shut down the Bay Bulls store because he thinks the rent and management salary is draining the main location dry. I try to tell him it's seasonal. But he doesn't buy it. The truth is, if it was Christmas, he'd see things differently.

"The people from Bay Bulls still pass that store and come here anyway. I don't see the point in having it. All he's selling up there is three inch potted plants."

"He doesn't just sell potted plants," I say. "Besides the accountant said in order to survive the second mortgage I had to expand."

I jam flowers into the centerpiece. I pick up a piece of fern and stab it in between the flowers.

"I think we need to throw in the towel."

"I'm fine with that," I say.

Sidney raises his eyebrows. "Wow that was easy."

"Admit it Sidney us getting back together was a mistake. A big mistake. We had so much garbage we needed to deal with and with this mess of a building we just added more bags to the pile."

He backs away, "No. No. I was talking about the shop, not us. Christ, we can't be having this conversation again."

"You're the one who started it."

"No. I did not. I was taking about giving up the shop, not us. Please . . . please . . . please don't do this to me again . . . please."

"You're never satisfied are you? First it was the Bay Bulls store and now this one too? NO! NO! NO! ABSOLUTELY NOT!" I feel like a lion defending her cub. I lower my voice, "What's wrong not enough money to buy drugs?"

"Juanita that was low. Below the belt. You know I don't do drugs anymore."

"You're right I'm sorry. Sidney we have double the garbage we had when we separated."

"What garbage."

"Like the underpants I found under the mattress."

"Christ Juanita that was a year ago. I told you I don't know how they got there."

I mimic Sidney. "Oh I haven't laid anybody, Deborah was helping me clean the house and got a shower, she must have forgotten her bra. Does the name Paula ring a bell?"

"Juanita I swear on Sid's life I didn't sleep with her. When I told her I was still in love with you she probably put them there out of spite knowing you'd find them one day."

"I don't care what you did, I care that you lie."

"I don't lie."

"Fine. Swear on Sid's life you haven't lied to me."

"I can't do that, because everyone tells white lies. You said that yourself."

"Swear on Sid's life that you aren't holding anything back from me."

I watch his chest heave as he says, "Fine. A while back when I was teaching, I hid your mail. It was a letter from an old boyfriend."

"What?"

"The guy's name was on the envelope. I had to open it."

"So where is it?"

"I burned it."

"When?"

"The year we got married."

"What did it say?"

He winces. "It said—he said—You were his first true love and true love never dies and he wanted you to fly out to be with him."

"Anything else?"

"Yes. I burned the plane ticket."

"Is that it?"

"I wrote back and told him, it was over, only a fling, and to screw off and get lost."

"Nothing else?"

"I signed your name to the letter."

Alone Again

Sidney and I shake hands with the attorney. "Let's go celebrate. Let's go dancing."

I look at him in shock. He hates dancing but much to my surprise he's serious and that's exactly what we end up doing.

Sidney is smiling twirling me around. I smile back.

"I always loved your smile."

"Thanks," I grin.

"How about we go somewhere and make out?"

I laugh, "In your dreams."

"Dreams are good things."

"Since when did you start believing in dreams?"

"After I fell in love with a dreamer."

We walk outside and Sidney throws his coat around me, "Warm enough?"

I nod.

"Excuse me. Mr. and Mrs. Simon? I'm Jenna, remember me? I used to babysit for you."

"Oh Jenna! Hi, how are you?"

"I'm great. I'm engaged and getting married next year. I want to have a marriage just like yours!"

Sidney and I glance at each other and grin.

"Isn't that nice. Juanita. Do you hear that. We are the perfect couple." His grin widens.

"Yes we two lovebirds are definitely role models," I say.

He kisses me on the lips.

"Knock it off," I whisper. "We're in public."

"So," Sidney says. He backs up, peels a little rubber and swerves to the right.

For two miles we share silence but it's a pleasant silence because we finally accept each other for who we are.

Sidney doesn't shut off the car. He keeps it idling and throws on a tune. "This will always be our song. Do you remember when I played this and you asked the name and I said, Our Song, and you thought I meant it was our song? You didn't even know who Elton John was."

I laugh.

We hug.

"Can I come in?"

"No. You know what the attorney said, if we get together the divorce won't happen and the separation won't be legal anymore."

"How would he even know?"

"You. You'd be the first to tell him."

"It was nice of you to furnish the apartment and pay the rent. It's obvious you still love me."

"I did it for Sid. But I still think he should live with me."

"I can't lose you both. Besides we have joint custody so neither one of us can leave the province with him. If I lose you both, life won't be worth living. I'm not strong enough to make it alone, but you've been alone forever. You wear it well. I don't."

"School is next week. Who gets to take him shopping for new clothes?"
Sidney takes a coin from his pocket, "Heads or tails?"
"My choice would be both, but if I can have that I'll pick heads."
The coin flutters on the dash. I win.
"Best two out of three?"
Half an hour later, after twelve coin tosses, I say, "How about we both take him?"
"Split the bill down the middle?" he asks.
I nod.
"Do you ever get nervous here all alone?"
"Sometimes."
"Maybe you should give me another chance."
"I'm not that lonely," I laugh.
"You should at least get a dog."
"Why."
"It's a big house. At night the place looks dark. It's too bad they didn't let you have lit signs . . ."
"What?"
"Have you heard this song? Just listen to the words. It sounds like us. It reminds me of you. It's Photographs and Memories by Jim Croce."
The title sounds familiar. That's it—he had that written all over one the photo albums he kept. I listen to one verse. "Sidney you need to stop listening to this stuff. It's too depressing." I shut the radio off. "Your car windows are wide open and the neighbors could be trying to sleep."
"Promise me you'll get a dog."
"I promise."
"When?"
"Tomorrow."
He stays in the parking lot until I am safe inside.
I head straight to bed but I toss and turn all night. I feel alone. Part of me wants to go downstairs and work, but part of me is too scared. Maybe if I had window coverings for the downstairs workshop I wouldn't be afraid to work at night.

Maybe I'll get some of those, after I get a dog.

At sunrise, I look in the phone books. I find a breeder for German Shepard dogs. Even though he's the price of two mortgage payments. I buy him.

The dog is barely six months old. He already has a name, Claudius. His mother is some prize winning show dog. I rename him Cloud.

Cloud becomes a large part of my life. He's great with Sid and very protective of us both. When Sid isn't with me, he sits by the door to the downstairs and whines until I bribe him with beef.

Tonight Sid is with his father and I have a date. It's with a guy Sidney introduced me to. Apparently, Sidney has a regular girlfriend who thinks we are too close. Sidney thinks if I have a boyfriend we can hang out again as couples. I only said yes because Sidney expected me to say no. It's with a guy he used to work with at the TV station.

As I soak in the tub, Cloud jumps in with me. I pull out the plug and grab him by the collar while I get into my housecoat. I kick the bathroom door shut with my foot. He shakes twice, destroying the entire bathroom. I towel dry him as much as I can and lead him down into the workshop. I shut the door, stand in the entry and wait for him to stop whining. He doesn't so I trudge back up the steps and head to the shower.

It takes me twenty minute to dry my hair. I take one final look at myself and head downstairs. I shut the top floor door and when I reach the lower landing, I hear Cloud sniffing at the bottom of the design room door. I see his paws digging under the door. "Be a good boy. I'll be back before you know it."

I go outside and twist the key into the lock, shake the other doorknob to the shop, to double check it's locked and drive away.

My breath quickens as I pull into a parking spot near the door. I can hear music playing. I'm nervous. At least I had sense enough to meet him here, I think as I shut off the van. I stare at the door to the lounge. What if he's not here? What if he forgot? I walk to the door of the lounge trying to remember what he looks like. It's dim inside. Everyone looks similar. People form clusters around the bar. Some size me up. Maybe he got tired of waiting. Maybe he's in the bathroom. I feel like every eye in the place is judging me. I make a beeline for the door.

The closer I get to home, the worse I feel. I hate being single already. The dread of going back to that empty house consumes me. Where do single people hang out? I know! I'll go to a movie.

I head to the mall and line up for a ticket. Half of the people in line seem to be alone.

Inside the lights dim. I munch on popcorn and think this is great. What a perfect way to pass time. A place where it isn't so weird to walk in alone. No chance of being hit on. I'm coming here every chance I get.

One week later, with five movies under my belt, I pull into the gas station. A Rod Stewart impersonator fills up my tank. I hand him a fifty-dollar bill. "Keep the change." I start up the van.

"Turn on your radio and you'll see your left speaker is dead."

"I know," I say. *Wait! Did I have the radio on when I pulled in?* I don't remember.

"Want me to fix it?"

"Now?"

"Why not? It'll only take five minutes if it's a loose wire."

"What if it's not a loose wire?"

"It is. I can tell." He leans in, turns the radio on, and bangs his fist on the dash.

"It works!"

He bangs it again. It stops working.

"What did you do that for? You had it working!"

"The first time you hit a bump that was gonna happen anyway. Pull over to the side, away from the pumps."

I sit on a back seat in the van while he removes the console between the front seats.

He glances up every now and then. "So how's single life?"

"Pardon?"

"I can't believe you married such a stuffed shirt. I just pictured you with someone a little more fun and a lot better looking. Better looking, like me."

"How do you know me?"

"You don't remember me do you?"

"No I don't. Who are you?"

"I'm Gerry Prowler. I went to school with you."

"I don't remember you."

"I'm sure you don't. You only had eyes for him. But I know everything about you."

I look through my purse for nothing in particular and snap it shut.

"Didn't you know I had a crush on you?" he asks.

I snap my purse open and close it repeatedly.

"There hear that? It's working, good as new. See how handy a real man can be?"

"Thank you," I say, "how much do I owe you?"

"Nothing. You're going to marry me, so it's free."

This guy's got to be nuts.

"So tell me something I don't know about you."

"Shouldn't you be pumping gas? Won't you get into trouble? Reprimanded? Fired?"

He wipes his knees, jumps from the van and reaches back to shut the door.

"I don't pump gas. I'm a mechanic."

"But you pumped mine."

Slam.

I get into the driver's seat. He props his elbows on my window sill.

"That's not all I want to pump."

I feel utterly shocked.

"I see you're not used to honest guys. I think you're absolutely gorgeous and I plan to fuck you."

I hit the gas and almost wrench his arms off. I decide to spend another night at the movies.

Stalked

I sit in the movie theater thinking what a rotten movie it is. They should be paying me to watch this crap. I leave at ten-thirty—before it's over. The mall is closed, except for the lounge on the upper floor. I'm parked just across the road. I should probably go to earlier shows I think as I drive home.

I lock the front door behind me. Something's is not right. The door to the stairs is open, so is the workroom. Where's Cloud? Pricks of shock pierce my chest. A thumping sound upstairs startles me. I turn and struggle to open the dead bolt. I'm slammed against the front door. I scream and fall. Cloud slurps my face and nose. I crouch beside him looking around. How did he get out of the workroom? Cloud runs upstairs and runs back down to me again and back up. I know I shut that workroom door and dead bolted it. Cloud waits at the stop of the stairs, arches his butt, wiggles it and barks. And I know I shut that top door too, but it's ajar.

"Get him boy. Get him!"

Cloud returns with his ball.

I ignore him and mutter, "Some attack dog you turned out to be." I trudge upstairs and I flick on the bedroom light. Several dresser drawers are open. One is dumped on its side onto the floor. My clothes are strewn all over the place.

My legs feel weak as I back away. I cautiously walk past the living room, towards the kitchen phone. Living room plants are tipped over with their roots exposed. Soil is everywhere. I slide on a silk slip, trip on some socks, and catch myself by hanging onto the edge of the counter. My nerves are raw. "Stay here," I hiss at Cloud. He lies on the kitchen floor and chews on a pair of my underwear as I dial 911.

I'm a total basket case by the time the police arrive.

"What do you mean nobody broke in?"

"We don't see any signs of break and entry."

I wave my arms erratically around the room. "Are you blind?"

He looks at his partner and shrugs. One slightly nods his head towards me.

They think I did this? They think I'm crazy?

"I'm not the one who did this, I was at a movie and this is what I came back to." I grope inside my pocket and pull out my movie ticket receipt.

"Look whoever did this must have a key to the place. Can you think of a worker? Any disgruntled employees?"

I shake my head. "Lots of people have worked here, before and after the place was built."

"That's right. This is the place that collapsed. Did you sue anyone?"

"No."

One partner motions for the other to step away. Moments later he returns. "Tell you what. We'll keep watching this place. We'll be on patrol all night. One word of advice? You should think about changing that light bulb."

"What light bulb?"

"The red recessed lighting. People might think it's a brothel."

"A what?"

"A whore house. Ever hear of the red light district?"

"But this is the Goulds."

"All some guys need is a few extra beers and a red light."

I shut off the lights and flick on some lamps. "You don't suppose some pervert thinks this is one do you. Surely they can see the flower shop sign."

"Not at night. Anyway, we will keep an eye out. Any sign of trouble and you call 911 again okay?"

The next night I'm too scared to stay home. I go to an early movie. When it's over, I see it's only nine pm. The stores are still open for another half an hour. I wander around the mall. I hear music come from the top floor. I stand just inside the door and listen. I hide in the shadows and avoid looking at people as they enter. The band seems good. I can't tell if the lead singer is male or female. I turn around and walk out. As I do an arm slips around my waste, "Where do you think you're going?" He deftly pivots me in the opposite direction. I'm facing back towards the lounge door. I think, that was smooth. "Stay and have a drink with me." He propels me towards the entry.

"I can't I have to go."

"No you don't."

"How do you know I don't?"

"Anyone who spends all day walking around a mall buying nothing, has nowhere to go."

"You've been following me all day!"

"No not all day. A day starts just after midnight. So . . . what were the police doing at your place?"

A knot forms in my throat. There's nobody out here but the two of us. "How would you know the police were at my place at one am?"

He cups his ear. He points to the black door of the bar and says, "I work at a garage. A garage with a police scanner."

I take a deep breath and hold it. "What did you hear?"

"I'll answer that after you buy me a drink," he says. "Come on. I don't have all night. Tomorrow I'll be up before dawn catching a wave."

"As in surfing?"

"Geezuz no. This is Newfoundland, the only things that ride a wave are seagulls and fishing boats. My uncle and I are going out to catch a few cod."

A female voice sings, "Do you want my body? Do ya think I'm sexy? Come on baby let me know . . .."

"I love that song. It reminds me of us."

Chills crawl up my spine—us? What the hell does he mean by us?

He shifts to his right and looks to his left, "Oh there you are buddy. I didn't see you there. I'm Gerry Prowler, what's your name? Pleased to meet you my son." He shakes an imaginary hand.

"Who are you talking to?" Please someone, anyone, come outside the bar and save me.

"You look like you saw a ghost so I'd thought I'd introduce myself to him."

Why was I such an idiot? I must be mental for leaving Sidney.

"You know I don't date women on the rebound but for you I'm willing to make an exception. So how's next April 30th looking for you?"

"For what?"

"For our wedding. It's my birthday. I learned the hard way about forgetting anniversaries." He smirks and tips up the bottom of my chin. "Can't have you catching flies. Now what about that drink? You look like you could use a double."

Suddenly a bar full of people sounds good. I wonder how many drinks it takes to fill a man's bladder. I'll make a run for it as soon as he heads to the bathroom.

"Just one drink and you'll tell me the truth."

"About what?"

"How you know about the police—and everything else."

"I'll tell you everything, and then some." He slides his arm back around me and propels me towards the door. The band stops singing.

We sit at the bar.

I kick off my heels thinking, if I am going to run for it I won't get very far in these. He leans towards my face and whispers, "How did you know I had a foot fetish." He presses his lips against my ear and sings, "When you're in love with a beautiful woman you go it alone . . ."

Sidney flashes into my mind. I remember him turning up the radio for me to hear that song. We were in the parking lot talking about getting a dog. The windows were wide open. Was Gerry Prowler hiding on the side of the building eavesdropping?

I try to convince myself I am being stupid.

The band must have played the song earlier, that's why he's singing it to me. It's got to be nothing more than a strange coincidence.

"Okay lay it on me."

I try to stay calm. "How do you really know about the police?" my voice sounds hoarse.

"How do you think I knew your speaker was broken?" he grins. "I know lots about you. I even know you're scared of heights."

"How?"

"Because five years ago, you quit a school play when you found out you had to climb up a ladder."

"That's not why I quit."

"Hey, it's water under the bridge. The point is I've been obsessed with you, since eighth grade, but you were too infatuated with Mr. Uppity Ass to notice me, but that's all gonna change real soon."

"How's that?"

"By the time tonight is over, you'll be sticking to me like shit to a blanket."

His eyes are dancing yet serious at the same time. They remind me of the old cat we had back in Hearts Delight. That's how Crowley's eyes looked when he saw a mouse. He knew it was an easy target, easier than a bird. He never seemed to be able to wear down a bird, but the mice were easy prey. Crowley knew exactly where a mouse would be before the mouse did.

Gerry pulls me to the dance floor. His hand, slipped behind my back, propels me to do a turn, just the way Crowley would paw the mouse, and roll it, before he ate it.

But by the time the night is over my jaws are sore from laughing. Gerry is the funniest guy I've ever met and the complete polar opposite of Sidney. He's too outrageous to be faking it and I find his bad boy attitude appealing. A little bad just might be exactly what the doctor ordered and a little bad might do me the world of good.

About The Author

Juanita Ray, a dual citizen, born in Newfoundland Canada, is a well-educated, retired entrepreneur who has had several successful careers, and earned multiple certificates and awards. She is married to her soulmate Scott, and together they live at 'the jungle' in Southern California, with the horde, a 6-pack of dogs, 150 small birds housed in an outside aviary, and a 6-pack of adopted outside semi-feral cats (one loves to crash photo shoots), who have spent the last decade drooling while 'guarding' the aviary. Her newest rescue is a misfit Siamese cat with a dissociative identity disorder.

Juanita's hobbies include photography, creating music, writing lyrics, and painting everything in sight. Her favorite tools are drills, hammers, and her 10-inch miter saw. Her lifelong passion for animals has never waned. Neither has her allergies to cats and dust.

Juanita wants to thank you for reading this book. She invites you to leave a review online and share what you thought with others. Keep in touch with her by visiting the following websites, or sending her an email.

AuthorJRay.com
ToxicThoughts.com
Twitter @toxicthoughtsbk
Facebook @ToxicThoughtsSeries
Twitter/Facebook @authorJRay
SmorgasbordPublications@gmail.com

Intoxicated (Toxic Thoughts Series #3)

Printed in Great Britain
by Amazon

22092209R00209